# THE HERITAGE OF
# ITALIAN
# C·O·O·K·I·N·G

# THE HERITAGE OF
# ITALIAN
# C·O·O·K·I·N·G

## LORENZA DE' MEDICI

This edition published in 1993 by Limited Editions

First published in the United Kingdom in 1990 by
Ebury Press, an imprint of the Random Century Group
20 Vauxhall Bridge Road
London SW1V 2SA

By arrangement with Weldon Russell Pty Ltd
a member of the Weldon International Group of Companies

Produced by Weldon Russell Pty Ltd
107 Union Street
North Sydney NSW 2060 Australia

Copyright © 1990 Weldon Russell Pty Ltd

Publisher: Elaine Russell
Managing editor: Dawn Titmus
Editor: Ariana Klepac
Translator: Barbara McGilvray
Text researchers: John Meis, Susan Chenery
Copy-editor: Jill Wayment
Proofreader: Roderic Campbell
Picture researcher: Ancilla Antonini, Index
US cooking consultant: Mardee Haidin Regan
Design concept: Susan Kinealy
Designers: Catherine Martin, Birita Abols
Food photographers: John Sims, Romano Vada
Indexer: Jill Matthews, Hitech Editing
Production: Dianne Leddy

The right of Lorenza de'Medici to be identified as the author of this work
has been asserted by her in accordance with the Copyright, Designs and
Patents Act, 1988.

A catalogue record for the book is available from the British Library

ISBN 0 09 178181 7

Typeset by Savage Type Pty Ltd, Brisbane, Australia
Colour separation by Scantrans, Singapore
Produced by Mandarin Offset, Hong Kong
Printed in China

A KEVIN WELDON PRODUCTION

---

NOTE TO READERS

All recipes serve 6 people unless otherwise indicated.

| 1 quart | = | 2 pints |
|---|---|---|

*Terminology*

| skillet | = | frying pan |
|---|---|---|
| griller | = | grill |
| cheesecloth | = | muslin |
| semisweet chocolate | = | plain chocolate |

---

Front cover: *Vegetables and fruit*, Cristiano Berentz
(1658–1722); NATIONAL GALLERY OF ANCIENT ART, ROME

Back cover: *The birth of John the Baptist* (detail), *Ginevra
de'Benci and Lucrezia Tornabuoni*, Domenico Bigondi,
known as Ghirlandaio; SANTA MARIA NOVELLA

Opp. title page: *Cherries*, Bartolomeo Bimbi (1648–1725);
PITTI GALLERY, FLORENCE

Title page: *Refreshments*, Francesco Napoletano (sixteenth
century); PALATINA GALLERY, FLORENCE

*An elegant snack*, Cristiano Berentz (1658–1722);
NATIONAL GALLERY OF ANCIENT ART, ROME

# CONTENTS

*Afternoon in Fiesole*, Baccio Maria Bacci (twentieth century); UFFIZI GALLERY, FLORENCE

*Summer*, Giuseppe Arcimboldo (1527–93); PINACOTECA CIVICA, BRESCIA  Arcimboldo was famous for his elaborate fruit and flower paintings depicting human forms.

# INTRODUCTION

Italy's cuisine is one of the country's richest cultural heritages. It has often been remarked that not everyone in Italy may know how to cook but all Italians know how to eat! The national passion for food is a joyous expression of the Italian love of a good life. The Italian people have the happy ability to make eating together a festive occasion. Food is a celebration, and conviviality at the table greatly enhances a tradition that has emerged from a long and eventful history.

Inspiration for Italian cooks is everywhere. Italy's particular combination of mountains and sea, fertile river valleys and arid terrain produces a cornucopia of foods as varied and extreme as the contours of the land itself. In the North, icy-cold Alpine streams water lush pasture for land that produces fine veal and beef as well as rich dairy products. These waters are channeled into canals for irrigating extensive rice paddies. Grain fields, orchards and vegetable farms flourish. Picturesque lakes and the beautiful upper Adriatic Sea readily yield an extraordinary bounty of fish. Along the Riviera, sea breezes encourage aromatic herbs to fill the air with their perfumes. In the more arid central and southern regions olive groves are cultivated in the green foothills of the Apennine Mountains, which also provide herbage for sheep and goats. On the plains durum wheat is grown and the intense sun brings out the full flavor of the much-appreciated local fruits and vegetables. The heel and toe of the peninsula as well as the islands of Sardinia and Sicily are surrounded by the abundance of the Mediterranean and, of course, from tip to toe there are the vine-clad slopes.

As the heart and soul of Italian cooking is fresh, high-quality foods, it is providential indeed that the country has such a wealth of natural attributes. In the lively city and town marketplaces, frequented daily by the country's cooks, the dazzling displays of foodstuffs are truly a sight to be seen.

Then there are the accumulative ingredients of time itself, as essential for the creation of a gastronomic tradition as they are for the formation of a culture. The Republic of Italy is made up of twenty-three regions, many of which were independent kingdoms and republics before the unification of the country in the mid-nineteenth century. Each had its peculiar components of geography, climate, history and socio-political factors that formed local character in eating habits and cooking. There has long existed an extraordinary variety of regional dishes in Italy, unique among European cuisines for their sharp diversity.

Credit must be given to the ancient Romans for developing the peninsula's first culinary tradition, based on the Greek and Etruscan foundations of their civilization. In the

11

*The month of May, a meal in the outdoors* (detail), (fifteenth century), fresco; CASTELLO DEL BUONCONSIGLIO, TRENTO
One of a series of frescoes depicting the months of the year.

*The wedding feast at Cana*, Andrea
Boscoli (1560–1607); UFFIZI GALLERY, FLORENCE
Cana, the ancient town of Galilee, was the
site of Jesus Christ's first miracle—the
transforming of water into wine at a
wedding banquet.

ninth century of the Christian era the Saracens occupied the South and added an Oriental
flavor. But it was the period of the Renaissance that saw a tremendous rebirth of Italian
cuisine. It was at this time that the heritage of Italian cooking, as we enjoy it today, began
to be formulated and transmitted by means of the written word. We can only marvel today
at the fabulous menus of the opulent Renaissance banquets described in works of that time.
Important cookbooks continued to be written in the succeeding centuries and these must
be considered among the most precious contributions to the national heritage. Many of the
recipes then recorded have survived the passing of time and fashion intact and are still
in widespread use today. The recipes in this book are all indebted in one way or another
to these early cookbook writers whose names appear throughout this book.

The first cookbook written, *De Re Coquinaria (Concerning Culinary Matters)*, which
was probably compiled sometime during the first centuries AD, is attributed to a Roman
gastronome named Apicius. The author collected contemporary recipes and also created
some himself. Many are interesting only as an account of the epicurean excesses of
imperial Rome. Others, however, have an enduring appeal: such as a pasta pie with meat
and vegetables; prosciutto cooked in honey with dried figs and bay leaves; and a sweet
and sour sauce that, among other ingredients, contained mint, pine nuts, raisins, honey,
wine, vinegar and oil.

Two other important manuscripts on Italian cooking date from the late Middle Ages. Sadly, the authors' names are unknown. One is the *Libro della Cocina (The Book of Cooking)*, and was written by a Tuscan, and the other is *Libro per Cuoco (The Book for the Cook)* and the author was a Venetian. Totally different in style and form, they are significant for the development of cookbook writing when examined side by side. The Tuscan was the first Italian to organize his recipes under headings of individual foods, giving several ways to prepare *fava* (broad) beans and three versions of fish soup. He also includes a section of recipes for those who are unwell: his cure for the common cold, for instance, was a kind of porridge. He does not, however, give any measurements for ingredients or information about cooking techniques. In this respect the work of the Venetian is an advance in cookbook writing: weights and measurements are given as well as cooking times for ingredients and their order of execution. His more technical style qualifies him as the progenitor of the long lineage extending to present-day cookbook writers.

There was a great leap forward in this field with the first of the great Renaissance writers on food and cooking: Maestro Martino da Como, who was the personal cook to the Patriarch of Aquileia. His book, *Libro de Arte Coquinaria (Book of Culinary Art)*, greatly enlarges the traditional repertoire of recipes. There are lengthy discourses on how to prepare all kinds of fish, and chapters on seasonings and desserts. There is, too, advice on the selection of the best raw materials — for instance, rice from the Po Valley and cured

*Lunch in the garden of Massimiliano* Sforza (sixteenth century); CASTELLO SFORZESCO LIBRARY
The Sforza family was the ruler of Milan in the fifteenth century, and was a great patron of many artists including Leonardo da Vinci.

*Springtime*, Adolfo Tommasi (1851–1933); GALLERY OF MODERN ART, FLORENCE
Tuscan peasants used to have to give half their produce to the landowners, so they would often grow several crops at once.

Shovel of Vincenzo Magalotti, called "The Exalted One" (sixteenth century);
ACCADEMIA DELLA CRUSCA, FLORENCE
The Accademia della Crusca was set up in 1582 in order to establish correct usage in the Tuscan language. The shovels symbolized this "sifting" of the good from the bad.

meats from Bologna. He shows great interest in perfecting cooking methods and, to this end, pays close attention to a range of practical matters. He takes care to give precise measurements and also gives consideration to cooking utensils, to how the dishes should be served and how they should look.

Not the least of his contributions was his influence on the great Renaissance humanist Bartolomeo Sacchi, known as Platina, who acknowledged Martino as his master and transcribed many of his recipes. Platina entitled his opus *De Honesta Voluptate ac Valetudine (Concerning Honest Pleasure and Well-being)* and it is an exhaustive treatise of 417 chapters on how food and eating should help achieve just that. While drawing on the wisdom of the classical Greek and Roman philosophers, he counseled against the culinary excesses of the Romans and, at the same time, offered his own sage advice. Something of a visionary, Platina was interested in nutrition and in eating that aided the digestion; he also extolled the benefits of exercise for anyone who wanted to eat well and live a healthy life. Platina's was the first *printed* food book to be published — in about 1474 in Rome, where he was a librarian at the Vatican — and it soon became a bestseller, being translated into French, German and English.

It was the period of the high Renaissance that produced the first cookbook writer to merit the title "chef." The title was bestowed upon the great Cristoforo di Messisbugo (a gentleman married to a noble lady) by the Emperor Charles V. Historians consider him the founder of *la grande tradizione* (the great tradition) of Italian cooking. He was in service as meat-carver to the Dukes of Ferrara. The title of his work is *Banchetti, Composizione di Vivande et Apparecchio Generale (Banquets, Composition of Meals and General Equipment)*. Besides giving 315 recipes for soups, meat, fish, sauces and desserts, he extends the tradition with detailed instructions for banquets and dinner parties, including how to incorporate entertainment such as music, dancing and theatricals into the meal and which wines to serve. Most interesting is the full menu of what surely must have been a banquet of immense proportions given in honor of the Duke of Ferrara by his son. Over 100 different dishes were served to a mere 104 people!

Meat-carvers in Renaissance times were highly honored in the courts. Another meat-carver in service to the nobility who left posterity a valuable book was the Florentine Domenico Romoli. *La Singolar Dottrina (The Particular Doctrine)*, published in 1560, is unique in the tradition of cookery books up to this time for the personal style in which it is written. He presents all the, by now, standard material but in a more conversational tone, introducing comments and criticisms often with typical Tuscan irony in a way that reveals his own taste and personality. He himself was known as "*Panunto*" ("Oilybread"), not without equal irony, maybe because he was inordinately fond of that still-popular Tuscan dish. He gives several recipes for variations of it. One, topped with slices of sweet pork sausage, he concludes with the following advice: "When you eat the part without meat, let it touch the top of your tongue and palate so that you can taste the flavor of the oiled bread."

The most celebrated cookbook of the sixteenth century is certainly the *Opera (Work)*, published in 1570, and written by Bartolomeo Scappi, who was probably from Bologna and worked as personal cook to Pope Pius V. It is still the most comprehensive work of its kind, remarkable not only for its more detailed analysis of the traditional subject matter but also for introducing new material. He records over a thousand recipes and was the first Italian

cooking writer to give instructions for using cheese, for making puff pastry, and for decorating cakes with a pastry tube. He even gives a recipe for preparing a rich pie that, he says, the Neapolitans call "pizza" — an enduring tradition that is in daily use all over the world today. The *Opera* is, in addition, the first cookbook to contain engraved copper plates illustrating not only the design of the kitchen and related workrooms but also the knives, spoons, pans and casseroles used in that period.

During the next two centuries the incomparable art and craft of Renaissance Italian cooking spread to the rest of Europe and returned to its native land influenced by the culinary traditions of these other countries. Most of the cookbooks of this later period have a decidedly French flavor. One Italian writer of the seventeenth century, however, remained true to his native culinary heritage and introduced a new concern for cookbooks — the food budget of a middle-class family. Although Bartolomeo Stefani was court chef to the Gonzaga of Mantua, the second edition of his book *L'Arte di Ben Cucinare (The Art of Good Cooking)* added a "note to the readers," in which he gives the cost of "ordinary food for eight people." His shopping list includes meat, pasta, cheese, eggs, pork fat, lard, ricotta, bread, salad, pepper, raisins and vinegar. It all added up to 6.19 lire in the currency of Mantua but, as he comments, when it comes to the cost of things, all the world is a village.

A new era in Italian cookbook writing was inaugurated in 1891, with the publication of Pellegrino Artusi's classic book, *La Scienza in Cucina e l'Arte di Mangiar Bene (The*

*The works of mercy; giving drink to the thirsty and food to the hungry*, school of Domenico Ghirlandaio (1449–94), fresco; CHURCH OF SAN MARTINO DEI BUONOMINI, FLORENCE This fresco would have been painted by pupils of Ghirlandaio under the master's supervision. One of his most famous pupils was Michelangelo.

*Science of Cooking and the Art of Eating Well).* As its subtitle indicates, it is a "practical manual for families," dealing with "hygiene, economy and good taste." In this work the grand culinary tradition of the past is certainly felt, but for the first time it has been reinterpreted for the present. Artusi, who was from Emilia-Romagna and lived in Florence, was not a professional cook himself but a gourmet with a passion for collecting recipes, which he tried out at home with the help of his faithful family cook, Marietta. He was a modern man in this sense, also. He prefaces most of the 790 recipes with introductory notes that are full of helpful hints as well as regional customs and humorous asides. *Artusi,* as the book soon came to be called, has been indispensable to generations of Italian home cooks, newlyweds and dilettantes in the kitchen.

In the end, however, the most vital contribution of all to the heritage of Italian cooking has come from the Italian people themselves, as household cooks and as consumers, in the marketplace as much as at the table. In the kitchens of country peasants and working-class families, resourcefulness and imagination have produced dishes that are classics of a simple, uncomplicated style of cooking. And in the houses of the aristocratic and import-

*Thirty-eight varieties of grape,* Bartolomeo Bimbi (1648–1725), fresco;
PITTI PALACE, FLORENCE
This painting is from the collection in the Pitti Palace, which belonged to the de' Medici family in the sixteenth century and was the repository of many of the de' Medici art treasures.

*Still life with musical instruments*,
Cristoforo Munari (1667–1720); UFFIZI
GALLERY, FLORENCE

ant merchant families of Italy — those who enjoyed the financial means, the leisure and the possibilities of travel that enabled them to devote considerable time to the pleasures of the table — cooks developed a cuisine that was diversified and refined, less local in character but nonetheless authentically Italian.

Italian taste in food has, thus, evolved over the centuries, from the elaborate banquets of Roman, Renaissance and Baroque periods to the lighter, simpler meals of today. In all this what has been constant is a taste for fresh, high-quality ingredients, prepared in ways that highlight the natural flavors. And a question of taste is what it finally comes down to: *de gustibus, non est disputandum* ("there is no disputing about tastes"). Or as Cicero, the Roman orator, remarked about taste: *cuicumque suum* ("each to their own"). Nevertheless, the art of Italian cooking is just another aspect of the art of living. Happily, there is a universal element in Italian cooking, as there is with all true art — a universality attested to by the widespread appeal this heritage enjoys throughout the world today.

*The wedding feast at Cana* (detail of guests), Paolo Caliari, known as Veronese (1528–88); LOUVRE, PARIS   Paolo Caliari is best known as a Venetian painter but was actually b

in Verona, hence his sobriquet "Veronese."

# MENU

Piroscafo REGINA MARGHERITA

## 19 MAGGIO 1900

## PRANZO

Riso con purè di piselli

Antipasto assortito

Costolettine alla Ville-roi

Manzo alla Godard

Carciofi alla Spagnuola

Pernici arrosto

INSALATA

TORTA CONVERSAZIONE

Vino Corvo

Formaggio Frutta

Caffè

# MENUS

Italian people know instinctively how to compose a perfectly balanced meal. This innate ability to bring together foods that complement each other comes from cultural patterns that are centuries' old. The art of combining dishes harmoniously to form a meal is known as the "menu."

For every genuine Italian meal there exists a menu, though it is often unwritten. The menu should not be confused with the *lista* (or bill of fare) handed to you in restaurants, which is merely the listing of the day's available dishes.

Visitors to Italy, when dining out, particularly in the small, rustic family-style *trattoria* (restaurant) would do well to take the waiter's advice (if it is offered) on the menu. The waiter well understands the subtleties of flavors; hence, it is not uncommon for a well-meaning waiter to let you know if you have made a bad decision!

The menu, understood not as a list of dishes but as the delicate combination in which they should be served, was given its first written rationale in the late fifteenth century by Bartolomeo Sacchi, better known as Platina, in his classic treatise, *De Honesta Voluptate ac Valetudine (Concerning Honest Pleasure and Well-being)*. A Renaissance humanist, he was as interested in questions of health and general well-being as in recipes and techniques of cooking. Platina counseled that the meal be introduced with light, delicate dishes such as salads, raw greens dressed with olive oil and vinegar, cooked vegetables, fruit, eggs and, according to the taste of the times, sweets. Soups, Platina suggested, should follow this, in order to ready the palate for boiled and roast meats. Cheeses, more sweets and confections should conclude the feast.

By the close of the Renaissance the menu had become more varied. By the seventeenth and eighteenth centuries it had burgeoned into a series of *servizi* ("services" or "courses"), each consisting of several dishes. An opulent eighteenth-century menu put together by an anonymous chef from Piedmont listed five services. Each service boasted at least six different dishes — for dessert there were eight — making a total of thirty-two dishes for a mere eight guests. Fortunately for the hostess there were seven waiters in attendance but whether the guests actually ate all the courses is a matter for speculation! The first service included four *antipasti* and two soups, with a beef dish served in between. The second service comprised six meat and poultry dishes, and the third, four roasts and two salads. The epicures were then allowed an interlude (*trasmesso*) before the fourth service. This consisted of vegetable fritters and six little molds and tarts to ready the palate for the last service, a sweet one. As a delicious conclusion to their meal, for the fifth service the guests sampled four compotes, and a platter of fresh fruit, followed by four ice-creams.

Menu served on board the *SS Regina Margherita* on May 19, 1900, for the Florio-Rubattino Society and the General Steamship Company of Italy
The menu consisted of: rice with pea purée, assorted *antipasti*, crumbed baby cutlets, beef alla Godard, roast partridge, green salad, "conversation" cake, Corvo wine, cheese and fruit, and coffee.

Menu served at the Franco-Italian banquet
held in honor of the Italian royal family's
visit to Paris on October 14, 1903 (colored
lithograph); BERTARELLI PRINT COLLECTION, MILAN
The banquet included: Renaissance
consommé and garnished salmon with
French–Italian sauce.

Although this undoubtedly is an example of a courtly menu, there was a tradition of
serving six courses which was honoured in upper-class homes up until the Second World
War, despite a growing disapproval of ostentation throughout the country from the end of
the eighteenth century. Pragmatism finally prevailed after the war and the elaborate *servizi*
of the past were reduced to one dish. Today, on special occasions, however, such as
weddings and banquets, a main course of meat will be prepared in three different ways:
braised, roasted and boiled, and the custom of including a *piatto di mezzo* (or interlude)
in the form of a vegetable mold or savory pie between the first and second courses has
been retained. A rather delightful custom to commemorate festive occasions is the tradition
of transcribing elaborate menus onto decorative cards for each guest at the table. Besides
acting as records of the history of gastronomy, these cards are often of considerable artistic
merit. It is somewhat unfortunate that the food took precedence over the artist. Sadly, in
a book on old Italian menus none of the designers is identified. Who knows who they may
have been or become?

Whether viewed as a tantalizing historical document or as social observation, the
menu should be interpreted according to three factors: *which* Italians are eating, *where* in
Italy and *when*. The first is a social class distinction. Culture and tradition followed economic and class lines. The wealthy may have indulged in extravagant feasts but standard
fare for the peasant or working class would have consisted of just one dish: in the South,
for example, spaghetti seasoned with tomato sauce or olive oil; in the North, polenta or
rice, accompanied by brown bread. The second is a geographical factor: each of the twenty-
three regions in Italy retains its own culinary distinctions. The last factor is a historical
consideration. The eating habits of Italians have evolved over the centuries and are still
evolving, having undergone significant changes since the Second World War. Any state-
ments about Italian eating habits and traditions must be qualified by these three basic
distinctions. To take an obvious example, dried pasta such as spaghetti, which today
appears on practically every menu, was eaten mostly in southern Italy up until the middle
of this century and usually only at the midday meal. Fresh pasta such as lasagne, which
today evokes images of home-made/family cooking, was enjoyed during the Renaissance
period only by the wealthy, leisured classes.

Today, a typical Italian meal will consist of three courses, although this is changing
in the larger cities, where it is no longer practical to return home in the middle of the day.
For the first course (*il primo*) pasta, soup or, in the North, perhaps a risotto will be served.
The second course (*il secondo*) will consist of meat and, more rarely, fish — particularly
on Fridays, the traditional abstinence day in Catholic countries (the custom lives on at the
table even though the Church has changed its law). For fish meals, dishes using *baccalà*
or *stoccafisso*, types of dried cod, are popular at family meals, particularly in the northern
region. The much-prized vegetable dish on the menu is known as *il contorno*, from the
Italian word meaning "to surround", as vegetables are traditionally served on the platter
surrounding the main course. Classical accompaniments are observed: small potatoes with
roast chicken and lamb, and white beans with pork. A crunchy green or mixed salad
served separately might take the place of a cooked vegetable. (Pasta is never served
together with a second course. Even at the family table the plate is always changed.) The
restorative final course will consist of a piece of local cheese or seasonal fresh fruit.

The palatable *antipasti* and the desserts are reserved for Sundays, feast days or for

*Dinner at Posillipo*, Giuseppe de Nittis (1846–84); GALLERY OF MODERN ART, MILAN De Nittis was a proponent of the *plein-air* style of landscape painting. Associated with the *Macchiaioli* group of Italian painters, he also exhibited with the French Impressionists in Paris.

special meals with guests. On these occasions the guests will relish a small vegetable mold or a fresh seafood salad served in a goblet. Platters of Italy's famous cured meats, salami and prosciutto, are more readily found in restaurants than with fine home cooking. The dessert will be wonderful fresh fruit. These days desserts for special occasions are likely to be bought from the local *pasticceria* (pastry shop), even though there is a fine Italian repertoire of simple and delicious home-made desserts.

Traditionally even a lighter meal, the daily evening meal consists of three courses. For example, instead of *pastasciutta* (pasta served with a sauce), for the first course *pastina in brodo* (a thin soup made with a meat broth and tiny pasta shapes added at the end of cooking), might be served. This would be followed by a slice or two of meat with a green salad or maybe just a *frittata* (an Italian omelet). A most civilized way of ending the day would be with cheese and fruit.

But perhaps the most important ingredient on the Italian menu is something that does not come from the kitchen and yet enriches the entire meal. This is the great Italian tradition, handed down through the centuries and still very much alive, of creating a festive and joyous occasion out of eating together. Until relatively recently businesses and schools closed down at midday and the entire family gathered for the main meal of the day, which the mother had spent most of the morning preparing. A glass of wine greatly enhanced the occasion. Now, despite the incursions of contemporary life, eating with family and friends remains the high point of the day. Conviviality at the table and the shared pleasure of good food and good company must be counted as one of the most enriching aspects of the heritage of Italian cooking.

*Still life*, Jacopo Chimenti, known as l'Empoli (1551–1640); MOLINARI PRADELLI COLLECTION, BOLOGNA  Empoli's paintings are rather rare: here are portrayed all the typical *antipasta*

foods — salami, prosciutto, *zampone*, eggs, seafood and vegetables.

# ANTIPASTI

One of Italy's most delightful cultural traditions is *antipasto*. The renowned English food writer Elizabeth David wrote in 1954, "Among Italian *antipasti* are to be found some of the most successful culinary achievements in European cooking." The dishes, with their blend of delicate flavors, serve to entice the appetite before the main course. The precursor to the French hors d'oeuvre, the word *antipasto* literally means "before the meal."

The rich heritage of *antipasto* probably had its origin in the Renaissance, when it was customary to begin and end a banquet with a series of cold dishes seasoned with both sweet and savory sauces, served on a sideboard. These dishes were known as *servizi di credenza* (side dishes), and *servizi di cucina* (hot dishes from the kitchen) were served between the *antipasti* delicacies.

The great sixteenth-century cook to the popes and remarkable writer on gastronomy, Bartolomeo Scappi, is thought to have introduced *antipasti* to the rest of the world in 1570 in the First Book of his celebrated *Opera*. Based on the work of the ancient Roman authors, Scappi's book nevertheless chided Romans on their excesses and suggested that meals should begin with fresh fruit to cleanse the palate. Today many of the cured meat dishes are accompanied by dried and fresh fruits. In the Fourth Book of the *Opera*, Scappi lists twenty-four dishes for the *primo servizio di credenza* (first course of side dishes) which were served at a banquet luncheon to stimulate the guests' appetite for the over one hundred dishes yet to come. Handed down over five hundred years, the legacy of Scappi's work remains intact. Many of his appetizers, such as fresh, filleted anchovies marinated in olive oil and vinegar, and dried roe of tuna fish dressed with olive oil and lemon juice, are still popular throughout Italy and the rest of the world.

In ostentatious Roman times, food was often presented at banquets in a spectacular fashion. Peacock or pheasant pâté would be displayed with the full glorious plumage of the bird carefully replaced after cooking. According to the taste of the sixteenth century, Scappi included sweet as well as savory *antipasti* in his *primo servizio di credenza offelle*, such as cookies containing jam, and *pinocchiata* (sweets made with eggwhites, sugar and pine nuts). Sadly, no further details of Scappi's banquets remain, other than a list of the dishes.

In Italy today, reminiscent of the elaborate Renaissance banquets, many restaurants, especially in Rome, adhere to the tradition of a sumptuous table of *antipasti* at the entrance or in the center of the dining room. To view and sample the colorful platters laden with an exquisite combination of flavors is a truly satisfying way to begin a fine meal. Some

*Still life*, (*circa* 1687), Giovanni Paolo Spadino (seventeenth century); PINACOTECA CAPITOLINA, ROME
The delicate flavors of cantaloupe and prosciutto are combined to form an *antipasto* that dates back to Renaissance times.

*Still life with eggs and game*, Roman fresco; NATIONAL ARCHEOLOGICAL MUSEUM, NAPLES Hardboiled eggs and cured meats form the traditional *antipasto* served for Easter Sunday lunch.

establishments deliver a selection of their special *antipasti* to the table while the diner is still mulling over the *lista* (menu of the day) and deciding what to order.

For the most part *antipasti* have remained restaurant and banquet food, and they are served at the family table only for special occasions, festive meals and feast-day celebrations. On these occasions the classical dishes dating from the sixteenth century may be served but with more elegant preparation and presentation. Recent trends towards lighter meals have brought *antipasti* into their own — traditional *antipasti* recipes are ideal as a main course for a light summer luncheon or a cold supper.

There are three main categories of traditional *antipasti: affettati*, delicious sliced cured meats; *antipasto misto*, a great variety of mixed dishes, often without meat; and *antipasto misto mare*, consisting of all kinds of seafood recipes using small fish and shellfish. *Affettati* are popular in the northern and central region restaurants of Italy where the tradition of curing meat — particularly pork (prosciutto) and, more rarely, beef (*bresaola*) — goes back to Roman times.

Salt was originally used for curing meat when the Romans found themselves with a surplus. Later honey, dried fruit and spices were added to make the meat more palatable. *Prosciutto di Parma* from the town of Parma in Emilia-Romagna, and *prosciutto di San Daniele* from San Daniele in Friuli, are considered the most delicious hams in the world. Served with melon or figs they are a wonderful way to begin a meal. They are produced by the judicious salting and air-curing of the pig's hind thigh in special rooms for at least nine months. The sweet prosciutto from these regions has a pinkish-red color and a delicate aroma. Also excellent are the prosciutti from Tuscany and Umbria which are more salty and often rubbed with a garlic and pepper mixture before curing.

Little has changed in the serving of *affettati*. The cured meats are served today as they have been since the Renaissance banquets. In fine restaurants the prosciutto is sliced by hand and then laid across slices of melon. For this dish, known as *prosciutto e melone*, the cantaloupe variety of melon (first cultivated in the papal garden of Cantalupo near Rome) is preferred. The delectable *prosciutto e fichi* is served with ripe, peeled figs. *Bresaola*, with its well-defined, intense flavor is served by itself, thinly sliced with a dribbling of fine, extra virgin olive oil, a squeeze of lemon juice, and ground black pepper.

The most common *antipasti*, however, are the endless varieties of regional salami, made from coarsely or finely ground pork and flavored variously with salt, pepper corns, white wine and chile peppers. Some are eaten fresh while others are matured. Tuscany and Umbria are prodigious producers of these meats. *Finocchiona* is a large pork sausage flavored with wild fennel; *coppa* is made from the boned shoulder of a pig and seasoned with nutmeg; marbled *sopressata* is a headcheese (brawn), and is a specialty of Siena.

Renaissance cooks found an elegant way of enhancing cold meats by presenting them in aspic. Jelly was made by boiling calf's and pig's feet, and was sometimes enriched by adding other porcine parts such as the ears, jowl and snout. The process was laborious but those wishing to make an attractive *antipasto* at home today can use powdered gelatin.

*Chinese bowl with figs, bird and cherries,*
Giovanna Garzoni (1600–70);
PITTI GALLERY, FLORENCE

Many of the classic *antipasti misti* came from humble origins and were testament to the triumph of style over poverty. Thrifty cooks devised ingenious and delicious ways for using every scrap of leftover food. Even further back in time, servants combined dishes from the remnants of their masters' opulent banquets. These peasant dishes now grace the most elegant tables and please the most refined palate. *Bruschetta* is made by broiling (grilling) a thick slice of country bread, rubbing it with a clove of garlic and dousing it with extra virgin olive oil. In Tuscany, where olive oil is almost sacred, this dish is called *fettunta* (literally an "anointed" slice of bread). Add fresh tomatoes mashed with a fork and you have a delicious light lunch. Another wonderful Tuscan *antipasto* with bread as a base is *crostini*. These "little toasts" are spread with a chicken-liver pâté or sautéed fresh *porcini* mushrooms. *Pizzette* (miniature pizzas) are also made with bread and are inspired by a popular culinary tradition of the South. These can be made by deep-frying bite-sized pieces of bread dough or, more simply, by placing little disks of buttered bread dressed *alla Napoletana* under the broiler (griller) with tomato, mozzarella, anchovy and seasoned with oregano. Polenta (boiled cornmeal), which was often used as a substitute for bread in the North of Italy, Lombardy and the Veneto, can be sliced when cold, broiled (grilled) and used as a base for an unusual *antipasto*, topped with a dab of fresh tomato sauce or a savory spread. The Roman soldier roasting his ration of wheat on his campfire to make

*The man of Artimino*, Giovanna Garzoni (1600–70); PITTI GALLERY, FLORENCE

polenta would, no doubt, have been interested to hear of the many ways his staple diet would be used in the future.

The innumerable dishes of the *antipasti misti* contain unexpected and delightful treats for the palate. Most *antipasti* are composed of vegetables, the cornerstone of Italian cooking, using all the colorful classics of the Italian garden. The artichoke (which originally grew wild in Sicily), bell peppers (capsicums), eggplant (aubergine), zucchini (courgettes) and tomatoes are all combined and treated with respect on the *antipasti misti* platter. Slices of fresh, crunchy greens are served raw in *pinzimonio* (the name for the sauce of olive oil), salt and pepper into which they are dipped. The bright, decorative *peperoni* (bell pepper) is a colorful jewel on the traditional *antipasto* table, with the lovely yellows, reds and greens of the sweet peppers, broiled (grilled) or stuffed, adding to the visual treat. Since no bell pepper recipes can be found in cookbooks before the twentieth century, it can be inferred that they were viewed as a rustic vegetable not considered suitable for the refined recipes of the Renaissance or even the nineteenth-century chef. These days the once-snubbed "peasant" vegetable is in evidence everywhere. Peppers are delicious broiled (grilled), peeled and seasoned with olive oil, salt, anchovy and parsley. An ingenious way of using up leftovers from "poor" cuisine and an elaboration of the "rich" cuisine is *ripieni* (stuffed peppers). They are first roasted directly over a flame, then peeled and filled with all manner of ingredients. Sausage meat is a particular favorite. For a different presentation, slices can be spread with a filling, rolled and served sprinkled with parsley.

*Fava* (broad beans) are delicious eaten raw before a meal. In Lazio a handful of fresh broad beans with a chunk of the sharp, local cheese, *pecorino Romano*, washed down with copious glasses of cool Frascati wine is a wonderful way to stimulate the appetite. On May Day, when these beans are in full season, Romans can be seen sitting at tables outside the taverns in the old neighborhood of Trastevere, up to their ankles in pods, celebrating the traditional workers' holiday. A more stylish variation of this popular dish is to serve these raw beans with shavings of fine Parmesan cheese, lightly dressed with olive oil and lemon juice.

Dating from the Etruscans, cheese is a long-honored traditional appetizer. On his menu for a mid-sixteenth-century banquet, Bartolomeo Scappi included *fior di latte*, a mozzarella-like cheese made from cow's milk. Sprinkled with sugar it was served along with the numerous other cold dishes that began the banquet. *Fior di latte* is still served in southern Italy where it comes fashioned in a decorative braid. A famous and effective dish combines slices of fresh tomatoes and mozzarella, dressed with olive oil and garnished with fresh basil leaves. *Torte di formaggio* (cheese "cakes"), a handsome and appetizing way to serve cheese by layering compatible cheeses with herbs and nuts, are popular items available at fine delicatessens.

*Antipasto misto mare* is Italian *antipasti* at their best. Fish restaurants in Italy provide a marvelous and remarkable array of seafood. Heaped high on the platter the guest will find baby clams, periwinkles, mussels (fresh, breaded or baked), sweet, succulent scallops with olive oil, garlic and parsley, and tiny juicy shrimps (prawns), marinated with olive oil and lemon. These can all be combined to make the delectable *insalata di frutti di mare* (shellfish salad). If the choice was just one from the wealth of Italian appetizers, this delicious seafood salad, beautifully presented in luscious tomato or aromatic orange cups, would do the most honor to the table.

*The cheese-seller*, Giuseppe Maria Mitelli (1634–1718); NATIONAL LIBRARY, FLORENCE "Come taste my excellent cheese, Try it with sweets or with drinks, Use it to season your dishes, The cheese from Piacenza will fulfil all your wishes."

*Laid table* (detail), Carlo Magini (1720–1806);
SANGALLI COLLECTION, BERGAMO

# LARGE HARDBOILED EGGS

*Uova sode grosse*

This recipe is taken from Vincenzo Tanara's *L'Economia del Cittadino in Villa* (*Economy in the City Home*), published in Venice by Tramontin in 1687. The dish was included in a rather elegant banquet mainly because of its spectacular appearance. The preparation of these banquets required considerable expertise. In general, women were never asked to prepare them as they were considered insolent witches, and it was said that even the dirtiest man was better than the cleanest of women! Such was the consideration given to females.

The modern recipe, needless to say, is simpler than the old one, but is equally suitable for an important dinner. To make it you will need six small ovenproof dishes or custard cups about 2 inches (5 cm) in diameter.

An egg as big as the head of a man may be made in this manner. Separate the yolks from the whites of twenty-five eggs, and beat the yolks well with a whisk, one at a time. The well-beaten yolks are put into a pig's bladder; the bladder is sealed and immersed in a boiler full of boiling water until the yolks are quite firm. This great hardboiled yolk is then removed from the bladder and placed in another much larger one, which already contains the stiffly beaten whites of the eggs, and this is then sealed, taking care that the yolk is well covered by the whites. The bladder is tied up with string and dangled in the boiling water until the eggwhite hardens; then this last bladder is also removed, leaving a huge hardboiled egg.

*¼ cup (2 oz/60 g) butter, at room temperature*
*6 eggs*
*salt and freshly ground pepper*
*juice of ½ lemon*

Butter 6 small ovenproof dishes. Separate the eggs, placing an egg yolk in the center of each dish.

Season with salt and pepper. Work the remaining butter and the lemon juice together; and put a small piece of butter on each yolk.

Beat the eggwhites until stiff peaks form. Using a pastry bag fitted with a fluted tip, pipe the eggwhite around each yolk to encircle it. Put the dishes under the broiler (griller) — but not too close to it — and cook for approximately 5 minutes, until the eggwhite becomes firm and lightly colored. Serve.

*Large hardboiled eggs — modern recipe*

*Creamy stuffed eggs*

# CREAMY STUFFED EGGS

*Uova sode alla crema*

**H**ardboiled eggs were served as hors d'oeuvre at dinners in the fifteenth century, and often appear in cookbooks from that time. One such recipe is to be found in a work by Bartolomeo Platina called *De Honesta Voluptate ac Valetudine* (*Concerning Honest Pleasure and Well-being*). Unlike the following recipe, Platina's concoction was heavy and elaborate — so much so that at the end of his description he wrote: "these do more harm than good!"

*3 oz (90 g) ricotta*
*6 hardboiled eggs*
*2 tablespoons (1 oz/30 g) butter, softened*
*¼ cup (2 fl oz/ 60 ml) mayonnaise*
*a few chives, chopped*

Push the ricotta through a sieve. Halve the eggs lengthwise; remove the yolks. Push the yolks through a sieve.

In a bowl, cream the butter. Add the yolks, ricotta and mayonnaise and mix well. Using a pastry bag, pipe the filling mixture into the hollows of the eggwhites.

Garnish with the chives and serve.

33

*Piazza delle Erbe in Verona*, Angelo dall' Oca Bianca
(1858–1942); GALLERY OF MODERN ART, GENOA

# OX HEAD IN A CAP

*Testa di bue rivestita*

This is a dish recommended for *primo servizio* (first course). In the Renaissance these foods, which are the equivalent of our hors d'oeuvre, consisted of little savories such as fried ravioli, miniature *focacce*, small roasted animals or birds (often served with fur or feathers intact), hams and salamis. This recipe was discovered by Clotilde Vesco who was a keen scholar of Renaissance gastronomy. She found it in a volume in the Riccardiana Library in Florence, and later published it in a book written by her for Maria Pacini Fazzi in Lucca. As always, the ingredients given in the recipe are deliberately vague because it was assumed readers would be well versed in culinary matters. Animals' heads were considered a delicacy, as they still are, and lambs' heads were especially popular. The modern recipe is a specialty of Lombardy and today it is still served in all the typical Milanese restaurants. The Cibreo Restaurant in Florence also prepares a particularly delicate and flavorsome version.

> If you want to make ox-head in a cap for thirty people, you must have everything and all the *battuti* [chopped herbs and vegetables] incorporating all the flavors which this dish has always had, and wrap it in a pig's caul tinted yellow with saffron and tie it with string so that it will not break. Put it on a grate over the coals and turn it often until it is well cooked on all sides. This dish must be carried intact to the table, and placed in the center of the table to be cut.

*1 calf's head, about 3 lb (1.5 kg)*
*1 tablespoon vinegar*
*salt*
*2 medium sweet onions*
*1 whole clove*
*2 bay leaves*
*1 tablespoon fresh thyme leaves*
*2 tablespoons all purpose (plain) flour*
*⅓ cup (3 fl oz/90 ml) extra virgin olive oil*
*juice of 1 lemon*
*freshly ground pepper*
*10 oz (300 g) borlotti beans, boiled until tender*
*1 tablespoon chopped parsley*

Put the calf's head in a bowl and rinse under a thin stream of cold running water for a few hours. Bring a large pan of water to a boil. Submerge the head and cook for about 10 minutes; drain. Again, fill the saucepan with water. Add the vinegar and a little salt and immerse the head once more. Halve an onion and add the onion halves, the clove, bay leaves and thyme. Sprinkle the flour over the surface of the water and bring it to a boil. Cook over low heat for about 2 hours. Drain the head and carefully remove the bones.

Cut the meat into thin strips about ¼ inch (0.5 cm) long and put them in a salad bowl. Whisk together the oil, lemon juice and salt and pepper to taste. Pour the dressing over the warm meat and toss well. Allow to cool. Slice the second onion very finely. Add the onion, beans, and parsley to the meat. Mix together gently and serve.

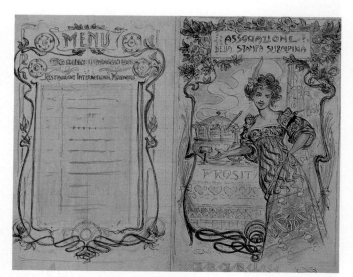

Printing proof of a 1902 menu for the Subalpine Press Association at the Molinari Restaurant in Turin (colored lithograph); BERTARELLI PRINT COLLECTION, MILAN
The Italian menu is not a list of the day's dishes, but the delicate art of combining various courses to form a harmonious meal.

*Ox head in a cap — modern recipe*

*Ham rolls (left) Little tomato pizzas (right)*

# HAM ROLLS

*Involtini di prosciutto*

The original version of this recipe includes a highly elaborate description of gelatin. In the cookery book of fifteenth-century Maestro Martino da Como, personal cook to the Patriarch of Aquileia, there is a recipe for making gelatin from pigs' trotters and snouts, which also describes its uses as an embellishment and flavor enhancer. Today things are simpler and excellent results can be obtained using granulated gelatin, or gelatin sheets.

*6 slices cooked lean ham*
*6 oz (180 g) liver pâté*
*1 cube (1 tablespoon/1 envelope) instant (powdered) unflavored gelatin*
*2 cups (16 fl oz/500 ml) clear beef stock*

Cut the ham slices into 2 inch by 4 inch (5 cm by 10 cm) rectangles. Mince the leftovers almost to a pulp; mix them into the liver pâté. Dissolve the gelatin into the stock; set aside to cool to room temperature (but do not refrigerate). Reserving ½ cup (4 fl oz/120 ml), pour the remaining stock into a wide shallow pan; refrigerate until set solid.

Spread the liver pâté on the ham slices and gently roll up each slice. Arrange the rolls on a serving plate and pour a thin layer of the reserved gelatin over and around them.

Chop the chilled gelatin into small pieces. Scatter between ham rolls and serve.

# LITTLE TOMATO PIZZAS

*Pizzette al pomodoro*

This is a modern version of *pizzelle*, the tiny Neapolitan pizzas of the old days which were fried in very hot oil and served with tomato or salted ricotta. These little pizzas, with their lighter ingredients and quick and easy preparation, are an excellent choice for today's busy cooks. They are delicious served with cocktails, or as a hot *antipasto* before dinner with a glass of chilled white wine.

*6 large slices bread*
*2 tablespoons extra virgin olive oil*
*6 oz (180 g) mozzarella, thinly sliced*
*6 ripe plum (egg) tomatoes, sliced*
*3 anchovy fillets packed in oil, cut into small pieces*
*1 teaspoon dried oregano*
*salt and freshly ground pepper*

Using a 3 inch (8 cm) round pastry cutter, cut a circle from each slice of bread. Brush on one side of each round only with half the oil. On each circle arrange a layer of cheese, a layer of tomato and a few pieces of anchovy. Sprinkle with oregano, and season with salt and pepper. Drizzle with the remaining oil. Place the pizzas on a lightly oiled baking sheet.

Bake in a preheated 400°F (200°C) oven for about 10 minutes or until the cheese melts. Serve very hot.

# SAUSAGE-STUFFED PEPPERS

*Peperoni ripieni alla salsiccia*

**B**ell peppers (capsicums) are found all over Italy from Piedmont to Calabria. Combined with sausage they make an appetizer which is homely, but at the same time so tasty that it would not be out of place even on the most refined table. Bell peppers came to Italy from Mexico after the discovery of America by Christopher Columbus in 1492, but they did not come into use in the kitchen until the seventeenth century.

*3 green bell peppers (capsicums)*
*2 tablespoons extra virgin olive oil*
*1 cup (2 oz/60 g) coarse, fresh breadcrumbs*
*1 cup (8 fl oz/250 ml) milk*
*6 oz (180 g) sweet Italian sausage, skinned*
*1 egg*
*salt and freshly ground pepper*
*1 tablespoon fine, dry breadcrumbs*

Wash and dry the bell peppers. Halve them lengthwise and remove the cores and seeds. Cook them in the oven at 400°F (200°C) for 10 minutes on a baking sheet which has been brushed with a little of the oil. Remove from the oven and allow to cool.

Soak the coarse breadcrumbs in the milk and squeeze out. Mix the sausage meat with the bread. Add the egg, season with salt and pepper and mix well.

Stuff the peppers with the mixture. Drizzle with the remaining oil, and sprinkle with the fine breadcrumbs. Bake in a preheated 400°F (200°C) oven for 20 minutes then serve.

*Bell pepper rolls*

# BELL PEPPER ROLLS

*Involtini di peperoni*

**T**hese wonderfully appetizing and colorful rolls are a traditional *antipasto* dish of southern Italy. In Italy they are best known as the most popular snack of a well-known restaurant on the magnificent island of Ischia, near Naples, where they are always available. In olden times the peppers were served halved rather than rolled up.

*6 large bell peppers (capsicums) (2 each of red,*
  *green and yellow)*
*salt and freshly ground pepper*
*½ cup (1 oz/30 g) coarse fresh breadcrumbs*
*⅓ cup (3 fl oz/90 ml) white wine vinegar*
*3 oz (90 g) olive paste*
*2 cloves garlic, minced*
*⅓ cup (3 fl oz/90 ml) extra virgin olive oil*
*1½ tablespoons chopped parsley*
*anchovy fillets packed in oil, for garnish (optional)*

Wash and dry the bell peppers. Bake them in a preheated 350°F (180°C) oven for 30 minutes, turning them carefully about 4 times, until easily pierced with a fork. Rub them one by one with a teatowel to remove the skin; cut each pepper in half and remove the seeds and ribs. Cut the peppers into 1¼ inch (3 cm) strips; sprinkle with a pinch of salt and pepper.

Soak the bread in the vinegar; squeeze it to remove excess vinegar. In a bowl, combine the bread, olive paste and garlic, until a thick cream forms. Mix in 2 tablespoons of the oil. Spread the mixture on the pepper strips and roll them up. Arrange the rolls on a serving dish and drizzle the remaining oil over them. Sprinkle with the parsley. If desired, garnish with anchovy fillets before serving.

*Sausage-stuffed peppers*

*The peasant family at table*, Giandomenico Tiepolo (1727–1804); VILLA VALMARANA, VICENZA   Tiepolo generally painted in the style of his more famous father, but had a taste for

genre scenes (such as this one), many of which are to be found in the guest rooms of the Villa Valmarana.

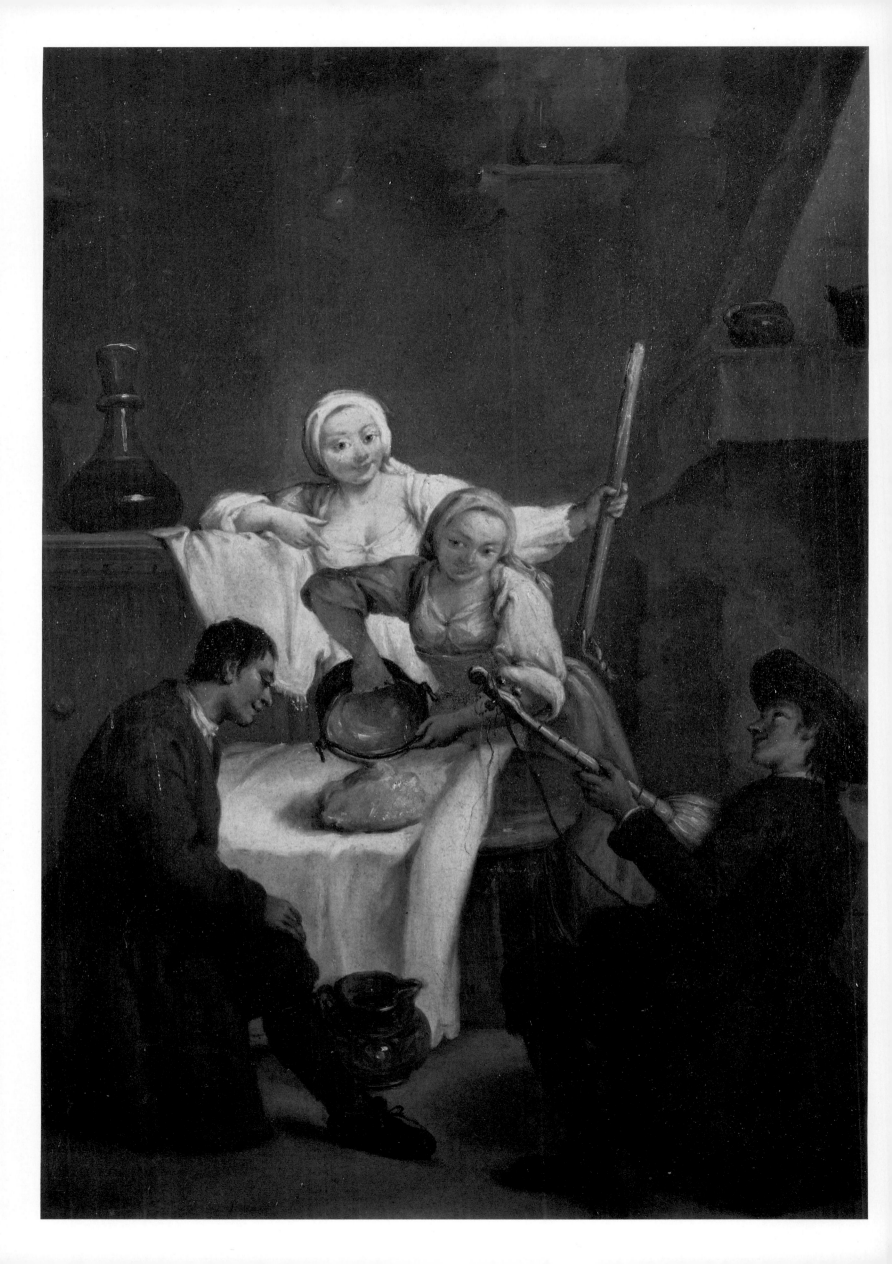

# PASTA, SOUPS, GNOCCHI, POLENTA AND RICE

If there is a national food of Italy, pasta is it. For an Italian no other food is so worthy of love and care: it nourishes, sustains, brings happiness and satisfaction. Throughout Italy's long and sometimes turbulent history pasta has remained the people's dish: economical, healthy and versatile — a simple, everyday food.

Pasta has been associated with the peoples of the Italian peninsula since time immemorial. It is one of those archetypal foods, like bread and beans, that seems to have been part of the gastronomic traditions of both Eastern and Western civilizations since before recorded history. Nowadays it is featured daily in countless ways from Alpine hamlets in the North to fishing villages on the southernmost tip of the Mediterranean coast. It crosses all boundaries and appears as frequently on the tables of country peasants as it does on the menus of elegant restaurants. Of the several types of dishes eaten as a first course, pasta is pre-eminent.

So great is the Italian passion for pasta that it is not surprising to find that pasta has even played its part in politics and revolutionary thought. The Futurists, who so delighted in attacking tradition in all its forms, saw the national predilection for pasta as an ideal target for one of their broadsides. The poet, Marinetti, who was one of the founders of Futurism, issued his manifesto *La Cucina Futurista (Futurist Cooking)* in 1932, in which he ridiculed pasta as "the absurd Italian gastronomic religion" and called for its "annihilation." His compatriots, however, seem not to have heeded his words and, instead, have continued to consume pasta in ever increasing quantities — so much so, in fact, that today the average Italian consumes more than fifty pounds (twenty-five kilograms) of pasta a year.

The word *pasta* simply means "dough" but can also refer to "pastry", as in *pasta sfoglia* (puff pastry) and *pasta frolla* (shortcrust pastry). As a single word, however, *pasta* signifies the paste — made from flour, water and salt, sometimes with eggs added — which is cut into various shapes of noodles, each one being known by a particular name, such as macaroni or *tagliatelle* or fettucine, and so on.

Pasta appears to have been a staple on the Italian peninsula at least several centuries before the Christian era. On the stucco reliefs of a fourth century BC Etruscan tomb at Cerveteri, north of Rome, are depicted, among other kitchen utensils, several that could have been used for making pasta, including a *rotella dentata* (fluted pastry wheel) almost the very same as the one still used for cutting pasta today. The Latin writers Horace and Cicero expressed their fondness for *lagani* (thin strips of dough made from flour and water) that seem to have been the prototype of lasagne. So many of Italy's most gratifying and useful dishes have survived the centuries intact, and pasta is no exception. Horace liked

43

*Polenta*, Pietro Longhi (1702–85); CA'REZZONICO, VENICE
Longhi became the chronicler of his time with charming informal scenes such as this one.

to season his with leeks and chickpeas: *lasagne e ceci* (lasagne with chickpeas) is still a popular dish in the southern region of Basilicata. Pasta also featured in the first cookbook ever written. The Roman gastronome, Apicius, describes a *timballo* (a sweet and savory pie made with pasta).

In the medieval manuscripts there are numerous references to macaroni, culminating in the enthusiasm Boccaccio expressed in his short story *Calandrino* for the culinary marriage of macaroni with cheese, a dish whose perfect simplicity is enjoyed everywhere today. In the first collection of recipes from the Renaissance, the fifteenth-century cook and writer Maestro Martino da Como gives precise instructions for making and drying vermicelli in the sun. Some one hundred years later, in his celebrated *Opera*, Bartolomeo Scappi transmitted yet another recipe there has been no good reason to change: *tagliatelle*. From these documents and from numerous others in the following two centuries, all written by chefs catering to the courts and aristocracy of their day, we can surmise that pasta had become an élitist food enjoyed by the wealthy and privileged. At their banquets it was lavishly served in the form of *pasticci*: huge pies with macaroni, meats, fish, vegetables, sweet and savory seasonings and sometimes baked in a pastry shell. Scappi includes over a dozen of these weighty pasta pies in his list of dishes for a Renaissance dinner. They contained kid, sweetbreads, hare, squab and veal tongue as well as trout and tortoise.

The "people's pasta movement" began toward the end of the eighteenth century in the southern region of Campania. Here not only was the soil ideal for growing durum wheat for pasta flour but the weather, particularly the sea breezes around Naples, was good for drying it too. Naples itself boasted several hundred pasta shops. Macaroni was sold from large wooden barrels and long strands of spaghetti were displayed bound in thick bundles and purchased by weight. There were street stalls, where pasta was cooked over charcoal fires and eaten on the spot — with the fingers, thus avoiding the perennial problem of wrapping it around a fork. In the nineteenth century the first pasta factories opened in the South. The hard durum wheat was ground into semolina flour in large hand-mills made of granite. Barefooted men and children kneaded the dough in immense troughs, stomping to the musical accompaniment of mandolins. They powered primitive machinery to cut the pasta, which was then hung out on long racks to dry. Pasta spread throughout the regions of the newly united Italy . . . and the rest is history.

The seemingly infinite variety of pasta dishes can be made from either *pasta fresca* (fresh pasta) or *pasta secca* (dried pasta), both of which are cut into countless shapes. Fresh pasta is most closely associated with the northern regions, in particular Emilia-Romagna and, to a lesser extent, the central regions of Tuscany, Umbria, Marche, Lazio and Abruzzi. Here it is traditionally made with numerous eggs and flour but without water or salt. In Piedmont, Liguria and Veneto fresh pasta is made with flour, water and a limited amount of egg. Fresh pasta in the South is made from a dough of *semola* (ground durum wheat) and water with no eggs at all.

There are two main kinds of fresh pasta: *pasta liscia* (strips of smooth or flat noodles) and *pasta ripiena* (stuffed pasta), made by folding the dough into pockets of various shapes and filling them with a variety of tantalizing ingredients. There are various colorful legends about how these classic noodles got their shape. One has it that they were invented on the occasion of the marriage of Alfonso d'Este to Lucrezia Borgia in 1503, by the Bolognese chef Cristoforo di Zeffirano, who was inspired by the blonde locks of the young bride. Most of these stories are the relatively recent product of nineteenth-century romanticism. The real reasons are nearly always more pragmatic: pasta is easy to cook, dress and eat — or, in the case of stuffed pasta, it is the pretty whim of a cook that has somehow caught the Italian imagination.

Types of *pasta liscia*, such as *tagliatelle* (wide ribbons of fresh pasta) and *taglierini* (narrow strips of fresh pasta), derive their names from the Italian verb *tagliare* (to cut), as they are made by cutting a thin sheet of dough into the desired shape. *Pasta liscia* is also cut into square shapes, like the handkerchief-sized lasagne of Liguria or thin rectangles like the *maccheroni alla chitarra* of Abruzzi, which are tiny long strips cut on an instrument with strings like a guitar.

*Pulcinella distributing pasta:*
PASTA AGNESI MUSEUM, ONEGLIA
Pulcinella was one of the characters in the Italian *commedia dell'arte*, a popular art form which led to the development of the comic characters Punch and Judy in England.

45

The great classic sauce for fresh flat pasta is a rich meat *ragù*. In the North this is made *alla Bolognese* from ground lean veal and tomatoes, which is seasoned with onion, carrot, celery, prosciutto, a pinch of lemon zest (rind) and nutmeg and very slowly simmered in butter. The southern version, *ragù alla Napoletana*, uses pork and is cooked in lard for an even longer time. In Rome during the post-war boom fettucine, slightly narrower and thicker than *tagliatelle*, was tossed in butter and cream with a large golden fork and spoon by Alfredo at his famous restaurant in Via della Scrofa, much to the delight of American tourists and movie stars. This method of serving fettucine now carries his name — *all'Alfredo*.

*The pasta-eater;* PASTA AGNESI MUSEUM, ONEGLIA
In his sixteenth-century work *Opera*, Bartolomeo Scappi included a recipe for *tagliatelle*. It is thought that pasta was an elitist food of the wealthy up until the eighteenth century.

*The pasta-eater,* PASTA AGNESI MUSEUM, ONEGLIA
In the nineteenth century pasta was sold
from large wooden barrels, often at street
stalls, cooked over charcoal fires and
eaten on the spot with the fingers.

Fresh *pasta liscia* is also used in several baked dishes. These enriched, baked *pasta liscia* dishes are less elaborate forms of the extravagant Renaissance and Baroque pasta pies, *pasticci* and *timballi*, and are usually served today for Sunday dinners and special meals. In Emilia-Romagna the dough is rolled out in thin rectangles, layered and coated with *ragù alla Bolognese* and béchamel sauce, sprinkled with Parmesan cheese, and baked into *lasagne al forno*. Sometimes spinach is added to the pasta dough to make *lasagne verdi*. In Southern Italy cannelloni, made from squares of fresh pasta, is cooked in boiling water, spread with ingredients that vary according to region (for example, in Naples they might use mozzarella cheese and tomato sauce), rolled up, and browned in the oven.

It is, however, the second kind of fresh pasta, *pasta ripiena* (stuffed pasta), that has, over centuries, stimulated the creativity of cooks, who have cut, filled and shaped these pockets of dough into a multitude of ingenious surprises. This form of pasta is common in northern and central Italy but almost totally absent in the South — southerners did not have the luxury of an abundance of eggs to make a dough suitable for stuffing. The best-known and loved stuffed pasta is ravioli, small square pockets of dough filled with an assortment of ingredients.

Variations on this theme are numerous: *agnolotti* from Piedmont are squares with ruffled edges, stuffed with meat and cabbage; *agnolini* from Emilia-Romagna are halfmoon shapes with a meat and vegetable stuffing; *tortelli* are larger squares, popular in central Italy, filled with a mixture of spinach and ricotta cheese. The tiniest stuffed pasta is *cappelletti* which are small rings of pasta, characteristic of Bologna, filled with a rich mixture of pork, chicken or turkey, mortadella, prosciutto, Parmesan cheese and seasoned with nutmeg. The versatile *cappelletti* can be served with a butter or cream sauce, or in a broth as the traditional dish for Christmas Eve. There is a romantic, and probably apocryphal story, that *cappelletti* acquired their shape by being molded directly in a woman's navel.

Dried pasta, on the other hand, originated in the South of Italy, although it is now widespread. Convenient and delicious, it is in no way inferior to fresh pasta. The dough, which is made commercially from superior semolina flour (without eggs), is forced through holes in dies of the desired shape, before being dried, usually in automatic dryers but sometimes, by smaller, high quality manufacturers, in special closets for at least two days.

Dried pasta comes in a bewildering assortment of shapes which, for the sake of simplification, can be reduced to two general types — one type is long and stringy, and the other is small and short. Included in the first category are spaghetti and *spaghettini*

*The Pulcinella family*, print
The ancestry of the shape of spaghetti can be traced back to the twelfth century, when an Arab explorer reported that Sicilians made a pasta called *tria* — "little strings."

(thin spaghetti, also called vermicelli in the South), and *linguine* (sometimes called *bavette*) which are flat and a little wider than spaghetti, similar to the fresh pasta *taglierini*. The ancestry of the shape of spaghetti can be traced back to the twelfth century, when an Arab explorer reports that in Sicily they made a pasta called *tria*, meaning "little strings," which was molded around knitting needles.

Among the seemingly endless varieties of small and short pasta, the tubular *penne* — so called because their ends are cut at an angle like pen quills — are perhaps the most widely appreciated. Macaroni, a tubular pasta as long as spaghetti but thicker, is sometimes broken into shorter pieces before cooking. These smaller types of pasta are formed and twisted into numerous shapes that originated in the lively imagination of creative cooks and took hold in local custom. There are also other delightful types such as *conchiglie* (seashells), *farfalle* (butterflies), *fusilli* (spindles), not to mention many others; some belong to particular regions of the South, such as the traditional pasta of Puglia, *orecchiette* (little ears), which is still made at home.

Each of the different lengths and shapes of dried pasta enhances and complements a particular type of sauce, which it catches and retains according to its form. The fine strands of *spaghettini* are perfect for the light and subtle sauces of shellfish, for example, cooked in olive oil so that the strings remain separate and slippery. Tubular pasta is more appropriate for robust and rich sauces of meat and vegetables, which its more substantial texture and shape can better accommodate.

Dried pasta of the short tubular kind has long been an ingredient in two baked dishes which have figured in Italian menus since classical times. The first is *timballo*, often made in a ring mold and filled with a palatable concoction of meat and vegetables, and the second is *pasticcio*, a piquant pie with similar ingredients but usually enclosed in a puff pastry shell. The stuffings and sauces for pasta are constantly evolving and changing as experimentation and innovation takes place in home-cooking as well as in restaurant kitchens.

*Neapolitan folk scene: the macaroni-seller* (1831)
The earliest existing reference to macaroni dates back to 1279 — it appears in a notary's list of items left by the deceased Ponzio Bastone.

## SOUPS

In Italy soup dishes range widely from elegant to rustic to basic simplicity. They all have one thing in common — they are hauntingly satisfying.

All the variations come from two basic types: *minestra in brodo* and *zuppa*. The robust combination of rice, little pasta shapes or vegetables cooked in a meat broth and served floating in the liquid is *minestra in brodo. Zuppa* on the other hand, is a particularly dense soup that is often poured over bread.

Some *minestre* made with vegetables are rather thick and substantial and are called "minestrone," an extremely hearty and filling addition to the menu. These nourishing vegetable soups are simmered very slowly for as long as three hours. Onions, carrots, celery, potatoes and other ingredients are added according to their cooking sequence until all the flavors have perfectly and happily blended. The regional and local versions of minestrone are countless. In the North rice and Parmesan are added. No Italian soup would be complete without Parmesan to help give soups their particular Italian character. In Tuscany beans and fresh olive oil are added instead of rice and cheese and in the South, lots of tomato and garlic. In Genoa a couple of tablespoons of *pesto* (a "paste" of basil, pine nuts, Parmesan, and olive oil), before serving, greatly enlivens the dish.

Other *minestre* are simple and light. *Stracciatella* is made by boiling little bits (or, as its name indicates, "rags") of eggs and grated Parmesan cheese beaten together, in the best home-made meat broth. In Emilia-Romagna, peasant housewives created a soup that has become famous as *passatelli*. Eggs, Parmesan cheese, breadcrumbs and a pinch of nutmeg are kneaded together and "passed" through a special tool so that the little strands fall directly into the boiling broth. The nineteenth-century cookery writer, Artusi, gives a heavy recipe for adding ground beef to the mixture as well as one where semolina is cooked in milk and added to the usual ingredients. Traditionally these soups are served as an enticing first course for the family evening meal. Despite their humble origins, they are delicate and appropriate for elegant suppers.

*Zuppa* is the original peasant soup, invented by mothers who had to combine whatever was at hand to make a complete meal for their families. *Zuppa di pesce* for example, is a substantial fish stew and today is served as the main course. Veneto has a hardy *zuppa* with tripe. Perhaps the most well-known and complex of these soups, the Tuscan *ribollita*, is prepared from day-old minestrone made with beans and *cavolo nero* (a dark variety of cabbage), thickened with bread and then "reboiled."

As one can see from the recipe for *ribollita, zuppa* is a close relative of bread soups, like the Tuscan *pappa al pomodoro* (stale bread softened with broth and tomatoes), another rustic invention of frugal home cooks as a tasty means of using up every last crumb. In fact, there is an old Italian adage, equivalent to the English "six of one, and half a dozen of the other," that says "*se non è zuppa è pan bagnato*" — if it isn't zuppa, it's moistened bread.

*GNOCCHI*

A very popular classic Italian first course is the unpretentious gnocchi, which is not unlike pasta in the flavors it combines. Its seemingly straightforward simplicity is somewhat deceiving, however, as a certain culinary skill is required to make these little dumplings so they are light and firm enough not to fall apart in the boiling water in which they are cooked. The word "*gnocchi*" means "dumplings;" in the singular, it is slang for a "soft-headed" person. In a popular nineteenth-century rhyme people from Verona are teasingly called *gnocchi* on the principle that you become what you eat.

The nourishing gnocchi can be made out of several ingredients, depending on the region of origin, and are seasoned with a variety of sauces. The traditional way to shape gnocchi is to form the mixture into sausage-like rolls about a thumb's thickness, and then cut each one into half-inch (one centimeter) pieces. They are given their characteristic shape by pressing them against the inner curve of the prongs of a fork. They are cooked for just a few seconds in boiling water before being drained and dressed. Gnocchi made from bread dough can also be fried in olive oil.

Traditionally, gnocchi are a dish of northern and central Italy, though their specific origin is not known. Practically every region has its own special and distinctive recipe, a sure sign that they had their origin as a folk food. In old recipes gnocchi were referred to as "ravioli" (today's ravioli used to be called *tortelli*), and were made with semolina, spinach and ricotta. However, since the eighteenth century, when they were first introduced into Italy, gnocchi have mostly been made from the humble potato. A particularly well-known recipe is *gnocchi alla Cadorina*, made from the fine potatoes of Pieve di Cadore

*The pasta-seller,* PASTA AGNESI MUSEUM, ONEGLIA
Nineteenth-century Naples boasted hundreds of pasta shops. Long strands of spaghetti were displayed bound in thick bundles and purchased by weight.

in the Alpine area of the Veneto. These are mixed with a delicious and subtle combination of flour, eggs and butter and dressed with melted butter and smoked ricotta cheese.

The basic potato gnocchi take on many varied and interesting characteristics. In the Friuli-Venezia Giulia region the influence of neighboring Austria can be tasted in *gnocchi di prugne*, a large potato gnocchi, each individual dumpling encasing a red, dried plum. A compelling favorite in the capital of that region, Trieste, are *gnocchi con il cacao*: potato gnocchi served with bitter chocolate and candied fruit, and eaten as a first course. These hark back to the Renaissance banquets, which included sweet foods on menus among the *antipasti*. A curious kind of green gnocchi from Emilia-Romagna are *malfatti*, ("awkward"),

51

The effects of good government, Ambrogio Lorenzetti (1319–48?), fresco; PALAZZO PUBBLICO, SIENA
Lorenzetti's frescoes in the Palazzo Pubblico include one of the earliest Italian examples of realistic landscape painting, and demonstrate an early understanding of the principles of perspective.

referring to their ungainly shape. These are made from a mixture of chopped spinach, *mascarpone* cheese, eggs, flour and breadcrumbs. The Tuscans use much the same mixture but with the flatter taste of sheep's ricotta instead of *mascarpone*. The seasoning for these *ravioli nudi* (naked ravioli) is a simple but effective sauce of melted butter and Parmesan cheese.

*Gnocchi alla Romana*, which probably originated in Piedmont but are now associated with the capital, are thin and flat, made from coarse-ground semolina flour, cooked in milk and briefly baked in the oven until the Parmesan cheese on top becomes golden.

Sardinia has its decorative *malloreddus* — very small gnocchi made from semolina and flavored with saffron. When the Sardinian women have shaped the gnocchi, they press them with their thumbs in several places against the inner ribbing of a traditional basket, embossing the gnocchi with the basket's flaxen pattern. *Malloreddus* are usually served with a sauce made from fresh tomatoes, the local sausage from Campidano, and lamb.

Finally, the rich and delicious *gnocchi alla Siciliana* are fashioned from flour, sheep's ricotta, eggs and cheese, and are seasoned with the exotic Arab influences of the island, *uvette* (sweet and tiny dried grapes), pine nuts and fresh basil.

## POLENTA

*An eating house with a sign advertising macaroni (nineteenth-century), print;* NARDECCHIA COLLECTION

The golden polenta is a greatly revered Italian tradition. Over the centuries a virtual polenta cult has developed and to this day polenta remains an immensely beloved dish with enthusiastic groups of aficionados, who attribute to it all kinds of wondrous properties. It is even said by some to be the cure for heartache! In her valuable volume *The Classic Italian Cookbook*, Marcella Hazan has written that "to call polenta 'maize porridge' is a most indelicate use of language." For centuries this kind of cornmeal pudding was practically the staff of life in much of northern Italy, and even now it is still an important food in the northern and central regions of the country. Today it is a prominent first course, an accompaniment to many other dishes and is often eaten on its own. Leftover polenta is also another traditional way to make gnocchi.

Polenta is an ancient food whose ancestry can be traced back to the Roman *puls* or *pulmentum*, which was a mush of grains boiled in water and dressed with whatever was at hand. It sustained Caesar's legions on the march as well as many of the ordinary citizens who lived in crippling poverty. Polenta was made of spelt and millet until the first corn from the New World was unloaded in Venice. The first man to cultivate a corn crop was the patrician Venetian, Leonardo Emo Capodilista, at Fanzolo di Vedelago near Treviso in the Veneto, on the farm of his splendid Palladian villa. He used it to feed his numerous dependants and soon polenta made from corn became the staple of people too poor to afford bread, especially those living in the remote mountainous regions of the North.

During the following century polenta became personified as a kind of gastronomic "king of fools;" comically depicted crowned and enthroned on its platter, as well as more romantically in the frescoes of Venetian artists such as Pietro Longhi and Giandomenico Tiepolo. In an early seventeenth-century satire on the great epic poem, *Orlando Furioso* (by Ariosto), the hero dies an ignominious death from an overdose of polenta.

The preparation of polenta has become almost a ritual. In country kitchens of the North it is still made in a *paiolo* (a copper pot that hangs over the fire), and is stirred frequently with a special long wooden stick for over half an hour. When ready, it is poured onto a white cloth, shaped with a damp wooden spatula (it is traditionally signed with a cross in the center) and sliced with a string.

The flour for making polenta can be coarsely or finely ground and sometimes in the Veneto a very fine, white cornflour is used. There are polenta dishes with the consistency of porridge and those which are solid enough to be sliced like bread. Polenta recipes have acquired a great deal of diversity over the centuries and even a certain amount of sophistication. At the family table polenta is often eaten on its own, piping hot with a little cold milk poured over it or simply dressed with butter. It can be enriched with a cream cheese like gorgonzola and a variety of other ingredients including mushrooms. When cold, slices can be fried, grilled or baked and seasoned with meat and tomato sauce. Most frequently it appears as the inseparable companion of some of the great traditional dishes — in the Veneto with *baccalà* (dried cod fish); in Lombardy with little birds that in Brescia are roasted on skewers, and in Bergamo in a pan; in central Italy with sweet pork sausages. In Piedmont polenta is truly a dish fit for a king. Slices are fried, topped with an egg cooked "sunny side up," and covered with shavings of white truffles.

## RICE AND RISOTTO

As in other matters, Italians have their own distinctive ways of using rice: their risotto in all its marvelous forms is one of them. In her classic book, *Italian Food*, Elizabeth David says she wishes she knew "who was the genius who first grasped the fact that Piedmontese rice was ideally suited to slow cooking and that its particular qualities would be best appreciated in what has become the famous Milanese risotto." Like polenta, rice has traditionally formed a gastronomic dividing line between northern and southern Italy. Whereas pasta from the South has invaded the North, rice dishes (with a few classic exceptions) remain firmly on the northern side of the Po River, where the water supply in the Padana Valley is ideal for its cultivation. There are several hypotheses about when and by whom rice was introduced to Italy from the Orient, but the first historical evidence is a letter written in 1475 by the Duke of Milan in which he promises to send twelve sacks of rice to his neighbor in Emilia-Romagna, the Duke of Ferrara: proof that the paddy fields of the Padana were already in full production. Today Italy is the largest producer and exporter of rice in Western Europe.

In the North — Piedmont, Lombardy and the Veneto — rice is used mainly for soups and the incomparable risotto. *Risi e bisi* (rice and peas), a traditional Venetian dish, lies in a culinary middle-ground between the two. It is made from fresh sweet peas cooked briefly in butter, *pancetta* (a kind of bacon), onion and parsley, mixed with the rice, with butter and Parmesan cheese added at the end. The rice is boiled (which it never is for risotto) in a broth so that it absorbs the flavor. It comes out in a more liquid form than in risotto but less so than in a soup. There is a divergence of opinion as to whether it should be eaten with a fork or a spoon, though it is equally fulfilling either way.

In regional cookbooks of the North there are usually several recipes for boiled rice. The *bomba di riso* is an interesting and sustaining traditional dish. Literally a "rice bomb," the rice is formed around the sides of a dome-shaped mold, the center filled with a variety of ingredients such as meats, mushrooms and cheese and then baked in the oven. A perfect and classic dish for a summer's luncheon is a rice mold of crunchy garden vegetables and fresh herbs served cold. Today however, the most celebrated way to prepare rice is as a risotto.

In her indispensable *Gastronomy of Italy*, Anna Del Conte cites a reference by the Renaissance cookery writer, Cristoforo di Messisbugo, to a rice dish "very similar to a *risotto alla Milanese*," and a recipe written by Giovan Felice Luraschi, in 1829, for risotto "just as it is made now," which may well be what Elizabeth David wishes to know.

By the end of the nineteenth century, the practice of cooking rice slowly in broth so as to absorb its flavor had become widely popular. In his influential cookbook *La Scienza in Cucina e l'Arte di Mangiar Bene (The Science of Cooking and the Art of Eating Well)*, first published in 1891, Artusi included recipes that remain unchanged nearly a hundred years later: *risotto alla Milanese*, seasoned with saffron; *risotto nero*, colored black by cuttlefish ink; and *risotto con ranocchi*, cooked with *rane* (the little frogs that proliferate in the rice paddy fields).

Risotto has a unique texture, not found in common long-grain rice. Italians use their *arborio* and *carnaroli*, which are thicker and shorter, and have the particular combination of starches that, together with close attention to the cooking, give the dish its unusual definition. It should come to the table creamy but not mushy, each grain tender but *al dente*.

In Venice it is said that there is no creature on land, in the sea or in the air that has not eventually ended up in a risotto. It is, indeed, true that almost any ingredient can be added to the rice for risotto: savory sausages, seafood (especially shellfish) and vegetables with a bite (such as asparagus, artichokes and celery) combine particularly well. Modern books have made artistic and aromatic additions to this already rich heritage with fresh herbs, lemon and even strawberries.

South of the Po Valley rice is less favored but is treated with formality. In Rome a traditional appetizer is *supplì* (rice croquettes with mozzarella cheese and prosciutto). A classic dish of Naples is a *sartù*, a rice *timballo* filled with little meatballs, chicken livers, sausages, peas and mushrooms. Finally, there are many recipes from the South for rice prepared as a versatile and excellent sweet.

*Neapolitan folk customs: selling and eating pasta*, M. de Vito (nineteenth century), watercolor; NATIONAL MUSEUM OF SAN MARTINO, NAPLES

# RIGATONI IN MUSHROOM SAUCE

*Rigatoni ai funghi*

In Roman times *porcini* mushrooms were considered to be delectable morsels. In autumn and winter when they are in season, fresh ones should be used for this dish. Otherwise champignons or fresh wild mushrooms may be substituted, but their flavor will be less strong. The *pancetta* is taken from the fat part of the pig's belly, and can be bought rolled or in a flat piece. Unlike English bacon, the Italian *pancetta* is never smoked but simply cured with salt and pepper. Unless the recipe requires otherwise, *pancetta* is usually sliced wafer-thin. It is excellent served on a slice of coarse-textured bread (*pane di campagna —* country bread) as a snack.

*1¼ lb (600 g) ripe tomatoes*
*2 garlic cloves, crushed*
*¼ cup (2 fl oz/60 ml) extra virgin olive oil*
*6 oz (180 g) pancetta, chopped*
*10 oz (300 g) fresh porcini mushrooms,*
  *champignons, or button mushrooms, sliced*

*⅓ cup (3 fl oz/90 ml) dry white wine*
*salt and freshly ground pepper*
*1¼ lb (600 g) rigatoni*
*1 tablespoon chopped parsley*

Immerse the tomatoes in boiling water for a few seconds; peel and chop.

In a deep skillet, fry the garlic gently in the oil until translucent. Add the *pancetta* and mushrooms and cook over moderate heat for about 5 minutes. Pour in the wine and stir well. Add the tomatoes and season with salt and pepper. Cook slowly over low heat for about 30 minutes, until all the liquid has evaporated.

Bring a large pan of salted water to a boil. Add the rigatoni and cook until *al dente*. Drain and arrange on a serving dish.

Carefully mix half the mushroom sauce into the rigatoni. Pour the remaining sauce on top. Sprinkle the parsley over and serve.

*Rigatoni in mushroom sauce*

*Rigatoni in lemon and cream sauce*

# RIGATONI IN LEMON AND CREAM SAUCE

*Rigatoni al limone*

The fresh and tasty flavors of the kitchen garden were often used in the old days as they were conveniently at hand, and could be used in quick-to-make, nourishing meals. Cream was made at home by farm women of the North nearly every day, after the cows were milked.

1¼ lb (600 g) rigatoni
1 cup (8 fl oz/250 ml) heavy (double) cream
¼ cup (2 oz/60 g) butter
grated zest (rind) 2 lemons
1 cup (4 oz/120 g) freshly grated Parmesan cheese

Cook the rigatoni in plenty of boiling salted water until *al dente*. Meanwhile, in a small saucepan, heat the cream with the butter, lemon zest and Parmesan.

Drain the rigatoni and turn into a serving dish. Dress with the prepared sauce and serve.

# LINGUINE WITH BROAD BEANS

*Linguine con le fave*

The dish *linguine con le fave* is a Roman specialty. Broad beans have always been used in Roman cooking and today are still one of the most commonly used vegetables in Italian recipes. If they are unavailable, peas may be used instead.

½ small onion, sliced
2 tablespoons extra virgin olive oil
13 oz (400 g) shelled broad beans
½ cup (4 fl oz/120 ml) clear chicken stock
¼ cup (2 oz/60 g) butter
salt and freshly ground pepper
13 oz (400 g) linguine *(long flat noodles)*
1 cup (4 oz/120 g) freshly grated Parmesan cheese

Sauté the onion gently in the oil over low heat until translucent; do not let it brown. Add the beans and stock and cook for about 20 minutes until beans are tender. Add the butter, and salt and pepper to taste.

Bring a large pot of salted water to a boil. Cook the *linguine* until almost *al dente*. Drain. Add the *linguine* to the beans and cook for a couple of minutes, stirring now and again. Transfer to a serving dish, sprinkle with the Parmesan and serve.

Linguine *with broad beans*

*Spaghetti with anchovy sauce*

# SPAGHETTI WITH ANCHOVY SAUCE

*Spaghetti con le acciughe*

This is a classic dish combining spaghetti and fish. Anchovies are plentiful in the waters off the Italian coasts which are literally teeming with fish. Anchovies are sometimes preserved in oil and canned, but in Italy they are usually preserved in salt — a practice that dates back to Roman times. If necessary, the anchovies can be replaced in this recipe by sardines or, for a more elegant dish, by shrimps (prawns).

*1 ¼ lb (600 g) fresh anchovies, or 3 oz (90 g)
    anchovies, cured in salt*
*1 lb (500 g) ripe plum (egg) tomatoes*
*salt*
*⅓ cup (3 fl oz/90 ml) extra virgin olive oil*
*1 garlic clove, crushed*
*½ cup (4 fl oz/120 ml) dry white wine*
*1 oz (30 g) finely chopped parsley*
*1 ¼ lb (600 g) spaghetti*

Using a small, sharp knife make a cut right along the underside of each anchovy and remove the innards, lift out the backbone and remove the head. Wash the fish thoroughly under running water; drain on paper towels. Cut the anchovies into small pieces, retaining a few whole ones for the garnish. Put the tomatoes into boiling water for a minute or two, then peel. Roughly chop the flesh, sprinkle with salt and set aside to drain.

Fry the garlic clove in the olive oil just until the garlic begins to color. Add the anchovies and wine. Season with salt and mix in the tomatoes. Cook for about 10 minutes. Just before removing the pan from the heat, add parsley. Keep warm.

Meanwhile, cook the spaghetti in plenty of boiling salted water. Drain when cooked *al dente*. Stir in the anchovy sauce and serve at once, garnished with the whole anchovies.

# TAGLIATELLE WITH EGG AND BREADCRUMBS

*Tagliatelle all'uovo e pangrattato*

In middle-class homes this dish was (and still is) often served in a freshly made, puff or shortcrust pastry case, either open or closed according to the whim of the cook. In the eighteenth century, Francesco Leonardi and in the nineteenth century, Vincenzo Agnoletti, provided recipes for numerous kinds of *timballo*, as this type of preparation was called in the old days.

*Tagliatelle with egg and breadcrumbs*

*1 lb (500 g) spinach, trimmed*
*2½ cups (10 oz/300 g) all purpose (plain) flour*
*salt*
*3 whole eggs*
*⅓ cup (3 oz/90 g) butter*
*1 cup (4 oz/120 g) fine, dry breadcrumbs*
*2 hardboiled eggs, chopped*

Wash the spinach in several changes of water. Cook it in a small amount of boiling water for a few minutes until wilted. Drain and squeeze as dry as possible. Chop finely in a food processor.

Sift the flour into a mound on a work surface, make a well in the center and add a pinch of salt, the whole eggs and the spinach. Knead the mixture into a soft, smooth ball. On a lightly floured board, roll out the dough as thin as possible. Roll up this pasta sheet into a long roll and cut it with a knife into ¼ inch (0.5 cm) wide tagliatelle.

Bring a wide, shallow pan of salted water to a boil. Cook the tagliatelle until they start to rise to the surface.

Meanwhile, melt 3 tablespoons (1½ oz/45 g) of the butter in a small saucepan. Add the breadcrumbs and fry gently for a few minutes. Add the remaining 3 tablespoons (1½ oz/45 g) butter and heat just until melted. Keep warm.

Drain the tagliatelle. Transfer the pasta to a hot serving dish and toss with the melted butter and breadcrumbs. Scatter the hardboiled eggs on top and serve.

*Minestrone with pasta*

# MINESTRONE WITH PASTA

*Minestrone di taglierini*

Since ancient times soups both thick and thin, pasta in broth, minestrone and other vegetable soups have always had a place on the Italian table, and the tradition continues today. Indeed, soups are more common on the everyday table than spaghetti or rice. *Minestra* is a generic term for the course between the *antipasto* and the main course, hence it also covers pasta (*minestra asciutta* — dry *minestra*); but the word is mainly used to describe soups. A *minestra in brodo* (pasta in clear broth) does not necessarily include vegetables; minestrone is made with chopped vegetables and rice or pasta and *zuppa* is the term used for a soup that is poured over slices of bread for serving.

*1 small onion, minced*
*1 garlic clove, minced*
*1 celery stalk, minced*
*¼ cup (2 fl oz/60 ml) extra virgin olive oil*
*10 oz (300 g) shelled fresh young peas*
*3 tablespoons yellow cornmeal (polenta)*
*8 cups (2 qt/2 l) clear beef stock*
*10 oz (300 g) fresh taglierini or linguine pasta*
*freshly ground salt and pepper*
*1 handful basil leaves*

In a skillet sauté the onion, garlic and celery in the oil for 5 minutes over low heat. Add the peas, sprinkle with the cornmeal and mix well. Pour in the stock. Cook, covered, for half an hour over low heat.

Add the pasta and the salt and pepper and cook until *al dente*. Pour the soup into a tureen, sprinkle with the basil and serve.

*Hearty peasant soup*

# HEARTY PEASANT SOUP

*Zuppa del contadino*

Clever peasant cooks will create tasty dishes with whatever is easily available to them such as bread, dried pasta, and tomatoes, now obtainable all year round, which at one time were preserved in sterilized jars or dried beneath the roofs of the houses.

*1 lb (500 g) ripe tomatoes*
*1 onion, chopped*
*1 garlic clove, chopped*
*2 tablespoons extra virgin olive oil*
*8 cups (2 qt/2 l) clear beef stock*
*salt and freshly ground pepper*
*10 oz (300 g) ditalini (tiny pasta tubes for soup)*
*6 slices coarse country bread*

Immerse the tomatoes in boiling water, then peel and chop them. In a large saucepan over low heat sauté the onion and garlic gently in the oil until translucent. Add the tomatoes and the stock, season with salt and pepper. Simmer for about 1 hour. Add the pasta and cook until *al dente*.

Toast the pieces of bread in the oven. Place 3 slices in a soup tureen, add the boiling soup, garnish with the remaining 3 slices of bread and serve.

# NEAPOLITAN HERB SOUP

*Zuppa di erbe alla Napoletana*

In his book titled *L'Apicio Moderno* (*The Modern Epicurean*), published in Rome in 1790, Francesco Leonardi outlines the history of Italian cooking from Roman times until his own. Among other things, he was cook to Catherine of Russia, and hence an expert in Russian cuisine as well as other European cuisines. Above all, he was interested in regional cuisines. His book is divided into six volumes, and this recipe is from the first. The modern recipe is also typical of Neapolitan cooking.

> The area around Naples is so beautiful and well cultivated that it gives more than a little pleasure to anyone to gaze upon it, and all the herbs that are produced there have the sweetest taste, so that the Neapolitans never boil them to make soups, except for chicory, cardoons and a few other species. Moreover, it is true that in the kitchens of the great are served soups of herbs boiled and arranged in bunches or otherwise, and the most flavorsome way is to put them uncooked into the broth, either alone or several kinds mixed together. Certainly the soup will not have the symmetry one would wish in the tureen, but that will be compensated for by the excellent flavor and taste of the herbs that are cooked in the broth. Furthermore, everyone can prepare the herbs to his own taste.

Tomato plant with fruit

3 eggs
salt
2 ripe medium-sized tomatoes
6 medium-sized zucchini (courgettes), diced
3 tablespoons extra virgin olive oil
8 cups (2 qt/2 l) clear chicken stock, boiling
1 tablespoon chopped basil
1 tablespoon chopped parsley
freshly ground pepper

Beat the eggs in a bowl with a pinch of salt.

Immerse the tomatoes for a minute in boiling water. Peel and dice them.

In a nonreactive saucepan, sauté the zucchini gently in the oil over moderate heat for 2 minutes, stirring with care. Pour in the hot stock and bring to a boil. Cook for 2 minutes.

Off the heat, add the beaten eggs, basil, parsley and pepper. Set over very low heat for 1 minute, whisking constantly until thickened. Add the tomatoes, season with pepper and serve.

*Vegetable soup*

# VEGETABLE SOUP

*Zuppa di verdure*

From the earliest recipes, Italian soups have included a whole variety of herbs, which was a reflection of Italians' interest in and knowledge of the nutritive and curative properties of herbs. Even today in spring, you will still see hundreds of people in the fields gathering wild herbs and greens for the cooking pot.

½ onion, finely sliced
⅓ cup (3 fl oz/90 ml) extra virgin olive oil
10 oz (300 g) cabbage, finely chopped
1 lettuce, finely chopped
10 oz (300 g) Swiss chard, finely chopped
10 oz (300 g) spinach, finely chopped
1 celery stalk, finely chopped
8 cups (2 qt/2 l) clear beef stock
salt and freshly ground pepper
8 oz (250 g) shelled fresh peas
6 slices coarse country bread
2 garlic cloves
1 tablespoon chopped parsley

In a large saucepan sauté the onion in half the oil over high heat until translucent. Reduce the heat to low and add the cabbage, lettuce, Swiss chard, spinach and celery. Cook gently, stirring from time to time, for about 15 minutes. Pour the stock over the vegetables, season with salt and pepper and bring to a boil. Reduce the heat and simmer for about 2 hours. Add the peas and cook for a further 15 minutes.

Toast the bread slices in the oven. While still hot, rub each well with the cut side of a garlic clove to flavor them. Place the bread in a soup tureen. Pour the soup over, sprinkle with the parsley and remaining oil and serve.

*Neapolitan herb soup — modern recipe*

61

# BROAD BEAN SOUP

*Zuppa di fave*

**B**road beans are among the oldest foods of the Mediterranean region, and were used by the Romans in both fresh and dried forms. This is a typical Roman Easter soup, for it is around Easter time that fresh broad beans begin to appear in the vegetable markets, the most famous being the market in Campo dei Fiori. Open-air vegetable markets are popular all over Italy because the produce is fresh and prices are slightly lower than in the shops.

*3 oz (90 g)* pancetta, *chopped*
*1 onion, chopped*
*1 carrot, chopped*
*1 celery stalk, chopped*
*⅓ cup (3 fl oz/90 ml) extra virgin olive oil*

*1¼ lb (600 g) plum (egg) tomatoes, peeled and diced*
*3 oz (90 g) beef (rump roast), cubed*
*1¼ lb (600 g) shelled fresh broad beans*
*8 cups (2 qt/2 l) clear chicken stock*
*salt and freshly ground pepper*
*3 slices bread, cut into small dice*

In a skillet, sauté the *pancetta*, onion, carrot and celery gently in the oil until translucent. Add the tomatoes, beef and, finally, the beans. Add the stock and cook over low heat for about 30 minutes. Season with salt and pepper.

Toast the bread dice in a preheated 350°F (180°C) oven until golden. Serve the soup accompanied by these croûtons.

*Broad bean soup*

*Cream of artichoke soup*

# CREAM OF ARTICHOKE SOUP

*Crema di carciofi*

In contrast to the *minestra* and minestrone types of soup, cream soups constitute a more sophisticated beginning to a meal, and here the French influence is evident. In fact, cream soups are more commonly served in the homes of upper middle-class families, who, in former times especially, would have been more likely to travel and exchange culinary ideas.

*6 large artichokes*
*juice of 1 lemon*
*1 cup (8 fl oz/250 ml) béchamel sauce*
*3 cups (24 fl oz/750 ml) milk*
*salt and freshly ground pepper*
*3 slices bread*
*2 tablespoons (1 oz/30 g) butter*

Clean and trim the artichokes, removing the stalks and tough outer leaves and cutting off the tops. As each artichoke is prepared place it in a bowl of water acidulated with the lemon juice to prevent darkening.

Bring a saucepan of salted water to a boil, immerse the artichokes in it and cook gently for 10 minutes. Drain, and when cool cut into slices.

Put the béchamel in a saucepan and gradually stir in the milk and then the artichoke slices. Let the mixture simmer for 10 minutes, then strain the soup through a sieve. Adjust the seasoning and return the soup to a boil.

Remove the crusts from the bread and cut it into strips. Heat the butter in a skillet and fry the bread strips until golden. Pour the soup into a hot tureen, garnish with the bread strips and serve.

*To make Sicilian gnocchi for twelve people — modern recipe*

# TO MAKE SICILIAN GNOCCHI FOR TWELVE PEOPLE

*Per fare gnocchi alla Siciliana per dodici persone*

This is a recipe by Giuseppe Lamma, a seventeenth-century Bolognese cook who served middle-class families, the aristocracy, nuns and friars. But as he never actually worked for royalty, his recipes are elaborate but not excessively so, and would have been within the reach of a wider public. This recipe is taken from *La Tavola Imbandita da Giuseppe Lamma* (*Banquets Prepared by Giuseppe Lamma*) by Giuseppe Roversi, the discoverer and annotator of Lamma's works; an elegant and scholarly edition was published in 1988 by Grafis Edizioni. The modern version of this dish is made with a few variations in Emilia-Romagna (where it is called *raviolo nudo* [nude ravioli], because it has no wrapping of pasta), in Tuscany, and in Sicily.

Take a handful of sorrel and one of basil, and a little parsley and chop all this with a knife, then pound it in a mortar together with twelve shelled walnuts. Add four ounces of grated Parmesan, two pounds of dry ricotta, the yolks of six fresh eggs and a handful of dried prunes mixed with four ounces of breadcrumbs, a quarter of an ounce of pepper and a quarter of an ounce of cinnamon and three ounces of raisins which have been soaked, and three ounces of shelled pine nuts and very little salt. Have a copper pot handy with plenty of water and salt, put in an onion stuck with cinnamon stick and cloves and let it boil a little. Then remove the onion, and with a spoon dipped in the water take pieces the size of a walnut from the mixture and boil them. Lift them out with a slotted spoon and put them in a dish, pouring over them a pound of melted butter and six ounces of grated Parmesan and one ounce of powdered spicy *mostaccioli* and serve them nice and hot.

64

⅓ cup (2 oz/60 g) golden raisins (sultanas)

2 lb (1 kg) ricotta

8 egg yolks

1½ oz (45 g) pine nuts, chopped

1¾ cups (7 oz/200 g) freshly grated Parmesan
cheese

3 tablespoons very finely chopped parsley

1 handful very finely chopped basil

salt and freshly ground pepper

1½ cups (6 oz/180 g) all purpose (plain) flour

¾ cup (6 oz/180 g) melted butter

Soak the raisins in a small bowl of water for about 30 minutes. Drain and pat dry.

Push the ricotta through a sieve into a bowl. Add the egg yolks, raisins, pine nuts, half the Parmesan, the parsley and basil. Season with salt and pepper and mix well. Add 2 tablespoons of flour and mix. Using a teaspoon, form the mixture into gnocchi the size of a small egg and roll them in the remaining flour.

Bring a pot of salted water to a boil. Add the gnocchi and cook until they rise to the surface. Scoop them out with a slotted spoon. Toss with the remaining melted butter and sprinkle with the rest of the Parmesan before serving. Serves 12.

# FRIED GNOCCHI

*Gnocchi fritti*

Frying has always been a popular method of cooking in all regions of Italy. Famous fried dishes are: the *fritto misto alla Piemontese*, a dish from the Piedmont area where the cooks used to fry together ingredients such as meat, liver, *amaretti* biscuits, apples and potato croquettes in clarified butter; the *fritto misto bolognese*, another very rich mixed fried dish with gnocchi from Bologna; the Tuscan version, made chiefly with vegetables; and the Neapolitan version with its infinite variety of croquettes or fish.

¼ oz (8 g) yeast

½ cup (4 fl oz/120 ml) milk

1½ cups (6 oz/180 g) all purpose (plain) flour

salt

7 oz (200 g) salami, thinly sliced

1 cup (4 oz/120 g) Parmesan cheese, sliced

4 cups (1 qt/1 l) olive oil, for frying

Dissolve the yeast in the milk.

Heap the flour in a mound on a work surface. Make a well in the center, pour in the milk and yeast mixture, and add a little salt. Work the mix-

*Fried gnocchi*

ture into a soft dough. Shape the dough into a ball and set aside covered, in a warm place, until doubled in volume. With a rolling pin, roll out the dough into a rectangle. Fold the rectangle into 4 and roll out once more into a rectangle. Repeat this process 4 times. Finally, roll the dough into a single thin sheet and cut it into 2 inch by 4 inch (5 cm by 10 cm) rectangles.

Place a slice of salami and a slice of Parmesan on one half of each piece of dough. Fold each rectangle over to enclose the filling, moistening the edges a little so they will hold together securely. Heat the oil to 350°F (180°C) and fry the rectangles of dough, a few at a time. When they are puffed and nicely browned, drain them, and place them on a paper towel to absorb excess fat. Arrange on a platter and serve.

*The Al Molo Coffee Shop*, print

Baked polenta with cream and mushrooms

# BAKED POLENTA WITH CREAM AND MUSHROOMS
*Polenta gratinata ai funghi*

In olden times polenta was eaten alone, or at most with a couple of slices of cheese or a little milk. Traditionally it was food for the poor, considered unworthy of the aristocratic table. But these days it is enriched with a variety of ingredients and forms the basis of many tasty dishes. It can also be served as a main meal and is very practical, because it can be made ahead and reheated at the last minute. For a more homely country-style meal, mild sausages may be used in this recipe in place of the mushrooms.

*6 cups (1½ qt/1.5 l) water*
*salt*
*2½ cups (14 oz/400 g) yellow cornmeal (polenta)*
*2 cups (16 fl oz/500 ml) heavy (double) cream*
*1 cup (4 oz/100 g) freshly grated Parmesan cheese*
*¼ cup (2 oz/60 g) butter*
*1 lb (500 g) fresh porcini mushrooms,*
*    champignons, or button mushrooms, sliced*
*freshly ground pepper*
*1 tablespoon chopped parsley*

Bring the water to a boil with a little salt. Sprinkle the cornmeal into the boiling water, stirring with a wooden spoon. Simmer, stirring all the time, for about 30 minutes. Pour the polenta into a large baking dish rinsed in cold water; spread it 1¼ inches (3 cm) thick and set aside to cool.

Mix the cream with the Parmesan. Heat the butter in a small skillet, add the mushrooms and sauté for 5 minutes over moderate heat. Season with salt and pepper, sprinkle with parsley and remove from the heat.

Preheat oven to 350°F (180°C). Turn out the polenta and slice it in half horizontally into 2 thin sheets. Pour a small amount of the cream mixture into the baking dish and place the lower half of the polenta on it. Pour over half the cream and replace the top half of the polenta. Scatter with the mushrooms and the remaining cream. Bake for 30 minutes in the preheated oven. Serve hot.

# POLENTA WITH VEGETABLES
*Polenta con le verdure*

Corn was brought to Europe by Christopher Columbus in the fifteenth century, and quickly became popular in Italy where it was used to make polenta. At that time polenta was often eaten as a substitute for bread. The custom of enriching polenta with vegetables is associated with the Brianza region of Lombardy, near Milan. Served this way, polenta becomes almost a one-dish meal rather than just an appetizer.

*3 oz (90 g) borlotti beans*
*½ red onion, finely chopped*
*2 oz (60 g) pancetta or rindless bacon, diced*
*4 carrots, diced*
*2 celery stalks, scraped and diced*
*7 oz (200 g) cabbage, thinly shredded*
*6 cups (1½ qt/1.5 l) water*
*salt*
*3¼ cups (13 oz/400 g) yellow cornmeal (polenta)*

Soak the beans in cold water for at least 8 hours. Drain and transfer them to a saucepan. Cover with cold water and bring to a boil. Simmer gently

Polenta with vegetables

66

*Polenta gnocchi with sage and butter sauce*

for 1½ hours. Drain and set beans aside.

Put the onion and *pancetta* in a saucepan and fry gently for a few minutes without coloring. Add the carrots, celery and cabbage and cook gently for a few minutes to blend the flavors. Add the water. Bring to a boil. Season with salt, reduce the heat and cook for about 30 minutes.

Sprinkle in the cornmeal and continue cooking for 40 minutes, stirring constantly. When the polenta is nearly cooked, add the beans.

Rinse a bowl in cold water. Turn the polenta mixture into it and press down well, leveling the surface. Turn out onto a dish and serve.

# POLENTA GNOCCHI WITH SAGE AND BUTTER SAUCE

*Gnocchi di polenta al burro e salvia*

Shaping polenta into gnocchi was one of the few ways of making it acceptable to the old aristocratic Italian families; in this way a peasant dish could become a stylish one that could be served at a family lunch.

Gnocchi are still very popular and many versions exist: the base used may be cornflour, semolina as in the famous "Roman gnocchi," ricotta and spinach (more common in Emilia-Romagna), choux pastry, or potatoes. And the sauces served with them are numerous. Sage and butter, featured in this recipe, is certainly one of the simplest, and also one of the most flavorsome.

*6 cups (1½ qt/1.5 l) water*
*salt*
*3¼ cups (13 oz/400 g) yellow cornmeal (polenta)*
*⅓ cup (3 oz/90 g) butter*
*1 handful sage leaves*

Salt the water lightly and bring it to a boil. Scatter the cornmeal into the boiling water, stirring continuously with a wooden spoon, and cook for about 30 minutes, until the mixture comes away easily from the sides of the saucepan.

Preheat the oven to 400°F (200°C). Use 2 tablespoons (1 oz/30 g) of the butter to coat a baking dish. Make the gnocchi by shaping the polenta into large egg shapes, using a tablespoon dipped in cold water. Place them in the baking dish.

In a small saucepan fry the sage in the remaining butter. Pour over the gnocchi and heat in the oven for 20 minutes before serving.

67

# RICE BOMBE

*Bomba di riso*

This recipe comes from Bartolomeo Scappi's cookbook entitled *Opera* which first appeared in Venice in 1570. The book not only provides recipes but also describes how to serve the food, the preparation of menus, kitchen layout and the equipment then considered necessary for good cooking. This recipe, like many others of the time, combines sweet with savory. The modern version of it is a well-known specialty of the Lombardy region.

Open-air restaurant in Milan, 1908

> To make a dish of rice in the style of Lombardy with poultry meats, Milanese sausage and yolks of egg: Take clean rice and cook it in the broth in which you have cooked capons, geese, and *cervellate* [local sausages made with brains and spices]. It has to be cooked so that it is firm (*al dente*). Now take a part of the rice and put it on a large terra-cotta or silver plate and sprinkle some cheese, sugar, and cinnamon over it; on top of this put a few knobs of fresh butter, the breast meats from the capons and geese, the sausages, all cut into small pieces, and again scatter cheese, sugar, and cinnamon over it. Three layers are to be made in this fashion, and the final one moistened with melted fresh butter and sprinkled with cheese, sugar, and cinnamon. It is to be put in an oven that is not too hot, for half an hour, until it colors, then sprinkled with rosewater and served hot.

*4 oz (120 g) dried* porcini *mushrooms*
*½ cup (4 oz/120 g) butter*
*7 oz (200 g) boned chicken breast, diced*
*7 oz (200 g) Italian-style sausage*
*salt and pepper*
*2 cups (1 lb/500 g) Arborio rice*
*8 cups (2 qt/2 l) clear chicken stock*
*½ cup (4 fl oz/120 ml) dry white wine*
*1 cup (4 oz/120 g) grated Parmesan cheese*
*1 egg*
*2 tablespoons fine, dry breadcrumbs*

Soak the mushrooms in a bowl of water for 30 minutes. Drain and squeeze dry then chop coarsely. Melt 1 tablespoon (½ oz/15 g) of the butter in a saucepan over moderate heat. Add the chicken and sausage meat and cook for a few minutes. Add the mushrooms, ¼ cup (2 fl oz/60 ml) water, and salt and pepper. Cover and cook over low heat for about 1 hour adding more water as necessary to keep the meat moist.

Heat 2½ tablespoons (1¼ oz/45 g) of the butter in another saucepan. Add the rice and cook for a couple of minutes, stirring frequently. Gradually add the chicken stock, a ladleful at a time, stirring constantly so that the rice is always covered with a film of stock.

After 10 minutes, add the wine and 2½ tablespoons (1¼ oz/40 g) of the butter. Cook for a couple of minutes to dry the rice. Remove from the heat and mix in the Parmesan cheese. Mix in the egg. Tip the rice out onto a board and spread it out to halt the cooking process.

Use the remaining tablespoon (½ oz/15 g) of butter to grease a 6 cup (1½ qt/1.5 l) mold. Sprinkle the mold with the breadcrumbs. When the rice is cold, fill half the mold with it. Make a hole in the center of the rice and fill it with the meat. Cover with the remaining rice; smooth the surface. Bake in a preheated 400°F (200°C) oven for about 20 minutes. Unmold onto a dish and serve.

*The rice shop* (fifteenth century), illumination from the Theatrum Sanitatis, code 4182; CASANATENSE LIBRARY, ROME

*Rice bombe — modern recipe*

# MOLDED RICE SALAD

*Riso in forma in insalata*

The Romans traded in rice and used it for medicinal purposes, but they did not grow it. It was probably first grown in Italy by the Aragonese in the fifteenth century. Rice presented in this manner, with an attractive garnish, is a particularly refreshing dish for hot summer days. It is also an excellent example of Italian cooking — light and nutritious, yet tasty and fragrant.

*12 cups (3 qt/3 l) water*
*2 cups (1 lb/500 g) Arborio rice*
*3 oz (90 g) fresh basil*
*1 cup (4 oz/120 g) freshly grated Parmesan cheese*
*⅓ cup (3 fl oz/90 ml) extra virgin olive oil*
*1 lb (500 g) small fresh (cherry) tomatoes, sliced*

Bring the salted water to a boil in a large pot. Pour in the rice and stir for a few minutes. Cook the rice for exactly 15 minutes then drain and transfer to a bowl. Chop or shred the basil leaves, reserving a few whole leaves for the garnish. Add the chopped basil, Parmesan, and olive oil to the rice; mix well.

Transfer the rice to a 6 cup (1½ qt/1.5 l) mold; press down a little. After a few minutes, turn out onto a serving dish. Decorate the rice mold with the tomato slices and the basil leaves. Serve at once.

*Molded rice with mushrooms and Swiss chard*

# MOLDED RICE WITH MUSHROOMS AND SWISS CHARD

*Riso in forma con bietole e funghi*

Molded rice is an interesting and attractive way to serve rice, and is well suited to a sophisticated and important dinner. This recipe is a modern, simplified version of a typical old Neapolitan dish called *sartù di riso*.

*10 oz (300 g) Swiss chard, trimmed*
*2 tablespoons extra virgin olive oil*
*1 onion, very finely chopped*
*⅓ cup (3 oz/90 g) butter*
*salt*
*6 oz (180 g) fresh* porcini *mushrooms, champignons or button mushrooms, sliced*
*2 cups (1 lb/500 g) Arborio rice*
*1 cup (4 oz/120 g) freshly grated Parmesan cheese*

Cook the Swiss chard in boiling salted water for 5 minutes. Drain well and squeeze out as much moisture as possible. Chop finely; sauté in the oil for 5 minutes.

In another skillet, cook the onion with ¼ cup (2 oz/60 g) of the butter and a pinch of salt until translucent. Add the mushrooms and cook for a few minutes over moderate heat.

Bring a large pot of salted water to a boil. Add the rice and cook for 15 minutes without stirring. Drain and transfer the rice to a bowl and add the mushroom mixture and the Parmesan. Mix well.

Butter a 6 cup (1½ qt/1.5 l) ring mold with the remaining butter. Fill it with the rice and press down carefully. Bake in a preheated 400°F (200°C) oven for about 20 minutes until hot. Turn the rice out onto a serving platter, arrange the hot Swiss chard in the center, and serve at once.

*Molded rice salad*

# COUNTRY RISOTTO

*Risotto alla paesana*

This risotto, which could be called a "dry minestrone," is especially tasty since it contains sausage and *pancetta*, both with strong flavors of their own. Sausages are of ancient origin. The Romans were expert sausage makers, and the flavors would then, as now, vary considerably depending on the region, and could be mild or strong (like, for example, the highly spiced Neapolitan variety).

8 cups (2 qt/2 l) clear beef stock
10 oz (300 g) shelled fresh borlotti beans
2 tablespoons (1 oz/30 g) butter
2 tablespoons extra virgin olive oil
6 oz (180 g) mild sausage, skinned
3 oz (90 g) pancetta, *chopped*
a few sage leaves, chopped
1¾ cups (13 oz/400 g) Arborio rice
1 large onion, chopped
1 celery stalk, chopped
1 carrot, chopped
1 garlic clove, chopped
salt and freshly ground pepper
⅓ cup (1½ oz/45 g) freshly grated Parmesan cheese

Bring the stock and beans to a boil. Simmer, covered, on low heat for 1 hour. Drain, reserving both the beans and liquid.

In a large saucepan heat the butter and oil. Crumble the sausage meat into it. Add the *pancetta* and the sage and gently fry over low heat until browned. Add the rice and mix well to blend the flavors. Cook for 10 minutes, adding some of the reserved stock as required, a little at a time so that the mixture is always covered with a film of liquid. Stir in the onion, celery, carrot, garlic and beans and cook stirring constantly and continuing to add stock as necessary for 5 minutes. Add the salt and pepper. Remove from the heat. Add the Parmesan and set aside, covered, for 2 minutes then serve.

*Country risotto*

*Lunch on the beach*, Pietro Fabris (late eighteenth century); NATIONAL LIBRARY, NAPLES  The tradition of serving molds and pies is an inheritance from more opulent times.

# EGGS, PIES, PANCAKES AND MOLDS

Italian cooking is full of surprises. It is the unexpected that makes eating Italian food such a memorable experience. One of the rewarding aspects of discovering Italian food is the sheer pleasure of observing the brilliantly colored dishes as they are lovingly presented at the table. Nowhere are these qualities more evident than in the tradition of molds and pies.

Many of these dishes are inherited from more opulent times. The small savory dishes were served in many Italian homes during the nineteenth century and even until the Second World War as *piatti di mezzo* (a dish between the first and the main course).

However, traditional Italian food moves with the times. A good dish will never disappear from the menu, it will simply re-emerge to perform another function. Many of the original *piatti di mezzo* are now considered an ideal main course for a luncheon or light supper.

The tasty, though not overwhelming *piatti di mezzo* of the nineteenth century often took the form of a *sformato* (a colorful vegetable mold) or a *pasticcio* (a pie of pasta with vegetables and meat, sometimes baked in a pastry shell). Otherwise it might have been one of a number of other forms of filled pastry such as: *crostate* (tarts with dough laid over the filling), *sfogliate* (a cake made with puff pastry) or *crespelle* (crêpes). Or else it might have been one of the numerous tasty and elegant renderings of the versatile egg, such as Italianized soufflés, a *rotolo di frittata* (a rolled omelet), or hardboiled stuffed eggs served in aspic. Artusi includes twenty-five of these aromatic *piatti di mezzo* in his chapter on *trasmessi o intermezzi* (dishes served between courses). Several of them, like *gnocchi alla Romana* and polenta with sausage, remain commendable whole meals.

The *sformato* (mold) is another dish which came through the centuries intact. Originally served at the Baroque banquets of the seventeenth and eighteenth centuries, its popularity increased markedly in the nineteenth century, when it became a common family dish. Artusi gives over a dozen recipes for these picturesque vegetable molds. Artichokes, cardoons, cauliflower, green beans, fennel, fresh peas, spinach and zucchini (courgettes) were employed among the traditional ingredients. The vegetable is cooked, put through a food mill to obtain a coarse purée, bound together with eggs and white sauce and finally cooked again in the oven (Artusi recommends using a *bagno-maria* — double boiler). A *sformato*, which is a fine way of using vegetables slightly past their prime, is not unlike a soufflé but it has the texture of a pudding. It is often served with a sauce which, if the *sformato* has been made in a ring mold, can be poured into the center. The sauce could be, depending on the principal vegetable ingredient, a thick meat sauce, a rich cream

*Birth of the Virgin: two maids carrying a basket of eggs* (detail), Agnolo Gaddi (active 1369–96), fresco; PRATO CATHEDRAL This fresco is one of a series depicting the story of the Virgin.

*Room next to the kitchen for special preparations* from Bartolomeo Scappi's book *Of the Art of Cooking with the Master of the House and Carver* from Scappi's *Opera* (1570); LEVY PISETZKY COLLECTION, MILAN One man is rolling out the dough while the other holds it down to stretch it out as thinly as possible.

and mushroom sauce or a light tomato sauce. Today, *sformati* are again appearing on the menus of fine restaurants.

The *pasticcio* was created by the great chefs of the Renaissance. The sweet pie pastry was often filled with delicacies such as game or sweetbreads. Maestro Martino da Como gives a recipe for *pasticcio d'anguilla*, a sweet and savory pie made with eels and other fish; and Bartolomeo Scappi includes several in his *Opera* made with artichokes, truffles, loin of beef and veal livers, all baked in a kind of *pasta sfoglia* (puff pastry layered with lard instead of butter). Scappi also gives the recipe for the princely *torta reale di piccioni* (royal pigeon tart), with squab meat, cream or cheese, baked in a crust of *marzapane* (marzipan) dough. The Neapolitans, he informs us, had a rather lovely name for this pie — *pizza di bocca di dama*, literally, "lady's mouth pizza" — a delicacy suitable for the highest born of ladies.

The French embraced *pasticci* in the sixteenth century, calling them *timbales*. In the eighteenth century the Neapolitan, Vincenzo Corrado, Italianized this word to *timballo*. Hence, the dish journeyed to France only to return with a new name. In *Il Cuoco Galante (The Gallant Cook)* Corrado gives recipes for *timballi* stuffed with, among other ingredients, macaroni, gnocchi and cream, *pasta fresca* (fresh pasta), rice with truffles, and spinach. This rich mixture is baked in a puff pastry or *mezza frolla* (shortcrust) dough without sugar. A reverential and beautiful description of this dish was written by Giuseppe Tommasi di Lampedusa in his classic novel *Il Gattopardo (The Leopard)*, where it is served at an aristocratic dinner party at a country estate: "The burnished gold of the crusts, the fragrance of the sugar and cinnamon they exuded, were but preludes to the delights released from the interior when the knife broke the crust; first came a spice-laden haze, then chicken livers, hardboiled eggs, sliced ham, chicken and truffles in masses of piping hot, glistening macaroni, to which the meat juice gave an exquisite hue of suede."

Today *pasticci* or *timballi* are made in several regions from North to South. There are two particularly sumptuous ones: the *pasticcio di polenta* from the Veneto, filled with squab, ham, Parmesan cheese and dried mushrooms; and the *pasta incasciata* pie of Sicily, made with rigatoni and as many other ingredients as can be fitted into it — little meatballs, salami, eggs, eggplant (aubergine), local cheese — and seasoned with tomato sauce, oregano and pepper. Both are encased in a sweet pastry crust.

*Frittelle* (fritters) are a piquant classic *piatto di mezzo*, which are now in demand for any meal or snack. In the eighteenth-century cookbook, *L'Apicio Moderno (The Modern Epicurean)*, Francesco Leonardi gives a recipe for *rissole alla Napoletana*, better known today as *panzarotti*. These are delightful little fried pies, made with bread dough and stuffed with the usual Neapolitan combination of tomato, mozzarella, anchovy fillets, egg and prosciutto, seasoned with basil and oregano. Traditionally they are fried in *strutto* (pork fat) and, in keeping with their name, each one puffs out like a "little belly."

The modest egg provides an inexhaustible source of amiable light dishes to eat as *piatti di mezzo*, and many recipes now appear on the traditional *antipasto* table. By the time of the Renaissance culinary treatment of the simple and nutritious egg had achieved a certain sophistication. Maestro Martino da Como dedicates a chapter to it entitled "Every way to cook an egg." In fact, he only provides fourteen recipes, which hardly covers the possibilities of this versatile food. His technique for the perfect softboiled egg is, perhaps, also the most poetic. His advice is to drop it in cold water, bring to a boil and in the time it takes to say the *paternostro* (Lord's Prayer) it will have been cooked (and perhaps blessed

as well!). Most of Maestro Martino's recipes have survived the ravages of time in one form or another.

One of the most delicious egg recipes written by Maestro Martino is one for a *frittata* (omelet). The *frittata* is the most distinctively Italian way of cooking eggs. It is a type of omelet that differs from the French variety in several respects. A *frittata* is cooked slowly in a pan on top of the stove over very low heat, until the eggs are firm and set but still moist. It is not served folded over, but flat and round. Other ingredients such as cheese, ham and vegetables can be incorporated into the eggs before cooking. To his fifteenth-century cheese *frittata* Maestro Martino also adds fresh herbs, parsley, borage, mint, marjoram and a little sage, which makes it equally appealing to contemporary tastes.

*The kitchen* (detail), Vincenzo Campi (1536–91); BRERA GALLERY, MILAN
Campi's paintings often depicted the everyday life of ordinary people in the sixteenth century.

*Banquet after the hunt*, Carlo Cane (1618–88);
CASTELLO SFORZESCO MUSEUM, MILAN

# STUFFED EGGS

*Ova piene*

This recipe for stuffed eggs comes from Maestro Martino da Como, the fifteenth-century cookery writer. In it the eggs are enriched by the addition of raisins, herbs and spices. In those times eggs were considered very important and often provided the basis for a meal. In his book, Maestro Martino gives recipes for simple buttered eggs, *frittate* (omelets), which he recommends should be very soft-textured, filled with herbs, and cooked on one side only, and lightly boiled eggs (sometimes cooked in milk), which he suggests could be sprinkled with a mixture of grated cheese and orange juice. The modern version of the recipe features a béchamel sauce.

Boil your fresh eggs in clean water until they are well cooked and hard. Then shell them and cut them in half so you can take out all the yolks, being careful not to break the whites; pound some of the yolks with a small quantity of raisins, a little good vintage cheese and a little fresh cheese as well. Add parsley, marjoram and mint, all finely chopped, mixing in a little bit of eggwhite according to the quantity you wish to make, with sweet or hot spices according to taste. And after you have mixed all these things together, you shall color the mixture yellow with saffron and fill the above-mentioned whites with it, then fry them very slowly in oil. To make a suitable sauce to go over them, take a few leftover yolks mixed with raisins and pounded well together, dilute them with a small amount of verjuice and *sapa* (that is, cooked wine); rub through a sieve, adding a little ginger, a few cloves and a lot of cinnamon, and boil this sauce for a while. When you wish to send the eggs to the table, pour the sauce over them.

*12 hardboiled eggs*
*2 tablespoons (1 oz/30 g) butter*
*¼ cup (1 oz/30 g) all purpose (plain) flour*
*2 cups (16 fl oz/500 ml) milk*
*½ teaspoon saffron threads*
*3 tablespoons tomato paste*
*salt*

Shell the eggs and cut them in half lengthwise. Remove 2 of the yolks; put the other eggs, yolks up, in an ovenproof dish.

Melt the butter over low heat, add the flour and mix in thoroughly. Add the milk a little at a time, stirring constantly. As soon as the mixture comes to a boil, remove from the heat.

Dissolve the saffron in a very small amount of water. Add to the sauce along with the tomato paste. Mix well; add salt to taste. Pour the aurora sauce over the eggs. Put the two reserved yolks through a small sieve and scatter over the top. Bake in a preheated 350°F (180°C) oven for 20 minutes. Serve hot.

*Stuffed eggs — modern recipe*

# EGGS ON TOAST WITH A SPICY SAUCE

*Uova sul crostone*

In Italy eggs have always constituted a classic dinner dish contrary to the tradition of other countries where they are eaten for breakfast. Eggs in Italy have dark orange yolks and are relatively small in size. Country families often used to raise hens so fresh eggs were always available.

1 red and 1 yellow bell pepper (capsicum), peeled
  and finely chopped
2 tomatoes, peeled and finely chopped
1 small onion, finely chopped
1 garlic clove, finely chopped
½ red chile pepper, finely chopped
¼ cup (2 fl oz/60 ml) extra virgin olive oil
1 tablespoon fresh thyme
¼ cup (2 fl oz/60 ml) clear meat stock
salt and freshly ground pepper
6 slices sandwich bread

6 slices pancetta
6 eggs
2 tablespoons (1 oz/30 g) butter

Combine the bell peppers, tomatoes, onion, garlic, chile pepper and 3 tablespoons of the oil in a small, nonreactive saucepan. Add the thyme and the stock; season with salt and pepper to taste. Cook over low heat for a few minutes until the sauce thickens.

Toast the bread. Meanwhile, in a skillet, sauté the *pancetta* with the remaining tablespoon of oil for 3 minutes, stirring frequently.

Melt the butter in a large skillet. Fry the eggs in the butter, adding salt to the whites only and taking care to keep the yolks fairly soft.

Arrange the bread slices on a hot serving dish. Place a slice of *pancetta* and a fried egg on top of each slice. Cover with a little of the hot sauce and serve.

*Eggs on toast with a spicy sauce*

# EGGS ON POLENTA TOAST

*Crostoni di uova e polenta*

This dish was traditionally considered rustic fare until in recent times the custom of finishing it with a little grated white truffle has given it a touch of refinement. Truffles are a specialty of Piedmont, and in particular of the town of Alba, where they are particularly fragrant. For some time now they have also been found in Tuscany, using specially trained dogs. The Tuscan variety is not quite so highly prized; nor are the black truffles, which grow in neighboring Umbria.

*polenta (a quarter of the recipe on p. 66)*
*6 thin slices lean cooked ham, divided into 12
  triangles*
*12 very fresh egg yolks*

*salt and freshly ground pepper*
*6 thin slices* fontina *cheese, divided into 12
  triangles*
*¼ cup (2 oz/60 g) butter*

Spread the polenta 1 inch (2.5 cm) thick on a board moistened with cold water. Use a pastry cutter to make 12 circles slightly bigger than an egg yolk.

Scoop out a little of the center and place a slice of ham and an egg yolk in each hollow. Sprinkle with salt and pepper. Cover with a slice of *fontina*.

Arrange the "toasts" in a buttered baking dish. Dot with the butter. Bake at 400°F (200°C) for about 10 minutes until the whites are set; then serve.

*Eggs on polenta toast*

*Egg fritters*

# EGG FRITTERS

*Crocchette di uova sode*

Fritters belong to the great tradition of Neapolitan cuisine, which has always relied heavily on fried dishes — in the old days lard was used because it made them crisp. Today, however, fritters are fried in olive oil which is considered healthier. Bases that may be used for fritters are potatoes, chicken, vegetables, spaghetti and, of course, eggs. Sometimes the eggs are lightly boiled which makes them very difficult to shape into fritters because the yolk must remain liquid after frying. Sometimes they are hardboiled as in this version.

*8 eggs*

*1 cup (2 oz/60 g) fresh bread, crusts removed and soaked in milk and squeezed*

*2 tablespoons chopped basil*

*2 tablespoons chopped parsley*

*1 tablespoon chopped thyme*

*⅓ cup (1½ oz/45 g) freshly grated Parmesan cheese*

*salt and freshly ground pepper*
*1 cup (4 oz/120 g) fine, dry breadcrumbs*
*4 cups (1 qt/1 l) olive oil for frying*

Put 6 eggs in a saucepan and add cold salted water to cover. Bring to a boil and cook for 10 minutes. Drain and cool under cold running water. Shell the eggs.

Mix the bread with the basil, parsley, thyme and Parmesan; season with salt and pepper. Divide the mixture into 6 equal portions. Pat each portion into a circle. Place a hardboiled egg on it and wrap the egg in the bread mixture, forming a ball. Beat the remaining 2 eggs in a shallow dish. Dip the fritters in the beaten eggs, roll them in the dry breadcrumbs. Heat the oil to 350°F (180°C) in a deep skillet and fry the fritters for about 5 minutes until golden. Drain on paper towels, arrange on a platter and serve.

*Layered ham and eggs*

# LAYERED HAM AND EGGS

*Pasticcio di uova e prosciutto*

The repertoire of Italian cuisine has always been rich in dishes suitable for replacing meat or fish, especially in family cooking. For centuries cooks have been handing down by word of mouth innumerable recipes for dishes that can be quickly made at home for simple family meals. Most of these will make a satisfying meal if they are preceded by a bowl of broth and followed by fresh fruit. If desired, this *pasticcio* can be served with a vegetable such as spinach, sliced artichokes or broccoli.

*¼ cup (2 fl oz/60 ml) extra virgin olive oil*

*1 small onion, sliced*

*1 garlic clove, crushed*

*salt and freshly ground pepper*

*4 ripe medium-sized tomatoes, peeled and chopped*

*6 oz (180 g) cooked ham, sliced*

*6 eggs, beaten*

*1 tablespoon chopped parsley*

*1 handful basil leaves*

Heat 2 tablespoons of the oil in a large skillet. Add the onion and garlic; season with salt and pepper. Cook over low heat until translucent. Add the tomatoes and cook until the liquid has completely reduced. Transfer to a warm serving dish. Place the slices of ham on top of the tomatoes and onions and keep warm.

Heat the remaining 2 tablespoons of oil in a saucepan. Add the eggs, season with salt and pepper and scramble with a fork until set. Sprinkle with the parsley. Spoon the eggs on top of the ham. Garnish with the basil leaves.

# VEGETABLE GRATIN WITH EGGS

*Pasticcio di verdure e uova*

For centuries eggs have lent themselves to endless variations in Italian cooking. The oldest cookery books give an infinite number of recipes for them, and today whole books are devoted to egg recipes. A popular method of serving them in refined restaurants in the North is fried in butter, and covered with grated Parmesan and sliced truffles.

*1 cauliflower*

*1 yellow and 1 red bell pepper (capsicum)*

*¼ cup (2 fl oz/60 ml) extra virgin olive oil*

*1½ tablespoons chopped parsley*

*salt*

*1 tablespoon dry breadcrumbs*

*1 cup (4 oz/120 g) freshly grated Parmesan cheese*

*6 very fresh eggs*

Cook the cauliflower in lightly salted boiling water until just softened. Drain; set aside to cool. Bake the peppers in the oven at 350°F (180°C) for approximately 30 minutes. Rub them with a cloth to remove the charred skin and cut them into strips.

Coat an oval ovenproof dish with a little of the oil. Arrange a layer of peppers on the bottom, sprinkle with parsley and salt very lightly; cover with the cauliflower and pour on half of the remaining oil. Mix together the breadcrumbs and Parmesan. Sprinkle over the vegetables.

Put the dish into a preheated 400°F (200°C) oven for 10 minutes. Meanwhile, in a skillet, fry the eggs in the remaining oil. When a crisp golden crust has formed on the vegetables, remove them from the oven. Top with the eggs and serve.

A set of cutlery in the Liberty style (1885); MILAN

*Vegetable gratin with eggs*

*Spinach pie*

# SPINACH PIE

*Torta di spinaci*

**N**ot only were *pasteli* (vegetable or meat pies) referred to by the author of the *Liber de Coquina* (*Book of Cooking*), they were mentioned as early as the fourteenth century in the cookery book by an anonymous Tuscan writer, and also by Maestro Martino da Como in the fifteenth century. With its mixture of sweet and savory, this spinach pie is one of the oldest of Italian dishes. In summer when there is no spinach, Swiss chard may be used, and, of course, broccoli in season is another excellent substitute.

*2 lb (1 kg) spinach, trimmed*
*3 oz (90 g) pancetta, cut into small dice*
*1½ oz (45 g) golden raisins (sultanas)*
*6 oz (180 g) ricotta*
*2 eggs, beaten*
*⅓ cup (1½ oz/45 g) freshly grated Parmesan cheese*
*1½ oz (45 g) pine nuts*
*pinch of freshly grated nutmeg*
*salt and freshly ground pepper*

*1 tablespoon (½ oz/15 g) butter*
*13 oz (400 g) puff pastry (frozen pastry may be used)*

Cook the spinach in a very small amount of boiling salted water until tender. Drain; squeeze to remove as much water as possible. Chop coarsely. In a large skillet, sauté the *pancetta* gently until golden. Add the spinach and cook for a few minutes to let the flavors blend.

Soak the raisins (sultanas) in 1 cup (8 fl oz/250 ml) of lukewarm water. Drain and add the raisins to the spinach. Turn off the heat, and mix in the ricotta, eggs, grated Parmesan, pine nuts and nutmeg. Add salt and pepper to taste.

Grease a pie pan with the butter. Roll out ¾ of the pastry and use it to line the pan. Fill with the spinach mixture. Roll out the remaining dough and cover the top. Bake in a preheated 350°F (180°C) oven for about 40 minutes. Turn out onto a platter and serve.

# AN ELEGANT PIZZA

*Sfogliata ai sottaceti*

Since pizza with a bread dough base is considered a rather common dish and is rarely served at the table of middle-class families, more elaborate versions of it are made using puff pastry for the base. The type of cheese can also be varied, of course, and often *fontina* is used in place of mozzarella, particularly in the North. The old cookery books contained advice and recipes for preserving different foods, and at one time it was a matter of pride for a cook to have a huge quantity of pickled vegetables to use in sauces during the winter.

*6 oz (180 g) puff pastry (frozen pastry may be used)*
*3 tablespoons extra virgin olive oil*
*10 oz (300 g) tomato pulp, cut in strips*
*10 oz (300 g) mozzarella, thinly sliced*
*3 oz (90 g) stuffed green olives, drained*
*3 oz (90 g) artichoke hearts preserved in oil, drained and sliced*
*2 oz (60 g) pickled cucumbers, sliced*
*3 anchovy fillets*
*salt*
*1 tablespoon dried oregano*

Roll out the dough into a circle ¼ inch (0.5 cm) thick. Coat a pizza pan with some of the oil. Place the pastry in the pan.

Leaving a 1 inch (2.5 cm) margin around the edge, arrange the tomato pulp and mozzarella on top of the dough. Scatter with the remaining ingredients. Salt lightly and sprinkle with the remaining oil. Bake in a preheated 425°F (220°C) oven for about 20 minutes.

# MIXED VEGETABLE PIE

*Sfogliata di verdure*

In the old days vegetable pies were served as a first course. At elegant luncheons today, they still are, instead of pasta such as spaghetti or *penne* which are not considered sufficiently stylish. But generally they can feature as a main dish, particularly at country luncheons where guests are often presented with a great variety of vegetable pies and *frittate* (omelets) as a one-course meal, perhaps followed by a big basket of fresh fruit.

*1 red bell pepper (capsicum)*
*1 yellow bell pepper (capsicum)*
*1 green bell pepper (capsicum)*
*1 onion, sliced*
*3 tablespoons extra virgin olive oil*
*1 eggplant (aubergine), peeled and cubed*
*2 zucchini (courgettes), diced*
*2 tomatoes, peeled and chopped*
*salt and freshly ground pepper*
*1 tablespoon capers, drained*
*10 oz (300 g) puff pastry (frozen pastry may be used)*
*all purpose (plain) flour*

Place the bell peppers in a baking dish. Bake in a preheated 350°F (180°C) oven for 20 minutes. Peel off the skins, remove the seeds and ribs and cut the flesh into thin strips. In a large skillet, wilt the onion gently in the oil. Add the eggplant and bell peppers reserving a few strips of bell pepper for the garnish. Pour in a little hot water and then add the zucchini, tomatoes, and salt and pepper to taste. Cover and cook the vegetables for about 30 minutes. Add the capers and cook for 5 minutes. Set aside to cool.

Roll out the pastry on a lightly floured board. Use it to line an oiled 9 inch (22 cm) tart pan. Cover with a sheet of parchment (baking paper) or foil and fill with dried beans. Bake the pastry in the 350°F (180°C) oven for about 40 minutes. Remove the tart shell from the oven, remove the beans, and let cool to room temperature. Fill the shell with the vegetable mixture, garnish with the reserved bell pepper strips and serve.

*An elegant pizza — modern recipe (left) Mixed vegetable pie (right)*

*Layered artichoke pie for Lenten days — modern recipe*

# LAYERED ARTICHOKE PIE FOR LENTEN DAYS

*Pastello di carciofoli*

This is one of the 315 recipes that appear in Cristoforo di Messisbugo's book of cooking, first published in Ferrara in 1549. Cristoforo di Messisbugo was an administrator at the Este court — in other words, he was more than a cook, as his style of writing shows. The recipes are grouped together under the headings *Entrées for Lent, Sweetbreads, Sauces, Stews, Roasts, Sautéed Vegetables*; and advice is given not only on how to prepare the dishes, but also how many serving persons, dishwashers or scullery-maids are required, and especially "people to collect the things from the table, who should be gracious to the host and mindful more of his honor than of their own gain."

The modern recipe is one of the many variations of the Genoese artichoke pie.

> First you shall make a shell from the pastry which will be the same kind as for vegetable *grostoli* [fritters]. Then you shall put on top of it some good oil and a few pieces of boiled smoked trout and a little pepper. Then on top of this you shall place the artichokes, adding a little oil and pepper and a few more pieces of trout or pressed dried salted roe cut into tiny pieces. You then take a little pike or tench roe with two ounces of sugar and orange juice, or verjuice, and mix them well together with very little salt, putting them through a sieve so that you have just over half a glass of the mixture. This you pour into the pastry case, put the lid on and leave it to cook.

10 large artichokes
¼ cup (2 fl oz/60 ml) extra virgin olive oil
2 tablespoons chopped borage
1 tablespoon chopped fresh marjoram
salt and freshly ground pepper
13 oz (400 g) puff pastry
2 eggs, beaten

Trim the artichokes, removing the tough leaves. Slice thinly. In a large skillet, cook the artichokes in the oil over low heat for 10 minutes. Add the borage and marjoram and sauté for a few minutes to blend the flavors. Season with salt and pepper.

Roll out ¾ of the pastry and line an 8 inch (20 cm) diameter tart tin with it.

Off the heat, stir the eggs into the artichokes. Pour the mixture into the pastry case. Roll out the remaining pastry and cover the tart with it. Seal and trim the edges. Bake the tart in a preheated 350°F (180°C) oven for about 40 minutes, or until the pastry begins to brown, then serve.

# PEPERONATA TART

*Crostata di peperonata*

As early as the fourteenth century, recipe books such as the *Liber de Coquina* (*Book of Cooking*), by an unknown author from the Angevin court in Naples, contained recipes for *pasteli*: vegetable pies encased in an envelope of pastry or simply placed on a savory tart case as in this recipe.

2½ cups (10 oz/300 g) all purpose (plain) flour
⅓ cup (3 oz/90 g) butter, cut in small pieces
2 tablespoons water
salt
1 lb (500 g) onions, sliced
¼ cup (2 fl oz/60 ml) extra virgin olive oil
1 lb (500 g) tomatoes, peeled and chopped
4 red or yellow bell peppers (capsicums), peeled, seeded and chopped

Sift the flour into a mound on a work surface; make a well in the center and add the butter. Gradually work the butter into the flour with the tips of your fingers. Add the water and a pinch of salt and knead until the dough is smooth. Set aside to rest for about 30 minutes.

Fry the onions gently in the oil in a saucepan until translucent. Add the tomatoes and bell peppers and season with salt. Cover the pan and cook over low heat for about 30 minutes. If this *peperonata* is very liquid, remove the lid and finish cooking.

Butter a tart pan. Roll out the dough and line the pan with it. Flute the edges. Fill with the *peperonata*. Bake the tart in a preheated 350°F (180°C) oven for 40 minutes. Let it cool in the pan for a moment or two, then turn out and serve.

*Peperonata tart*

# LEEK TART

*Crostata di porri*

While it is certainly true that many dishes of the world originated in France, Italy in fact, is the creator of many more, as it has a more ancient cuisine. However, this leek tart is possibly a variation of *quiche lorraine*. Leeks are particularly popular in the North of Italy, where they are cooked in numerous ways. Most often they are boiled and served covered with grated Parmesan and melted butter: they are then called "*leeks Parmigiana*".

*1 lb (500 g) leeks*
*½ cup (4 oz/120 g) butter, softened*
*3 cups (10 oz/300 g) all purpose (plain) flour*
*1¼ cups (10 fl oz/300 ml) milk, warmed*
*freshly ground pepper*
*½ cup (2 oz/60 g) freshly grated Parmesan cheese*
*2 egg yolks*
*salt*

Trim off the dark green parts of the leeks and the roots. Wash well to remove all grit. Cook the leeks in boiling salted water for 10 minutes then drain. Sauté the leeks in 2 tablespoons (1 oz/30 g) of the butter over low heat for a few minutes.

In a saucepan, melt 2 tablespoons (1 oz/30 g) of the butter over moderate heat. Stir in ¼ cup (1 oz/30 g) of the flour until well mixed. Add the milk, a little at a time, stirring constantly until the sauce is smooth. Remove from the heat. Season with a little pepper. Whisk in the Parmesan and egg yolks. Set this béchamel sauce aside.

Heap the remaining flour in a mound and make a well in the center. Add the remaining butter, a pinch of salt and a small amount of cold water. Work the mixture into a smooth, soft dough.

Roll out the dough into a circle large enough to line a 9 inch (22 cm) tin with 2 inch (5 cm) sides. Prick the pastry with a fork. Cover with a sheet of parchment (baking) paper or foil. Fill the tart shell with dried beans and bake at 350°F (180°C) for about 20 minutes. Remove the beans and paper. Arrange the leeks in a neat row on the pastry. Pour the béchamel over the leeks. Return the tart to the oven and bake for about 20 minutes. Let it rest for a moment or two out of the oven before turning out and serving.

*Leek tart (left) Potato cake with basil (right)*

# POTATO CAKE WITH BASIL

*Tortino di patate al basilico*

In Neapolitan middle-class homes the potato cake, *gattò di patate* (from the French *gâteau* — let us not forget the Bourbon influence!) has always been a *pièce de résistance* of the lunch table. It often replaces pasta, which is considered to be a lower-class dish. There are many versions of it, and every cook shows off his or her preferred recipe.

6 plum (egg) tomatoes, peeled and chopped
2 lb (1 kg) potatoes
¼ cup (2 oz/60 g) butter
salt and freshly ground pepper
½ cup (1½ oz/45 g) freshly grated Parmesan cheese
3 eggs
¼ cup (1 oz/30 g) fine dry breadcrumbs
6 oz (180 g) fontina *cheese, thinly sliced*
1 bunch fresh basil, chopped

Salt the tomatoes and then set aside to drain for 2 hours.

Cook the potatoes in their skins in boiling salted water. Drain. Peel them, and while still hot, push through a potato ricer or food mill into a saucepan. Set the pan over low heat, add the butter and stir with a wooden spoon for a couple of minutes. Remove from the heat; transfer the potatoes to a bowl. Season with salt and pepper, add the Parmesan and the eggs and stir the mixture gently.

Butter an oval, ovenproof dish and sprinkle it with breadcrumbs. Spread half the mixture over the bottom of the dish. Arrange the *fontina* and basil on top of the potato mixture. Top this with the remaining potato purée, leveling the surface with the blade of a knife dipped in water. Arrange the tomatoes on top.

Bake in a preheated 350°F (180°C) oven for about 40 minutes. Serve at once while very hot.

# ROLLED STUFFED OMELET

*Rotolo di frittata*

Italians traditionally eat little meat. This is partly because before the Second World War meat was expensive and Italy was a poor country; and partly because it was possible to breed stock only in a few areas of northern Italy — the land being generally

*Rolled stuffed omelet*

wooded or having a very dry soil not suited to pasture. Meat is often replaced by eggs, *frittate* (omelets) or cheese dishes.

2 lb (1 kg) spinach
1 cup (4 oz/120 g) freshly grated Parmesan cheese
3 tablespoons extra virgin olive oil
2 hardboiled eggs, chopped
pinch freshly grated nutmeg
6 whole eggs, beaten
salt and freshly ground pepper

Remove the roots from the spinach (but not the stems) and wash it well. Cook in a small amount of salted water for 5 minutes. Drain and chop coarsely. In a bowl, mix the spinach with the Parmesan, 1 tablespoon of the oil, the hardboiled eggs and the nutmeg.

Beat the raw eggs with salt and pepper to taste. Heat 1 tablespoon of the oil in a non-stick skillet. Add the eggs and cook until almost set. Invert the *frittata* onto a plate and slide it back into the skillet. Remove from the heat immediately.

Spread the spinach mixture over the surface of the *frittata*. Coat a baking dish with the remaining 1 tablespoon of oil. Roll up the *frittata* and place it in the baking dish. Bake in a preheated 400°F (200°C) oven for 10 minutes then serve.

*Semolina soufflé (left) Baked mozzarella (right)*

# SEMOLINA SOUFFLÉ

*Soufflé di semolino*

The soufflé is French inspired, but of course it is subject to the influence of the country where it is made. This one could not be more Italian, since it is made with semolina. It is very light, and often is enriched with chopped cooked ham or cheese.

*4 cups (1 qt/1 l) milk*
*1½ cups (6 oz/180 g) semolina*
*salt and freshly ground pepper*
*2 tablespoons (1 oz/30 g) butter*
*4 eggs, separated*
*1 cup (4 oz/120 g) freshly grated Parmesan cheese*

In a heavy saucepan bring the milk to a boil. Scatter the semolina over the surface and cook, stirring, for about 20 minutes over moderate heat. Remove from the heat, season with salt and a little pepper, and stir in the butter. Set aside to cool.

Beat the eggwhites until quite stiff. When the semolina has cooled a little, stir in the egg yolks, one at a time. Stir in the Parmesan until well mixed. Lastly, fold in the beaten eggwhites.

Butter an 8 cup (2 qt/2 l) ovenproof dish. Pour in the semolina mixture. Bake in a preheated 400°F (200°C) oven for about 30 minutes. Serve the soufflé from the dish in which it was baked.

# BAKED MOZZARELLA

*Pasticcio di mozzarella*

The true mozzarella made from buffalo's milk is very hard to find these days because it is produced only in the Salerno, Caserta and Battipaglia areas. The cheese lends itself to many different recipes. Today the genuine buffalo mozzarella is often replaced by one made with cow's milk, but it has neither the taste nor the texture of the real thing. This is a quickly prepared, typical family dish, which can easily be served in place of meat. As always, it is important to use *pane di campagna* (coarse-textured country bread).

*¼ cup (2 fl oz/60 ml) extra virgin olive oil*
*1 cup (8 fl oz/250 ml) milk*
*6 slices coarse country bread*

*salt and freshly ground pepper*
*13 oz (400 g) mozzarella, sliced*
*6 anchovy fillets packed in oil, chopped*
*1 tablespoon dried oregano*
*½ cup (2 oz/60 g) freshly grated Parmesan cheese*

Pour the oil into a baking dish.

Pour the milk into a deep dish and briefly soak the slices of bread. Arrange the bread slices in the baking dish so they are slightly overlapping in a single layer. Season with salt and pepper. Cover the bread with the mozzarella. Arrange the anchovies over the cheese. Sprinkle with the oregano and Parmesan.

Bake in a preheated 400°F (200°C) oven for about 20 minutes. Serve at once.

# CRÊPES STUFFED WITH MUSSELS

*Crespelle alle cozze*

In the cookbook by an anonymous Tuscan writer of the fourteenth century, there is already mention of *crespelle* or *frittelle* and a little further on a reference to *crespelle, tortelli* and *ravioli* , thus crediting Italy, not France, with the creation of these crêpes. In France they appeared in the cookery books much later. *Crespelle* are refined crêpes that are very popular for elegant meals. They often take the place of lasagne, considered to be a more "common" dish. They are also very practical because they can be made beforehand and covered with a light béchamel sauce before heating.

*3 lb (1.5 kg) mussels*
*1 shallot, chopped*
*2 tablespoons (1 oz/30 g) butter*
*⅓ cup (1½ oz/45 g) all purpose (plain) flour*
*½ cup (4 fl oz/120 ml) dry white wine*
*salt and freshly ground pepper*
*1 tablespoon chopped parsley*
*2 eggs, beaten*
*2 tablespoons extra virgin olive oil*
*⅓ cup (3 fl oz/90 ml) milk, boiling*

Scrub the mussels and wash them under cold running water. Place them in a large pot. Cover and set over moderate heat until the shells open. Remove the mussels from their shells, reserving their liquid. Discard any that do not open. Strain the mussel liquid and set aside.

Combine the shallot and 1 tablespoon (½ oz/ 15 g) of the butter in a saucepan. Sauté gently until just soft. Add 2 tablespoons of flour and mix well to avoid lumps forming. Pour in the wine and the reserved mussel liquid; season with salt and pepper. Cut the remaining tablespoon of butter into small pieces and stir in until melted. Remove from the heat. Stir in the parsley and mussels.

Combine the remaining flour with a pinch of salt in a bowl. One at a time, stir in the beaten eggs. Add 1 tablespoon of the oil and the boiling milk. The batter should be creamy but fairly liquid.

Oil a small skillet and set over moderate heat. Pour in 2 tablespoons of the batter and tilt the pan to spread the mixture into a thin crêpe. Cook until lightly browned on one side, turn and brown the other side. Slide the *crespelle* onto a plate and repeat the procedure, greasing the pan with a little oil each time, until all of the batter has been used.

When all the crêpes are ready, lay them out on a work surface and divide the mussel sauce among them. Fold each one in 4 to make a fan shape. Layer them in a buttered ovenproof dish and bake in a preheated 400°F (200°C) oven for 10 minutes before serving.

*Crêpes stuffed with mussels*

*Fritters* (eighteenth century), a Castelli ceramic tile;
CASTELLO SFORZESCO, MILAN

# NEAPOLITAN FRITTERS

*Rissole alla Napoletana*

Francesco Leonardi, author of a six-volume work on cookery entitled *L'Apicio Moderno (The Modern Apicius)*, published in 1790, not only provides a wealth of recipes but also traces what may be called a history of Italian cooking from Roman times to his own period. He was cook to Catherine II, Empress of all the Russias, and had extensive experience in French, German and English cooking as well as Italian. His knowledge of Italian and foreign wines was considerable, and he includes an ample list of these. Many of his recipes are almost the same as those that are used today. These little fritters, for example, are very like the *panzarotti* which are still to be found in many food shops in Naples.

> Chop two fresh buffalo cheeses, add a little Parmesan, some *marzolino* and some grated *caciocavallo* [a cheese originally made from sheep's milk], and a slice of *prosciutto* which you have chopped and sweated a little in a saucepan over the fire, some chopped parsley, no salt, some crushed pepper, nutmeg, two uncooked eggs, and mix all these well together. Roll out a sheet of short pastry made with butter or lard (it matters little which) to a thickness of one *paolo* [an old coin], make little mounds of the above mixture on it and brush some beaten egg all around each one, then fold the dough back over the top, seal it well and cut it with a fluted pastry cutter into small halfmoon-shaped *ravioli*.
>
> At serving time, fry them in very hot pork fat and serve them as soon as they are nice and golden. In Naples these fritters, which we call *rissole*, are known as *panzarotti*.

1½ cups (6 oz/180 g) all purpose (plain) flour
¼ cup (2 fl oz/60 ml) water, lightly salted
3 oz (90 g) ricotta
1 egg
2 tablespoons chopped parsley
½ cup (2 oz/60 g) freshly grated Parmesan cheese
3 oz (90 g) mozzarella, cut into small dice
3 oz (90 g) salami, cut into small dice
freshly ground pepper
4 cups (1 qt/1 l) olive oil for frying

Heap the flour into a mound on a work surface. Make a well in the center and pour in the salted water, working the mixture until you have a soft dough.

Push the ricotta through a sieve into a bowl. Add the egg, parsley, Parmesan, mozzarella and salami. Mix thoroughly and add pepper to taste.

Roll out the dough to a 4 inch (10 cm) square and place little heaps of the ricotta mixture on it about 2 inches (5 cm) apart. Fold the dough over the top and press down between the heaps of filling to seal each one in a square. Cut out the squares with a fluted pastry cutter. Heat the oil to 350°F (180°C). Fry the *rissole* for about 5 minutes until they begin to turn golden. Drain on paper towels and serve very hot.

*Banquet scene* (French school of the fourteenth century), from Livy's *History of Rome*; STATE UNIVERSITY LIBRARY, GENEVA

*Neapolitan fritters — modern recipe*

*Eggs in aspic*

# EGGS IN ASPIC

*Aspic di uova sode*

Triumphant creations in gelatin have adorned the tables of the rich from the earliest times. Gelatin used to be made from good meat or chicken stock boiled with a pig's foot and a piece of calf's snout. Now we have powdered gelatin, but its flavor is certainly not as delicate.

*1 whole egg*
*⅓ cup (3 fl oz/90 ml) extra virgin olive oil*
*salt and freshly ground pepper*
*juice of 1 lemon*
*5 hardboiled eggs*
*6 oz (180 g) boiled chicken breast, cut into very*
  *thin strips*
*6 oz (180 g) lean cooked ham, diced*
*2 cubes (2 tablespoons/2 envelopes) instant*
  *(powdered) unflavored gelatin*

Beat the raw egg in a small bowl. Add the oil in a thin stream and whisk to make a mayonnaise. Season with salt and pepper; whisk in the lemon juice.

Shell the hardboiled eggs. Chop 1 egg and put it in a bowl. Add the chicken, ham, and mayonnaise, mixing with care.

Prepare the gelatin with warm water as directed on the packet and leave to cool but do not refrigerate. Take a 6 cup (1½ qt/1.5 l) pudding mold with straight, steep sides and coat with a thin film of the gelatin. Refrigerate until firmly set.

Slice the remaining 4 eggs. Arrange some of the egg slices in a circle at the bottom of the mold, like a crown. Fix in place with a thin layer of gelatin. Refrigerate at once, until set. Arrange the chicken, ham and egg slices in alternate layers in

the mold until all ingredients are used. Pour on the rest of the gelatin and refrigerate for at least 3 hours.

To serve, dip the sides of the mold in hot water for a moment. Invert the mold onto a serving plate to de-mold and serve.

# PEA AND HAM MOLD

*Sformato di piselli*

In Roman times peas were often dried, like lentils, beans and chick peas, and were even used for making flour. Later, during the Renaissance, people began to eat them fresh, and today they are sometimes served raw in a salad if they are really new and very fresh. Sometimes cooked ham is added to the vegetables in these *sformati* (molds), and if there is a bone from a raw ham left over when all the meat has gone, rather than throw it away, the cook adds it to the water for cooking the peas to give them more flavor. Ham bones are also often added to minestrone for the same purpose, especially in the North.

*4 lb (2 kg) fresh peas, shelled*
*¼ cup (2 oz/60 g) butter*
*¼ cup (1 oz/30 g) all purpose (plain) flour*
*¾ cup (6 fl oz/180 ml) milk, warmed*
*salt and freshly ground pepper*
*1 cup (4 oz/120 g) freshly grated Parmesan cheese*
*a little freshly grated nutmeg*
*4 eggs*
*6 oz (180 g) cooked ham, very finely chopped*
*1 tablespoon dry breadcrumbs*

Cook the peas in boiling salted water until tender. Drain. Purée the peas through a sieve.

Melt 2 tablespoons (1 oz/30 g) of the butter in a skillet over moderate heat. Add the flour and mix well. Add the milk, a little at a time, stirring

*Pea and ham mold*

94

constantly. Season with salt and pepper. Remove from the heat and add the Parmesan, nutmeg, eggs, chopped ham and purée of peas.

Use the remaining butter to coat a 6 cup (1½ qt/1.5 l) ring mold. Sprinkle the mold with the breadcrumbs and pour in the mixture. Bake in a preheated 350°F (180°C) oven for 1 hour. Unmold onto a serving platter and serve.

# MOLD OF GREEN BEANS

*Sformato di fagiolini*

**M**olded vegetable dishes used to be eaten only by wealthy families. Generally these dishes were served at dinner following the first course and before the main course of meat or fish. The *sformati* (molds) were generally accompanied by braised sweetbreads, hollandaise sauce or a light tomato sauce. Today they are eaten with these accompaniments as a main course instead of meat, especially in the evening.

*1¼ lb (600 g) fresh green beans, topped and tailed*
*¼ cup (2 oz/60 g) butter*

*3 tablespoons all purpose (plain) flour*
*1½ cups (13 fl oz/400 ml) milk, warmed*
*salt and freshly ground pepper*
*pinch of grated nutmeg*
*1 cup (4 oz/120 g) freshly grated Parmesan cheese*
*4 eggs*

Cook the beans in plenty of boiling salted water for 10 minutes. Drain well. Push them through a sieve or food mill to obtain an almost cream-like consistency.

To make the sauce, melt 1 tablespoon (½ oz/ 15 g) of the butter in a saucepan. Stir in the flour with a wooden spoon and mix thoroughly. Add the milk a little at a time, stirring constantly to dissolve any lumps. Season with salt, pepper and nutmeg and cook the sauce until thickened. Remove from the heat and stir in the Parmesan. Add the eggs, one at a time, and mix thoroughly. Stir the sauce into the bean purée.

Butter a 6 cup (1½ qt/1.5 l) ring mold. Pour in the bean mixture. Bake in a preheated 350°F (180°C) oven for about 1 hour. Turn out onto a plate and serve.

*Mold of green beans*

*Still life with fish* (detail), Vincenzo Campi (1536–91); BRERA GALLERY, MILAN Campi was a follower of the "populist" movement which depicted the humble scenes of life.

# FISH AND SHELLFISH

Italy has been shrouded in the legends of the sea since ancient times. The heartening sight of the fisherman bringing in his catch in the early morning light has remained unchanged for centuries. Unchanged, too, are many of the traditions for preparing and cooking the succulent catch. The legacy of seafood, inherited from the Greeks, took root in imperial Roman times. Since then generation after generation has celebrated the harvest of the sea.

The beautiful Mediterranean Sea has long been kind to the people of Italy, yielding an extraordinary wealth of edible sea-creatures. The Italian people are only too happy to take this glistening bounty into the kitchen, and there, create an array of sensational seafood dishes. The few inland regions take immense pleasure from the icy Alpine-fed rivers and lakes, which provide an abundance of freshwater fish. Since medieval times, for Italians in remote mountainous areas the tradition has endured of importing dried cod.

Today the bustling and variegated fish section of any market and the often spectacular window displays of fish restaurants are a colorful and shimmering testimony to the important place this food enjoys on the Italian table.

Crustaceans, mollusks and all manner of fish, large and small, have found their way into *antipasti*, robust soups, sauces for pasta and risotto, pizza and onto the table variously fried, roasted, grilled, boiled or baked to provide a memorable main course.

The ancient Romans were prepared to go to any lengths to ensure a continuous supply of fresh fish. Not only were the fish brought alive to market but they were transported in tanks of water taken from where the fish were caught — surely a back-breaking enterprise! One can now only imagine the dazzling sight of the aquarium in Trajan's market — freshwater and saltwater varieties teeming in the enormous tanks, with their rainbow hues reflected through the waters they swam in.

In medieval Italy the many monastic communities, which observed partial and even total abstinence from meat, devoted considerable energy to raising fish in monastery ponds, while Brother Cook drew on all his skills to prepare them for the refectory table. Fish was also prominent on Renaissance menus. In the sixteenth century, Bartolomeo Scappi provided various sea-food recipes, such as: sturgeon heads in aspic; baked pasta pies filled with squid; *orata* (gilthead sea bream) cooked with prunes, cinnamon and saffron; and, that time-honored delicacy, the eel, fried in a sweet and sour sauce. In addition, he described several ways to deal with a sea turtle, instructing his readers how to clean it without breaking its delicate eggs. The eggs, he suggested, should be set aside for frying afterwards.

*The sign of Aries* (detail), *The fishmonger* (fourteenth century), fresco; RAGIONE PALACE, PADUA
In medieval Italy monasteries observed partial or total abstinence from meat, thus they devoted considerable time and energy to raising pond-fish.

*Market scene in Veneto with fishmongers*
(*circa* 1835), colored lithograph;
BERTARELLI PRINT COLLECTION, MILAN
Fish is popular throughout the Veneto
region and is often cooked with rice in a
risotto or made into a stew and eaten with
polenta slices.

One of the great Italian classics is *zuppa di pesce* (fish soup). This edifying, robust dish is rather more of a stew than a soup and usually constitutes the main course of a meal. Like all *zuppe*, this flavorsome fish soup is traditionally served in deep plates, poured over a slice of broiled (grilled) country bread. Practically every major town along the coast has its own version, usually with a local character, although the variations between recipes is often minor. What they all have in common, however, is the use of a bony but rather ordinary fish, more a source of flavor than flesh, which is upgraded by the addition of a more prized variety, such as shellfish.

The Venetians make a broth from the more humble species for their *brodetto di pesce* (fish broth) before enlivening it with morsels of a superior species. The illustrious former maritime republic of Genoa boasts two celebrated renditions of this dish. First there is *buridda alla Genovese*, which is a splendid stew that calls for angler fish, octopus, squid, a handful of mussels, shrimps and clams, with a large margin of liberty for what might be left over from the morning market's flavorsome bits and pieces. Then there is *ciuppin*, which uses much the same ingredients although the fish, after being cooked, is boned and puréed. From Livorno, on the Adriatic coast, comes the famous fish soup, *cacciucco*, the densest of all fish soups. Based on rascasse (*scorfano* or dogfish) and other coarse (though exotic sounding) indigenous fish, the texture is refined with the usual crustaceans. Often, as a delightful surprise, one small *aragosta* (spiny lobster) for each diner will be added. *Peperoncini* (chile peppers) are added to the broth to give it a distinctive flavor. The fish is placed over a slice of broiled (grilled) bread rubbed with garlic and the thick broth is poured over it. Most distinguished of the *zuppe di pesce* is the mixture of mollusks such as *datteri* (date-shells), *cannolicchi* (razor-shells), *telline* (wedge-shells), *vongole* (clams), and *tartufi di mare* (sea-truffles). This wonderful combination is a specialty in several regions, where the ingredients are available.

It is the custom, in restaurants, for the proprietor to proudly present the whole fish on a platter both before and after it is cooked. This is particularly true if it is the handsome *orata* (gilthead sea bream), with its distinctive golden spot on each cheek and between the eyes, a fish that is the most prized of its family. As with so many of the whole fish dishes, its delicate flavor is highlighted in the simplest way possible. It is exquisite baked in paper (so no juices can escape) with olive oil and parsley or with slices of *porcini* mushrooms when they are in season. The steel-blue *dentice* (dentex or sea bass) adds vivid color to the restaurateur's platter. With its silver sides and reddish hue, it is a fine fish indeed. It is best broiled (grilled) or, if large enough, stuffed and baked. The head and neck are considered especially delectable.

The *triglia* (red mullet), which has been held in the highest esteem since ancient times, is another fish suitable for presenting on a platter. Unique in both its flavor and luminous crimson color, it has been valued for its visual pleasure as much as for its taste. The Greeks considered it sacred to Hecate and, according to Alan Davidson in his definitive *Mediterranean Seafood*, during the first century AD the Romans "went mad over it." All the celebrated Latin writers of the day — Cicero, Horace, Juvenal, Martial and Seneca — commented on the "red mullet fever" which spread among the rich. Large specimens (mention is made of mullets weighing at least five pounds — 2.5 kilograms) were proudly displayed in captivity. According to Pliny, "the readers in gastronomy" enjoyed watching through a glass bowl the changing color of a dying fish. Today red mullet is prepared in

numerous ways: in Venice it is marinated in white wine, in Livorno it is simmered in tomato sauce, and in Abruzzi it is seasoned with bay leaves. The essential point is not to mask its distinctive taste with too many other flavors. It is excellent simply broiled (grilled) with a congenial herb such as wild fennel or thyme.

Two other popular and excellent fish — the *tonno* (tuna) and *pesce spada* (swordfish) — are far too large to be presented on a platter! They are, however, quite something to be seen whole in markets. Tuna is the more versatile of the two. The best-quality *tonno sott'olio*, preserved in olive oil, is sold by weight from large tin containers and appears in an array of *antipasti* dishes and pasta sauces. There are also numerous traditional recipes for cooking it fresh as a main course, particularly in the southern regions, whose waters are rich spawning grounds for a wide variety of species — the immense bluefin, the longfin albacore, and a little tuna called *tonnetto*. Commercial tuna fisheries in the Mediterranean area date back to the early Greeks. In Sicily the flashing blue tuna are still trapped in long nets extending out to sea and then gaffed. This ancient ritual, called the *mattanza*, was described by Aeschylus and is still a popular spectacle in May or June, especially along the coast of Trapani.

*Marine fauna*, Roman mosaic;
NATIONAL ARCHEOLOGICAL MUSEUM, NAPLES
The ancient Romans went to extreme lengths to ensure a continuous supply of fresh fish: they transported live, freshly caught fish to market in huge tanks of water.

*Tuna-fishing*, Trapani school
(seventeenth–eighteenth century),
ceramic tiles; PEPOLI MUSEUM, TRAPANI

The ancients served tuna with their classic tingling sweet and sour sauces of honey, herbs and vinegar. The fifteenth-century cook and writer Maestro Martino da Como, in a lengthy section in his book *Libro de Arte Coquinaria (Book of Culinary Art)*, describes the best methods of cooking fish. He recommends using the *ventresca* (the belly of the fish) — the fatter, firmer, and more compact the better. His recipe calls for boiling the tuna and then steeping the flesh in vinegar. Because tuna has a strongly pronounced natural flavor, traditional Italian methods of preparing it favor a light touch — olives, capers, and tomatoes are classic complements.

The tradition of hunting swordfish by harpoon along the coast of Sicily is a ritual that has been handed down through the generations since antiquity. With all its attendant action and drama, it is a veritable battle between man and beast. During the August main holiday (*Ferragosto*) an annual festival is held in Messina, where local fishermen show off their considerable prowess and skill for the tourists, who are then able to feast on swordfish steaks cooked on grills along the harbor. In the markets the fishmonger deftly slices fat, white steaks from a huge, fresh fish, whose sword is displayed alongside. Francesco Leonardi, the eighteenth-century chef to the aristocracy of Naples during the era of the Bourbons, and author of *L'Apicio Moderno (The Modern Epicurean)*, recommends flavoring pieces of swordfish, cut to the thickness of a thumb, in a marinade based on truffles or plums (depending on the season), before sautéing them in the liquid and deglazing the pan with champagne. Marinated swordfish steaks are delicious broiled (grilled), or, as in an old Calabrian recipe, steamed with capers, olive oil, lemon and vinegar.

While the big fish may be impressive, Italians are also expert at preparing small fish with the greatest care and skill. The tiniest of these are *alici* (fresh anchovies), which are often served as an antipasto. In her book, *Italian Food*, Elizabeth David is unstinting in her praise of them: "Fresh anchovies and fresh sardines are two of the most delicate fish of the Mediterranean. Anchovies in particular are difficult to get hold of. They are caught only at the time of the waning moon." In the sixteenth century Scappi included them in his list of cold dishes for the *primo servizio di credenza* (first course served from the sideboard), and today their delicate flavor is perfect for a light luncheon. Perhaps the best way to experience the anchovy is raw, simply filleted, splitting open their attractive blue-green back and silver sides and marinating them for several hours in lemon juice. They are also a treat cooked briefly in olive oil, garlic and herbs.

Fresh, silvery *sarde* (sardines) are utterly delicious. A classic from Palermo is *pasta con le sarde* (pasta with sardines), in which rigatoni is matched with a sauce of wild fennel, pine nuts, raisins and fried sardines, then baked in the oven with more sardines laid on top. As a main course fresh sardines are most wonderful when unadulterated. Broiling (grilling) is an excellent way of retaining the intrinsic flavor; but sardines can also be deep fried or rolled in breadcrumbs and baked. The traditional way of preparing them was, however, much more elaborate: it involved stuffing them with a rich mixture, possibly including olives, cloves, capers, pine nuts, raisins, *pecorino* cheese, breadcrumbs and eggs. The sardines can be rolled up into tasty small balls, as Bartolomeo Scappi suggested in the sixteenth century, or cooked lengthwise as in the celebrated Sicilian dish, *sarde a beccafico*. With this dish the sardines are brought to the table as tantalizingly plump and

*The fishmonger*, school of Carlo Saraceni (*circa* 1580–1620); CORSINI COLLECTION, FLORENCE Saraceni followed in the style of Caravaggio, painting realistic, unidealised everyday scenes.

103

round as their namesakes, the *beccafico* (literally, fig-peckers — birds who feed on figs and whose tasty flesh is much sought after by local hunters).

Of the small crustaceans, the juicy jewels of the sea, shrimps (prawns) have long been sought after and put to many uses. In *L'Apicio Moderno* Leonardi gives a refined eighteenth-century recipe for preparing them "the Italian way," cooked in a sublime sauce of white wine, lemon and a bouquet of chopped herbs. Complementing their natural sweetness with aromatic herbs — marjoram, thyme, tarragon, basil and parsley — remains the perfect way to serve them.

The exquisitely tender small mollusks of the octopus family are eaten throughout Italy. The four varieties: *seppie* (cuttlefish), *calamari* (squid) and *polipetti* and *moscardini* (tiny octopus) can be no bigger than walnuts. Methods of cooking them individually vary from region to region. A favorite cuttlefish recipe has it stuffed with a mixture of parsley, garlic, eggs, cheese, breadcrumbs, bits of other fish and its own chopped-up tentacles. In Tuscany *seppie in zimino* are cooked with spinach, herbs and spices, and lots of ground pepper. This recipe is reminiscent of a Renaissance recipe reported by Scappi, who proposed simmering them with chopped greens and seasoning with cinnamon and saffron. Squid are also ideal for stuffing in similar ways to cuttlefish but, as they are chewier, it is more prudent and effective to stew them in wine, onion, garlic, tomatoes and herbs. All these mollusks are most commonly found nestling together with other bite-sized fish in a *fritto misto mare* — mixed fish fry.

*Fish*, Giuseppe Recco (1634–95);
SAN MARTINO MUSEUM, NAPLES
It is a time-honored tradition that the proprietor of a restaurant presents the selected fish to the patron on a platter both before and after it is cooked.

For centuries the picturesque streams, rivers and lakes fed by the waters of the Alps and Apennines provided the surrounding regions with an abundance of freshwater fish such as excellent trout, perch, carp, shad and sturgeon. Sadly, as with the rest of the Western world, Italy suffers from pollution, but that still does not stop scores of fishermen who, like their ancestors, are still bringing in their catch. They are not restricted to the rugged mountainous areas but can also be seen along the banks of rivers like the Arno, which flows through Florence. Although farmed trout is the variety now most commonly available, fresh salmon trout can still be found leaping in the northern streams. Classical writers reported glowingly of the Tiber's tasty trout (*pesce persico*), of perch from Lake Maggiore and huge *lasca* (a rare roach), from Umbria's Lake Trasimeno. During medieval and Renaissance times the Bishop of Perugia sent a gift of *lasca* to the Pope in the Vatican for his supper each Holy Saturday, the eve of Easter. As in fish stories the world over, the trout of former times seem to have assumed immense proportions. Scappi tells of trout fished from the lakes of northern Italy weighing in at an astonishing sixty pounds (twenty-seven kilograms) and more. Recipes called for these monsters to be cut into pieces and stewed with sugar and spices. In the seventeenth and eighteenth centuries it was stylish to prepare them *alla Francesca*, with thick and rich cream sauces. Today's taste prefers them simply and deliciously marinated in white wine and herbs and eaten hot off the grill.

*The eel-seller*, Filippo Palizzi (1819–99), print; MUNICIPAL LIBRARY, MILAN
The *capitone* eel is a huge variety of eel traditionally served as an *antipasto* on Christmas Eve. It is cooked in vinegar with bay leaves and garlic and then left to marinate for a few days.

A curiously ugly sea creature, but one that has been considered a great delicacy since the Middle Ages, is the *anguilla* or common eel. Spending much of its life in fresh waters, it spawns in the western Atlantic and grows to maturity in European rivers. Baby eels are snared by opportunistic fishermen, who await their return to the open sea. In Italy the Comacchio Lagoon at the mouth of the Po River is the lively center of the eel-fishing industry, as indeed it has been since the Middle Ages. The luckier eels are released to spawn in the Sargasso Sea, while the others are fished out to be canned.

The Comacchio eels, which are large and tasty, are first cooked to reduce the fat, then preserved in wine vinegar with bay leaves and, finally, packed and shipped throughout the country. The rich flesh of fresh eel is usually eaten cut into thick slices and roasted with herbs. On Christmas Eve — traditionally a day of religious abstinence from meat — the classic dish in Rome is *capitone*, a type of common eel that has been specially fattened. In a practice reminiscent of the Roman Emperor Trajan's day, the eel is bought live from tanks in the Roman fish markets. It is cleaned, sliced, rubbed with garlic, skewered with alternating bay leaves, marinated in olive oil and vinegar, and then roasted. In *Italian Food* Elizabeth David quotes the succinct comment of the nineteenth-century writer, George Augustus Sala: "Some people are prejudiced against eels. Combat the prejudice; subdue it."

Oddly, for a land with a commitment to fresh fish and a rich tradition of preparing it, one of the most significant seafood dishes in Italy is a dried fish — dried cod, which has been imported from Scandinavia and North America since the sixteenth and seventeenth centuries respectively. Cod is another example of a food of poor people which has survived the passing of time and fashion to become a national taste and an aristocrat of the table. Its popularity is largely due to the fact that it is not only economic and highly nutritious but practically imperishable. These are important qualities for a country in which many poor people lived in remote mountainous areas without refrigeration and were often obliged to abstain from meat for religious reasons. Not found in the Mediterranean, cod arrived by ship at the great port cities such as Venice and Genoa, packed in barrels, and was then transported inland over the Alps and Apennines along the so-called salt routes — well-traveled ways along which dried cod, as well as salted foods and later olive oil, were transported. The repertoire of recipes for cooking dried cod is vast and includes examples from regions the length and breadth of Italy.

The best-known and most widely used types of dried cod are *baccalà* and *stoccafisso*, each of which is cured by quite different methods. Despite this, they often are confused in Italian recipe books and restaurant menus, the word *baccalà* being indiscriminately used for both. *Stoccafisso* is cured in Norway, Iceland and Newfoundland by being hung from sticks and dried in the North winds. The result is a long, hard, stick-like object with the color and texture of parchment. Its preparation is time-consuming and arduous. It has to be beaten in order to loosen the fibers and then soaked for a few days in several changes of fresh water before it is ready for the many excellent ways of cooking. *Baccalà* is cured by salting; it is only partially dried, and then pressed in layers; it is usually sold in chunks. The flesh remains white and need only be soaked for a day. Fortunately the fish is prepared for cooking by the grocer before it is bought!

Cod made its first appearance in recipes in 1570. In Chapter 112 of the Third Book of his *Opera* entitled "many ways of cooking dried cod," Bartolomeo Scappi counseled against beating the fish, in favor of the gentler method of letting it soften on its own in tepid water over eight hours. He suggests boiling it with a chopped onion, or sautéing fillets in herbs, and serving them with a garlic sauce; or else frying the fish coated in flour, serving it accompanied by an orange sauce with, on a side plate, some *mostarda* (preserves of candied fruit). He also gives recipes for grander sauces seasoned with pepper, cinnamon and cloves, because, as he put it so beautifully, "this fish loves spices."

After Scappi's worthy effort, there is no further mention of cod in the recipe books for some 200 years, until it reappeared in 1790 in Leonardi's *L'Apicio Moderno*. Perhaps those earlier writers, often writing for the aristocracy, considered the humble cod too "common" to bother with. During the seventeenth and eighteenth centuries, however, cod became immensely popular in Italy and imports from Norway increased from a mere 100 tons to 11 000 tons.

Leonardi's recommendation was for perfect simplicity: to boil the *baccalà* and, just before serving, to pour over some *butirro nero* (butter heated almost to burning point) and garnish the platter with fried parsley.

Artusi, in the nineteenth century, was full of praise for the quality of *baccalà* in the markets of Florence (imported from Labrador). He recommends it as an alternative for days of religious abstinence, when there was a critical shortage of fresh fish. He gives nine recipes for dried cod, preferring it coated in egg and breadcrumbs and fried in butter, which, he says, entices one by its similarity (in appearance at least) to the more distinguished breaded veal cutlet.

Venice and Genoa, with their long history of sea-trading, are the most famous for their methods of preparing cod. The Venetian *baccalà mantecato* is the most refined rendition of *stoccafisso* to be found anywhere. Along with the French Provençal *brandade de morue*, it can be traced back to the Spanish version, *bacalao al ajo arriero*. In Venetian dialect "*mantecato*" means "worked" and refers to the amount of preparation involved in bringing this noted dish to the table. The finest, fattest fillets are steamed before being skinned and boned. The flesh is then energetically pounded for several minutes, while adding olive oil

*The fish-seller from Posillipo*, print
The fish and seafood of Naples have been famous for centuries. The Neapolitan markets display a surprising array of fresh fish.

*Tarantella in Mergellina* (detail), *Fish-seller and fishermen*, Filippo Falciatore (eighteenth century); INSTITUTE OF ART, DETROIT It is no wonder that fish constitute such a large part of the Italian diet since fifteen of the twenty Italian regions have a coastline — the remaining five have an abundance of freshwater fish.

little by little until a thick white cream ensues. Salt, pepper, chopped parsley and garlic are mixed in and the dish is served cold with slices of broiled (grilled) bread. In Liguria, fried *baccalà* is eaten with a pungent sauce of soft breadcrumbs, white wine vinegar and a heap of garlic. In the traditional dish of the Venetian province of Vincenza, dried cod poached in milk is paired with polenta.

The great Italian seafood tradition proves that, despite an increasingly sophisticated world, the legacies handed down from family to family are the root of Italian culture.

# TENCH

*La tinca*

This recipe by Bartolomeo Platina is contained in the tenth volume of *De Honesta Voluptate ac Valetudine* (*Concerning Honest Pleasure and Well-being*), published in 1474. In the introduction to the book he writes mainly about fish and the various ways of cooking them, and observes that fish are moist and cold like the element in which they live. They are also, he says, indigestible and not very healthy — in contrast to modern nutritionists who recommend them highly in the fight against cholesterol. Platina gives a brief description of each fish and explains how to clean it, before going on to give cooking suggestions. Tench, like carp, is a freshwater fish living mainly in the mud. This gives it a slightly muddy taste which, however, disappears when the fish is properly cooked, and the result is a very delicate flavor. The recipe was inspired by a very similar one by the fifteenth-century Maestro Martino da Como. The modern recipe calls for the fish to be marinated so that it loses this distinctive muddy taste.

I believe the fish that today is known as tench was at one time called *mena*. If it is large and you wish to cook it by boiling, eat it dressed with verjuice, spices and very finely chopped parsley, or, again if it is large, after you have removed the scales cut it along the backbone, turn it inside out so that its innards are on the outside, remove the entrails and bones and put in a mixture made from its eggs, chopped parsley, crushed pepper and garlic and a little saffron. There are some who make this mixture with black or red cherries or with sultanas, shelled pine nuts and a beaten egg. Finally, cook it over the coals on low heat, and as soon as it is cooked dress it with some vinegar pickle and oil, and moisten with verjuice or orange juice. Or, if the tench is small, cut it as before and after you have dredged it in flour, fry it in oil and when it is cooked, moisten with verjuice and orange juice. Whatever way you cook it, there is nothing worse than tench.

*1 small onion, chopped*
*2 garlic cloves, chopped*
*3 tablespoons extra virgin olive oil*
*½ cup (4 fl oz/120 ml) vinegar*
*½ cup (4 fl oz/120 ml) dry white wine*
*1 handful fresh sage leaves*
*salt*
*6 tench or trout, about 6 oz (180 g) each, cleaned*
*4 cups (1 qt/1 l) oil for frying*

Gently fry the onion and garlic in the olive oil over low heat until translucent. Add the vinegar, wine and sage; season with salt. Bring the mixture to a boil.

Fry the fish in the oil at 400°F (200°C) until golden. Drain, and transfer them to a deep dish and pour the marinade over them. Cover and set aside in the liquid for a couple of days. At the end of that time, drain the fish, arrange on a serving dish and serve.

*Fishing in the river* (fifteenth century), illumination from the Theatrum Sanitatis, code 4182; CASANATENSE LIBRARY, ROME

# TO ROAST BONITO

*Ad arrostire la palamite*

This simple recipe, from a collection by an unknown southern writer of the fifteenth century, could still be followed today by home cooks. The description of preparing the fish is especially amusing and is given in minute detail. The bonito is a kind of small tuna, rather slender in shape. The recipe book was compiled for aristocratic and upper middle-class households, and is full of meat, fish and vegetable pies which were very popular at the time. Most noticeable is the extensive use of spices, such as cumin, coriander, and the now very expensive saffron, no longer fashionable in Italian cookery, and of combinations of sweet with savory, such as in the recipe for fish entrails cooked with almonds, spices and sugar. The modern recipe is for trout with a simple lemon sauce.

To roast a bonito take out the intestines of the fish through its ears and put in some salt through the ears and in the mouth and put a wooden spit, shaped like a sword, in through the mouth and make it come out through the tail, and let it cook a little close to the fire. Then bind it carefully, as you would a pheasant, with pork fat and cook it properly and eat it with the juice of citrons or lemons or with rosewater.

6 fresh rosemary sprigs
¼ cup (2 fl oz/60 ml) vinegar
6 trout, cleaned
salt and freshly ground pepper

6 thin slices pancetta
⅓ cup (3 fl oz/90 ml) extra virgin olive oil
juice of 1 lemon

Dip the rosemary sprigs in the vinegar and insert them in the fish. Season with salt and pepper. Wrap each trout in a slice of *pancetta*. Thread each onto a skewer and broil (grill), turning often and brushing frequently with a little of the oil. After about 20 minutes transfer the fish to a serving plate.

In a small bowl dissolve a pinch of salt in the lemon juice. Mix in the remaining oil. Serve the sauce separately with the trout.

*Tench — modern recipe (left) To roast bonito — modern recipe (right)*

*Grilled salmon trout*

# GRILLED SALMON TROUT

*Trota salmonata alla griglia*

Trout is served mainly in the North of Italy. It has always been highly regarded, especially in times before the importation of salmon from Scotland. It has a more delicate flavor than salmon, and is suited to Italian cooking which is simple and oriented towards enhancing the natural flavors of food rather than covering them up with rich sauces. This is without doubt one of the best ways of cooking trout.

*6 salmon trouts, about 6 oz (180 g) each*
*¼ cup (2 fl oz/60 ml) extra virgin olive oil*
*salt*
*juice of 1 lemon*
*freshly ground pepper*
*¼ cup (2 fl oz/60 ml) dry white wine*

*1 tablespoon (½ oz/15 g) butter*
*1 tablespoon chopped fresh basil*

Arrange the fish in a single layer on a plate. Brush with a little of the oil. Season with salt, sprinkle with half the lemon juice and pepper lightly. Pour on the wine. Set aside to marinate for a couple of hours, turning now and again.

Heat a broiler (griller) until red-hot. Drain the fish of its marinade. Place the fish on a broiling pan (grill), and broil (grill) for a few minutes on each side.

Meanwhile, combine the remaining oil and the butter in a saucepan and heat, but do not brown. Turn off the heat and add the remaining lemon juice and the basil. Season with pepper.

Arrange the fish on a serving dish, pour the oil and butter sauce over, and serve.

# SWORDFISH AND CAPERS BAKED IN FOIL

*Pesce spada ai capperi*

**H**ere is another recipe for cooking fish in paper which is one of the oldest and simplest. Fish cooked this way retains all its flavor, as do certain cuts of meat given similar treatment. The only seasonings required are capers, chopped herbs or cut-up fresh tomatoes — it is not necessary to use too many fats.

*6 swordfish steaks (or tuna or snapper) about 6 oz (180 g) each*
*⅓ cup (3 fl oz/90 ml) extra virgin olive oil*
*a little wine vinegar*
*salt and freshly ground pepper*
*1 tablespoon chopped parsley*
*6 lemon slices*
*2 oz (60 g) capers, drained*

Take 6 sheets of foil and place a fish steak on each. Brush the fish with a little of the oil, and sprinkle on a small amount of vinegar. Season each steak with salt and pepper, scatter a pinch of parsley on top, and add a slice of lemon and some capers.

Fold and seal the fish parcels, making sure they are tightly closed. Place them on a baking sheet and bake in a preheated 400°F (200°C) oven for about 15 minutes, until cooked through.

Transfer the parcels to a hot serving dish and open them at the table, taking care not to let the juices escape.

*Swordfish and capers baked in foil*

*Grilled mullet with thyme*

# GRILLED MULLET WITH THYME

*Triglie al timo*

**I**n the sixth chapter of Maestro Martino da Como's *Libro de Arte Coquinaria* (*Book of Culinary Art*), a chapter devoted to fish, there are numerous recipes using herbs, often mixed with spices as well. Today we tend to leave out the spices and make more frequent use of the fresh taste of herbs.

Despite the disadvantage of having lots of bones, red mullet is one of the finest fish the Mediterranean has to offer, and also one of the most aesthetically pleasing because of its reddish color. It is a strong-flavored fish and therefore does not require the addition of other strong flavors. A sprig of fresh thyme or rosemary is sufficient to make it a very special dish, particularly if it is cooked in paper (*al cartoccio*).

*6 red mullet, about 6 oz (180 g) each, cleaned*
*¼ cup (2 fl oz/60 ml) extra virgin olive oil*
*12 fresh thyme twigs*
*6 slices lemon*
*salt and freshly ground pepper*

Clean and wash the fish. Oil 6 sheets of foil and place a fish on each sheet. Place a thyme twig inside each. Lay a slice of lemon and another twig of thyme on top of the fish; season with salt and pepper.

Close up the packages, rolling the edges of the foil together to seal. Preheat the broiler (griller) and broil (grill) the fish for 5 minutes on each side. Serve at once.

*Sea bream baked with mushrooms*

# SEA BREAM BAKED WITH MUSHROOMS

*Orata ai funghi*

As far back as the fourteenth century we find in a book by an anonymous Venetian author the recipe for a "tasty and truely perfect" mushroom pie in which fish pieces were mixed with the mushrooms. The great Venetian chef of the sixteenth century, Giulio Cesare Tirelli, described the gilthead sea bream thus: "The fishes that carry the crown are indeed the queen of the others because they are delicate beyond belief." The gilthead sea bream is one of the finest and most expensive fish available in Italy. It is eminently suitable for elegant dinners, especially when prepared according to this very simple recipe in which the fish scales are replaced by slices of cultivated mushrooms. Better still is to cover it with slices of small *porcini* (boletus) mushrooms or the very delicate *ovuli* (Caesar's mushrooms) when these are in season.

*1 gilthead sea bream, about 3 lb (1.5 kg)*
*salt and freshly ground pepper*
*6 oz (180 g) champignons or button mushrooms,*
  *thickly sliced*
*¼ cup (2 fl oz/60 ml) extra virgin olive oil*

Plunge the fish briefly into boiling salted water, drain and leave to cool, then remove the skin. Lay it in an oiled baking dish, season with salt and pepper, cover with the mushrooms and sprinkle with oil.

Cover the baking dish with foil, and bake the fish in a preheated 350°F (180°C) oven for about 20 minutes.

# SEA BREAM ON A BED OF VEGETABLES AND HERBS

*Pagello alle verdure*

In medieval times, this dish from the Ligurian region, belonged to the "cuisine of the poor." As much of the day's catch as possible would be sold for the tables of the rich, so the fisherman's family had to make do with the meagre remains. This recipe, using abundant vegetables and herbs, was one way of making a small amount of fish serve a large number of people.

The sea bream is a similar fish to the gilthead (or dorade), and one may be substituted for the other. For this dish dentex (or porgy) is also suitable. The vegetable flavors complement the fish perfectly, and the vegetables themselves can be used to make a delicate sauce to serve with it. As an accompaniment you might serve plain boiled potatoes sprinkled with chopped parsley.

*1 sea bream, about 4 lb (2 kg)*
*¼ cup (2 fl oz/60 ml) extra virgin olive oil*
*1 lb (500 g) ripe tomatoes, peeled and chopped*
*1 medium onion, chopped*
*1 celery stalk, chopped*
*1 carrot, scraped and chopped*
*2 tablespoons of parsley, chopped*
*2 garlic cloves, chopped*
*3 fresh sage leaves, chopped*
*1 tablespoon fresh rosemary leaves, chopped*
*salt and freshly ground pepper*

Clean, gut and scale the fish, leaving head and tail intact. Wash and pat dry.

Put a large shallow flameproof casserole over

*Sea bream on a bed of vegetables and herbs*

low heat. Add 2 tablespoons of the oil, the vegetables and herbs and cook for about 10 minutes. Lay the fish carefully on top and pour the remaining oil over it. Season with salt and pepper and cook for about 30 minutes.

# SEA BREAM BAKED IN A PARCEL

*Orata al cartoccio*

One of the classic dishes of Italian fish cookery is sea bream baked in the oven in a paper wrapping. At one time it used to be cooked in greased paper, but today parchment (baking paper) or foil is sometimes used instead. There are also special terracotta saucepans which produce the same effect: the fish is placed in the saucepan virtually without seasoning, sealed firmly and baked in the oven.

*1 gilthead sea bream, about 3 lb (1.5 kg)*
*1 tablespoon (½ oz/15 g) butter*
*2 tablespoons chopped parsley*
*salt and freshly ground pepper*
*6 oz (180 g) mushrooms, chopped*
*4 anchovy fillets packed in oil, chopped*
*¼ cup (2 fl oz/60 ml) extra virgin olive oil*
*juice of 1 lemon*

Clean the bream, scrape it with a small knife to remove the scales, wash and dry it.

Work the butter with 1 tablespoon of chopped parsley and place inside the fish with a little salt and pepper, half the mushrooms and the pieces of anchovy.

Mix the oil and lemon juice with the other tablespoon of parsley. Brush a sheet of greaseproof paper with the oil and lemon mixture, lay the fish on top and scatter the remaining mushrooms over it. Pour the rest of the oil and lemon mixture on top and cover with another sheet of paper. Seal the parcel well all round and place it on an oven tray.

Bake at 400°F (200°C) for about 20 minutes. Open the parcel and serve.

*Sea bream baked in a parcel*

113

Tuna cutlets in parsley and breadcrumbs

# TUNA CUTLETS IN PARSLEY AND BREADCRUMBS

*Costolette di tonno al prezzemolo*

The custom of frying fish in breadcrumbs is common in Italy, and it can make a very attractive presentation, particularly if the breadcrumbs are mixed with a little parsley. Stronger herbs such as rosemary or sage are also sometimes used. Italian parsley is flat and very flavorsome, in contrast to the more commonly used curly parsley which has less flavor and is thus more suited for use as a garnish.

*6 tuna steaks, about 6 oz (180 g) each*
*½ cup (4 fl oz/120 ml) white wine vinegar*
*¾ cup (3 oz/90 g) all purpose (plain) flour*
*1 egg, beaten*
*¾ cup (3 oz/90 g) dry breadcrumbs*
*1 tablespoon chopped parsley*
*¾ cup (6 fl oz/180 ml) extra virgin olive oil*
*salt*
*1 lemon, cut into wedges*

Wash the fish and pat dry. Place the vinegar, flour and egg in separate shallow bowls. Combine the breadcrumbs and parsley in another shallow bowl. Dip the fish steaks in the vinegar one at a time, drain them and dredge in the flour. Dip in the beaten egg and then in the breadcrumb mixture, coating both sides.

Heat the oil in a cast-iron skillet. Brown the cutlets for a few minutes on each side. Sprinkle with salt and drain on paper towels.

Serve at once, accompanied by lemon wedges.

# OVEN-BAKED TUNA WITH ARTICHOKES

*Tonno con carciofi*

Tuna has a rather pronounced flavor and has always been a widely popular fish, as the seas around Italy are full of them and because it represents good value for a fairly low price. At one time in Sicily there used to be special tuna-fishing areas known as *tonnare* where the fishermen used sharp spears. Today these have been abolished, and the fish are caught by more commercial means.

*6 large artichokes*
*juice of 2 lemons*
*¼ cup (2 fl oz/60 ml) extra virgin olive oil*
*6 tuna steaks, about 6 oz (180 g) each*
*2 tablespoons dry breadcrumbs*
*1 tablespoon parsley, finely chopped*
*2 garlic cloves, finely chopped*
*salt*

Trim the artichokes and remove the tough leaves and the spikes. Cut into wedges; place in a bowl of water acidulated with half the lemon juice to prevent darkening.

Oil a baking dish. Arrange 3 of the fish steaks on the bottom and sprinkle with 1 tablespoon of the breadcrumbs. Mix the parsley with the garlic and sprinkle half over the breadcrumbs. Add salt to taste. Pour on 2 tablespoons of the oil and cover with half of the artichokes. Make another layer of fish, add the remaining breadcrumbs, parsley and garlic and artichoke wedges. Pour on the remaining oil and the lemon juice.

Seal the dish with foil. Bake in a preheated 350°F (180°C) oven for 30 minutes. Take the baking dish to the table on a serving platter, and serve from the dish.

*Oven-baked tuna with artichokes*

*Tuna with olives and capers*

# TUNA WITH OLIVES AND CAPERS

*Tonno con le olive e capperi*

**A**t one time tuna, because of its strong, distinctive taste, was cooked with a variety of spices, raisins, pine nuts, and even honey and sugar. Nowadays these strong flavors are replaced by lighter tastes — capers or olives, for example, giving a more Mediterranean flavor.

*¼ cup (2 fl oz/60 ml) extra virgin olive oil*
*6 fresh tuna steaks, about 6 oz (180 g) each*
*1 tablespoon chopped fresh basil*
*1 tablespoon capers, drained*
*3 oz (90 g) green olives, pitted (stoned) and sliced*
*1 lb (500 g) ripe tomatoes, peeled and chopped*
*¼ cup (1 oz/30 g) dry breadcrumbs*
*pinch of dried oregano*
*salt and freshly ground pepper*

Heat the oil in a deep skillet. Add the tuna steaks and brown for a few minutes in the hot oil. Scatter on the basil, capers, olives, tomatoes, breadcrumbs, oregano, some salt, and a good quantity of ground pepper. Continue cooking for another 10 minutes, then serve.

# GRILLED SOLE AND RADICCHIO

*Sogliole al radicchio*

**R**adicchio is a salad vegetable which was widely used in ancient times and grew wild. This recipe uses the highly prized *radicchio di Treviso* — Treviso is a small town near Venice, where the *radicchio* is whitened beneath manure or sand so the leaves become tender and lose some of their characteristic slightly bitter taste.

*6 sole, about 6 oz (180 g) each*
*¼ cup (2 fl oz/60 ml) extra virgin olive oil*
*1 tablespoon chopped parsley*
*1 garlic clove, chopped*
*salt and freshly ground pepper*
*6 small red radicchio lettuces*
*1 lemon, cut in wedges*

Clean and gut the fish but leave the skin on. Wash and pat dry.

In a large bowl, mix the oil with the parsley and garlic; add salt and a good pinch of pepper. Add the fish and marinate for about 2 hours, turning often.

Wash and dry the *radicchio* and cut each one in half lengthwise. Preheat a broiling (grilling) pan under the broiler (griller) until very hot. Place the *radicchio* on the pan and cook for 2 minutes on each side, turning only once. Remove and keep warm.

Cook the fish on the same broiling (grilling) pan for 3 minutes. Turn and broil for 3 minutes on the other side.

Arrange the sole and *radicchio* on a serving platter with the lemon wedges and serve.

*Grilled sole and* radicchio

116

*Anchovies with oregano*

# ANCHOVIES WITH OREGANO

*Alici all'origano*

In the sixteenth century Bartolomeo Scappi included fresh anchovies in his list of cold dishes for the *primo servizio di credenza* (first course). In spring, schools of anchovies in their thousands crowd the seas and swim very close to the coast. The anchovy, like the sardine and the mackerel, is classed as a "blue" fish — not a great delicacy but very tasty. In the old days anchovies would appear only on the tables of the common people, but today they are also prepared in more sophisticated kitchens. Like sardines they used to be served cooked with raisins and pine nuts, especially in the South of Italy. They are very small fish, and another common way of preparing them is to bone them and soak them in lemon juice for several hours, which has the effect of "cooking" them.

*2 lb (1 kg) fresh anchovies*
*¼ cup (2 fl oz/60 ml) extra virgin olive oil*
*4 garlic cloves*
*½ cup (4 fl oz/120 ml) dry white wine*
*1 tablespoon dried oregano*
*salt and freshly ground pepper*
*juice of ½ lemon*

Trim and gut the anchovies and remove the heads. Wash them and drain on a tea-towel.

Combine the oil, garlic, wine, oregano, salt and pepper in a skillet. Bring to a boil and cook for 5 minutes. Add the anchovies and cook over fairly low heat for 5 minutes.

Remove from the heat, squeeze the lemon juice over the fish and serve.

117

*Salt cod with bell peppers*

# SALT COD WITH BELL PEPPERS

*Baccalà ai peperoni*

**D**ried salt cod has always been a much sought-after fish, especially so in the old days when the transportation of fresh fish was extremely difficult and most fish were consumed in the area where they were caught. Cod keeps for long periods, even in a hot climate, and is both nourishing and tasty. It was a useful reserve food for sailors to take onboard ship for long voyages. Until fairly recent times salt cod was mainly eaten in the northern parts of Italy, in particular the Veneto and Liguria regions.

*1 lb (500 g) dried salt cod, soaked in several*
 *changes of cold water until soft*
*⅓ cup (3 fl oz/90 ml) extra virgin olive oil*
*2 red bell peppers (capsicums), cut into strips*
*2 lb (1 kg) potatoes, sliced*
*salt*
*2 tablespoons dry breadcrumbs*
*1 tablespoon dried oregano*

Drain the cod and cut it into small pieces.

Heat the oil in a skillet. Add the bell peppers and fry gently for 15 minutes. Use a little of the oil to lightly grease a baking dish. Line the bottom of the dish with a layer of potato slices, and then a layer of cod. Scatter the bell pepper strips on top; season with salt and sprinkle on a little of the oil used for frying the bell peppers. Continue alternating layers of potatoes, cod and bell peppers until all ingredients have been used.

Combine the breadcrumbs and oregano. Sprinkle over the dish. Bake in a preheated 350°F (180°C) oven for about 40 minutes then serve.

# COD WITH PEAS

*Palombo alla pescatora con pisellini*

**C**od, although not held in very high regard, is nevertheless a common family food, possibly because of its reasonable price. Because it has a very light taste, it is often cooked together with vegetables such as peas or spinach. The marriage of vegetables with fish has always been popular throughout Italy: take for example the famous dish *seppie in zimino*, an ancient recipe still in use today, in which cuttlefish is cooked with a covering of spinach and a touch of tomato.

*1 tablespoon chopped onion*
*⅓ cup (3 fl oz/90 ml) extra virgin olive oil*
*1 lb (500 g) small young peas, shelled*
*⅓ cup (3 fl oz/90 ml) fish stock, heated*
*6 pieces of cod fillet, about 6 oz (180 g) each*
*¾ cup (3 oz/90 g) all purpose (plain) flour*
*1 garlic clove, chopped*
*salt and freshly ground pepper*
*¼ cup (2 fl oz/60 ml) dry white wine*
*1 tablespoon tomato purée*
*1 tablespoon chopped parsley*

In a large skillet fry the onion very gently in 2 tablespoons of the oil. Add the peas, mix well and continue cooking for 5 minutes, adding a little of the hot stock from time to time.

*Cod with peas*

*Dentex with almond stuffing*

Meanwhile, dredge the fish fillets in the flour. Heat the remaining oil in another skillet. Add the garlic and fish and fry over high heat for a few minutes on each side, until lightly browned. Season with salt and pepper. Sprinkle the wine over and cook until evaporated. Add the peas. Stir the remaining broth into the tomato purée and add to the skillet. Adjust the seasoning. Cover the pan and cook over low heat for about 5 minutes.

Transfer to a serving dish, sprinkle with the parsley and serve.

# DENTEX WITH ALMOND STUFFING

*Dentice alle mandorle*

Almonds were already used in cooking during the Renaissance. They still feature in numerous recipes, although the tendency now is to use them mainly in sweet dishes. They are still to be found, however, in a few recipes for fish, meat and even vegetables. A famous example is the recipe for spinach finished with a handful of chopped almonds.

*1 dentex or sea bass about 4 lb (2 kg), cleaned*
*⅓ cup (3 fl oz/90 ml) extra virgin olive oil*
*juice of 1 lemon*

*¼ cup (2 fl oz/60 ml) dry Marsala*
*1 bay leaf*
*salt and freshly ground pepper*
*6 oz (180 g) shrimps (prawns), peeled and deveined*
*6 oz (180 g) blanched almonds, finely chopped*
*3 tablespoons dry breadcrumbs*
*1 egg yolk*

Wash the fish and pat dry. In a shallow dish, combine 3 tablespoons of the oil, the lemon juice, Marsala, bay leaf and a pinch of salt and pepper. Add the fish to the marinade and marinate for 2 hours, turning it now and again.

In a skillet, warm 1 tablespoon of the oil over moderate heat. Add the shrimps and cook until browned. Drain and chop the shrimps. In a bowl, combine the shrimps with half the almonds, 1 tablespoon of the breadcrumbs, the egg yolk, and salt and pepper to taste. Mix thoroughly.

Remove the fish from the marinade; pat dry. Fill the belly cavity with the prepared stuffing. Mix the remaining breadcrumbs with the remaining chopped almonds. Coat the fish with the mixture. Set in a baking dish, and sprinkle with the remaining oil. Bake in a preheated 350°F (180°C) oven for about 30 minutes and serve.

119

Ancient dish with fish design (1206);
PEGLI ARCHEOLOGICAL MUSEUM, GENOA

# FISH IN A CLOAK

*Pesce a cappucciolo*

The work by Cristoforo di Messisbugo entitled *Banchetti Composizioni di Vivande e Apparecchio Generale* (*Banquets, Composition of Meals and General Equipment*) is not only a treasure trove of recipes, but also of serving methods, food quantities and menu construction, how to prepare the table, what is needed in the kitchen, and a thousand other considerations of the utmost importance, making it a very significant reference work on life in the fifteenth century. The writer undoubtedly had first-hand experience of the way the wealthy lived and of life at court. He kept company with people in high places, and gives us some fascinating descriptions, the most interesting without doubt being those of receptions held in honor of important figures of the period who visited the family he was serving. The recipe chosen here is typical of the time — fish cooked with sugar, spices and honey. The modern version is closer to contemporary tastes.

Of all the varieties of fish, I find *meggia* [dialect name for grey mullet], gilt-head sea bream, medium dentex, river perch and grayling are good cooked by this method which is called *cappucciolo*. You shall take one of the aforementioned fish and split it down the back and take out the innards, then you put it to soak in some vinegar and wine and salt and powdered coriander or crushed fennel seeds. Let it remain in the vinegar and wine bath just described for three or four hours, but no more than this. Then give it a good wash and dredge it lightly in flour and thread it onto a spit, and put it on to cook, turning the spit a little bit one way and a little bit the other way, that is to say a little turn of the point of the skewer and a little turn of the handle. When it is cooked you shall take some shelled walnuts, hardboiled egg yolks, raisins, and a little honey or sugar and some parsley and mint, and pound all this together, moistening every ingredient with verjuice. This you shall pass through a sieve, and then set it to boil in a saucepan so that it thickens a little. Then when you have opened up the fish, put this sauce on top of it. When you do not wish to go to the expense of this sauce, you shall use instead vinegar and parsley.

*1 dentex, sea bass, salmon or grouper about 4 lb (2 kg)*
*½ cup (4 fl oz/120 ml) vinegar*
*½ cup (4 fl oz/120 ml) dry white wine*
*1 teaspoon whole black peppercorns*
*2 hardboiled egg yolks*
*1 tablespoon chopped parsley*
*juice of 1 lemon*
*⅓ cup (3 fl oz/90 ml) extra virgin olive oil*
*salt*

Clean the fish and place it in a deep dish. Pour the vinegar and wine over it, sprinkle with peppercorns and leave to soak for about 3 hours.

Drain and dry the fish. Grill on both sides over charcoals or under a hot broiler (griller) until just cooked through.

Chop the eggs, add the parsley, lemon juice, oil, and salt to taste. Transfer the fish to a serving plate and serve the sauce separately.

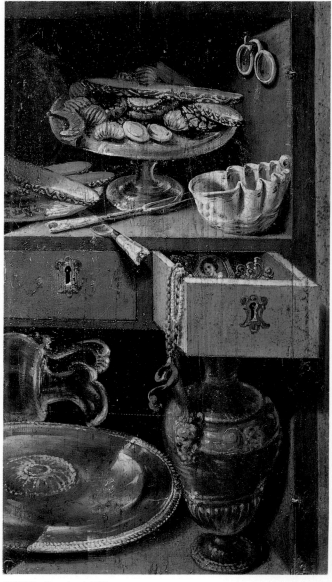

*Still life*, Baccio del Bianco; CASA BUONARROTI, FLORENCE

*Fish in a cloak — modern recipe*

# SHELLFISH SOUP

*Zuppa di frutti di mare*

Fish soups are a traditional part of Italian cuisine, each region having its own special recipes. They were usually made with fish that were not highly regarded. Sometimes, particularly if they were intended for the tables of the rich and powerful, they would be made with the best fish available — even shellfish. This recipe also contains sea-dates, a very delicate shellfish that is extremely rare these days.

*6 lb (3 kg) mixed shellfish (small clams, sea dates, wedge shells, venus shells, top-shells, mussels etc.)*
*¼ cup (2 fl oz/60 ml) extra virgin olive oil*
*1 garlic clove, finely chopped*
*1 small onion, chopped*
*½ cup (4 fl oz/120 ml) dry white wine*
*1 lb (500 g) tomatoes*
*salt and freshly ground pepper*
*1 fresh chile pepper*
*1 handful chopped parsley*
*6 slices bread, toasted in the oven*

Keeping the shellfish immersed in a basin of water, wash and brush them thoroughly under the tap. Transfer them to a wide pan. Cover and set over moderate heat until they open. Drain and reserve the cooking liquid. Remove the empty half-shells, retaining the halves with the meat still attached. Strain the cooking liquid through a piece of dampened cheesecloth; set aside.

Heat the oil in a skillet and brown the garlic and onion. Add the strained cooking liquid, the wine and the tomatoes; season with salt and pepper. Cook for about 15 minutes, adding the chile pepper. If necessary, add a little water; the soup should be fairly thin.

Add all the shellfish and cook for 1 minute. Sprinkle with the parsley.

Put a slice of the toasted bread in the bottom of each soup plate. Pour on the soup and serve.

*Shellfish soup*

*Shrimps with fresh herbs*

# SHRIMPS WITH FRESH HERBS

*Gamberi alle erbe aromatiche*

In Italy, herbs have always been used extensively in the kitchen, their fresh flavors replacing heavy and complicated sauces. They constitute an excellent seasoning for all types of food and are always used fresh. You will find them in abundance in the markets throughout Italy.

*2 lb (1 kg) shrimps (prawns)*
*1 garlic clove, crushed*
*¼ cup (2 fl oz/60 ml) extra virgin olive oil*
*salt and freshly ground pepper*
*1 bunch parsley, finely chopped*
*⅓ cup (1½ oz/45 g) bunch fresh marjoram*
*⅓ cup (1½ oz/45 g) bunch fresh thyme*
*⅓ cup (1½ oz/45 g) bunch fresh tarragon*
*⅓ cup (1½ oz/45 g) bunch fresh basil*
*¼ cup (2 fl oz/60 ml) dry white wine*

Finely chop half of each bunch of the herbs.

Peel the shrimps and remove the heads. Wash them and dry with a tea-towel.

Fry the garlic gently in the oil until golden brown, then remove it. Add the shrimps to the oil and brown them for 5 minutes. Season with salt and pepper, stir in the chopped herbs and moisten with the wine. Finish cooking for a few minutes and serve hot, garnished with the remaining fresh herbs.

# SALAD OF BABY OCTOPUS

*Polipetti al prezzemolo*

Several varieties of small squid, octopus and cuttlefish, offered in many Italian fish shops today, were mentioned as early as the fourteenth century by an anonymous Tuscan author who suggests serving them with sauces enriched with "gold, precious stones, selected spices." These baby shellfish, caught when they are no more than a couple of inches long, are wonderfully tender and delicate in taste. They may be fried, stewed with a little tomato or, to make the most of their exquisite flavor, served as a salad with oil, lemon juice and parsley.

*2 lb (1 kg) baby octopus or small squid or*
*   cuttlefish, cleaned*
*2 tablespoons vinegar*
*¼ cup (2 fl oz/60 ml) extra virgin olive oil*
*juice of 1 lemon*
*salt and freshly ground pepper*
*1 tablespoon parsley, finely chopped*
*1 garlic clove, finely chopped*

Rinse the octopus. Bring a pot of salted water to a boil. Add vinegar and octopus and cook for 15 minutes. Set aside to cool in the cooking liquid. Drain and pat dry. Cut the tentacles into small pieces and cut the mantle into thin rounds.

Mix the oil and lemon juice in a small bowl; season with salt and pepper. Stir in the parsley and garlic and mix well. Pour the dressing over the octopus and mix thoroughly. Set aside at room temperature for 1 hour before serving.

*Salad of baby octopus*

123

*Still life*, Jacopo Chimenti, known as l'Empoli (1551–1640); UFFIZI GALLERY, FLORENCE  Italians eat many varieties of bird, from tiny fig-peckers to the glorious peacock.

# MEAT, GAME AND POULTRY

I taly abounds in a rich array of simple yet delicious meat dishes. From Tuscany there is the tender and aromatic *bistecca alla Fiorentina* (Florentine beefsteak) — mouth-watering steaks grilled (barbecued) over a wood fire; from Parma, the sweet prosciutto traditionally served with melon or figs; the exquisite *mortadella* from Bologna; tender veal of Lombardy, served in a variety of appetizing sauces; succulent pork from Emilia-Romagna, and the highly prized delicacies of baby lamb and kid, to mention only a few. Yet visitors to Italy have often remarked that Italians seem to be practically vegetarian. It is certainly true that less meat is eaten in the country than in North America or northern Europe, probably because Italy, like most other industrialized countries of Europe, lacks the large grazing areas of North America or Australia. Thus, the available meat is expensive, and until well after the Second World War Italy was a poor country. In addition, Italy's superabundance of tasty salad ingredients and vegetables could convert the most avid carnivore. However, the meat Italians do have is mostly of a high quality and their recipes for preparing it are inventive as well as delicious.

By contrast, ancient books on gastronomy as well as old menus provide evidence of how carnivorous their ancestors were. These documents are, of course, records of how the wealthy ate. Bartolomeo Scappi lists more than forty meat dishes for a sixteenth-century menu, including numerous roasts, small game birds, elaborate presentations of peacocks and turkeys, whole and half suckling pigs, and milk-fed calves as well as various meat casseroles, pies, and loaves. This spirit of abundance lives on today at special occasions such as the wedding feast, where the main course might begin with braised cuts, followed by a selection of roasts and concluding with mixed boiled meats.

As far as the standard contemporary diet is concerned, the following regional generalizations hold true. Fine veal and beef are virtually limited to the northern regions, where there is comparatively abundant pasture. A notable exception is Tuscany's fertile plain, the Val di Chiana, where the *Chianina* cattle for an authentic *bistecca alla Fiorentina* are raised. These cattle are always white and are famous throughout Italy for the quality of their beef. These days, however, this choice beef is quite rare, even in Florence. Lamb and, to a lesser extent, kid are the meats of the more hilly and arid southern parts of the country. Pork is available throughout Italy, although processed pork products are mostly associated with the north-central regions. From Emilia-Romagna there are the *cotechino* and *zampone* of Modena, and the mortadella of Bologna as well as the prosciutto of Parma. Tuscany and Umbria are renowned for a variety of both sausages and salami.

Chickens, too, are bred throughout Italy but Tuscany has the reputation for breeding

*The month of June, milking and making cheese* (detail), (fifteenth century), fresco;
CASTELLO DEL BUONCONSIGLIO, TRENTO
Due to the lack of large grazing areas in Italy, Italians eat a lot less meat than people from other industrialized European countries.

*The offal-seller*, Giuseppe Maria Mitelli (1634–1718); NATIONAL LIBRARY, FLORENCE
As it is a cheap and nourishing food, offal is popular in Italy. Many kinds of offal are eaten including calves' heads, brains and sweetbreads; pigs' feet, tripe, tongue and lung; spleen, kidneys and, of course, tripe.

the finest free-range fowl. It is also the north-central regions that have the best game. Here the wooded terrain provides an ideal habitat for hare, birds, a few deer, and many wild boar.

The regional methods of preparing meat are determined by the availability of the different meats in that area. In the North (Lombardy, Piedmont and Emilia-Romagna) there is a preference for boiling and braising fine cuts; in the central regions roasting is preferred; in the South, broiling (grilling). All regions have their characteristic ways of using up every morsel of meat in loaves and little balls, as well as the more classic and elaborate preparations of sautéing chops and cutlets and stuffing rolls.

An inevitable surprise to visitors to northern Italy is the meat dish called *bollito misto* (mixed boiled meats) which is served in many fine restaurants. The English name does little justice to this fine specialty of the North. The dish is rolled in on a special trolley with separate containers for each meat covered in steaming broth. The meats are carved at the table according to the diner's pleasure and traditionally served with two classic sauces: *salsa verde*, a sharp green mixture of parsley, capers, anchovies, mustard, red wine vinegar, and olive oil; and *salsa rossa*, a milder red sauce of tomatoes, onions, and sweet peppers. The selection of meats will usually include brisket of beef, tongue, calf's head, veal, chicken, and, in Emilia-Romagna, *cotechino* and *zampone* sausages. The meats are simmered together for hours in a large pot of boiling water so that their flavors combine, and each one is added to the pot according to the time it takes to reach perfect tenderness. It is a dish that evokes the large family kitchens of the past, when the cook had time to tend her pots carefully while going about her other chores. Today a full *bollito misto* is usually served only at restaurants. It is not, however, complicated to prepare and a scaled-down version of delicious boiled meats is an excellent family meal.

Even on its own, a boiled *cotechino* or *zampone* sausage makes a memorable and tasty meal. These are both large pork sausages, specialties of Modena in Emilia-Romagna. *Zampone* is the most ancient and famous. Its name comes from *zampa* (pig's foot), the casing into which is stuffed a finely minced mixture of pork parts flavored with cinnamon, cloves, salt and pepper. The date of its origin is not known but by the eighteenth century it appears frequently in folklore. The historian Marco Cesare Nannini traces its invention back to 1511, when the city of Modena was under siege and the *Modenesi*, already celebrated sausage-makers for centuries, were forced to use their pigs' front hooves for casings. The Italian opera composer Gioacchino Rossini ordered *zampone* to be sent to him by mail from Modena. Giuseppe Garibaldi wrote from exile on the island of Capri to the firm of Bellentani in Modena, fine sausage-makers of that time, saying he was grateful to have had the opportunity to taste their sausage meat, which certainly deserved its reputation of being the best. Even the nineteenth-century French writer, Emile Zola, considered *zampone* a "delicious and divine dish." Today there are two gastronomic confraternities that hold this sausage in veneration. One is the Confraternity of Saint Anthony, which reveres all pork products, and the other is the *Ordine dei Cavalieri dello Zampone* (Knights of the Order of the Zampone), who are entirely dedicated to its cult, although in their investiture ceremony mention is also made of prosciutto.

The proper preparation of *zampone* also has some of the characteristics of a ritual. The sausage is first soaked for several hours in cold water. It is then wrapped in a cloth in order to keep the skin from splitting during its lengthy (at least four hours) simmering.

*The cook*, Bernardo Strozzi (1581–1644);
ROSSO PALACE, GENOA
Strozzi was a Capuchin monk who became the leading Genoese painter of the early seventeenth century. Apart from religious subjects, he painted portraits and genre scenes and was a master colorist.

Preferably, it is cooked in a special pan called a *zamponiera*, made to measure so that the sausage can lie completely covered in a minimum of water. Early winter is the traditional season for pig-slaughtering and in the North the much prized *zampone*, freshly made, has become the traditional dish to welcome the New Year. It is accompanied by stewed lentils that symbolize a shower of small coins auguring prosperity. *Zampone* served with *zabaglione* sauce (made of egg, sugar and Marsala) makes an unusual and elegant supper.

*Cotechino* is sometimes considered a poor cousin to *zampone*. It is made with much the same ingredients but the meat is more coarsely ground and is stuffed into standard pig-casing instead of the flavorful and esteemed skin of the foot. It is simpler and somewhat quicker to cook but nonetheless tasty and is therefore an excellent choice for more ordinary meals. Cabbage is an appropriate accompaniment. Both sausages are now commercially produced — the *zampone* often partially pre-cooked — and widely distributed and exported.

*Triptych of the country life* (detail), *The farmhouse* (1912–14) A. Magri
MATTER COLLECTION, CARPENEDO DI MESTRE
The *zampone* is a popular Italian sausage where meat from the shoulder, head, neck and calf of the pig is finely minced and pushed into the skin of a boned pig's foot.

A much smaller sausage, which slipped over the border from Austria into the Trentino-Alto Adige, is *würstel*. Although it kept its German name, it is now produced in northern Italy and is popular throughout the country. It is made from a mixture of beef and pork ground very finely, and there are as many family recipes for using it as there are for the basic Frankfurter, except that in Italy it can end up in a pasta sauce or on top of a pizza.

One of the classic meat dishes of the North is *brasato* (braised beef). Because it takes lengthy cooking, it is a traditional Sunday dinner dish or is reserved for important occasions. The piece of meat — rump roast is a good cut to use — is first browned in fat in order to seal the juices and then cooked very slowly for three to five hours in red wine and herbs. In Piedmont a good bottle of Barolo is used, and in Lombardy cinnamon, cloves, and bay are added. When brought to the table, it should be full of juices and so tender that it can be cut with a fork alone.

The well-known Milanese fare *ossobuco* is another braised meat dish. It consists of thick, cross-cut slices of veal shin with both bone and marrow intact after cooking (*ossobuco* means "bone with a hole"). Before it is served, a mixture of chopped parsley, garlic, and grated lemon zest (rind), called *gremolata*, is sprinkled on top and the dish is traditionally accompanied by *risotto alla Milanese*.

This method of cooking meat very slowly for a long time in a small amount of liquid so that it becomes extremely juicy and tender, is also ideal for game and poorer cuts of meat. *Brasato* is also called *stracotto* (cooked extra long) and *umido*, that is, stewed.

A quite different way of cooking meat, but with the same goal of maximizing flavor and tenderness, is the Italian method of preparing *scaloppine*, thin slices of milk-fed calf that are cut across the grain and flattened. Traditionally this "white" meat was found only in the North but now it is served everywhere. The veal is cooked only for a few minutes in a large frying pan and can be flavored in a variety of ways — with Marsala wine, or lemon, or sautéed artichokes. A popular Roman dish is *saltimbocca alla Romana*. A slice of prosciutto and a leaf of fresh sage are laid on top of a thin slice of veal, which is then rolled up and secured with a toothpick. These rolls (which are sometimes prepared flat) are gently browned in butter and then simmered in white wine. They are so delicious that, when served, they live up to their name and "jump into the mouth."

*Trippa* (tripe) is a veal dish that has many enthusiastic devotees, especially in the old neighborhoods of the major northern and central Italian cities. It is a popular dish in the full sense of the word. The practice of cooking the lining of the stomach of ruminants (animals that chew cud) and flavoring it with other ingredients goes back to ancient times. In the eighteenth-century cookbook, *L'Apicio Moderno (The Modern Epicurean)*, Leonardi gives a recipe for *trippa di manzo alla Romana* (beef tripe), in which strips of tripe are cooked in wine and herbs, then layered with grated Parmesan cheese within an encasement of bread and pasta, sprinkled with chopped mint, and baked in the oven. With the exception of the encasement, this is still how tripe is served in the old Roman neighborhood of Trastevere.

In Florence, tripe has a centuries' old association with the popular quarter of San Frediano on the "other" side of the Arno river, where *trippai* (tripe-makers) prepared this low-cost dish for the impoverished artisans who lived in the neighborhood. Well-heeled inhabitants from the center of town often crossed over the Ponte Vecchio in order to partake of this specialty. Even the water in which it was boiled, called *"il brodo di San Frediano"* (San Frediano broth), was prized. At around five o'clock in the evening craftsmen would send their young apprentices with a flask to be filled from the cauldrons.

*The young shepherdess*, Filippo Palizzi (1818–99); GALLERY OF MODERN ART, FLORENCE Lamb is the traditional food for Easter in Italy. It is served in many ways including roasted whole on the spit, pan-roasted with wine, or braised with sauce.

*Still life with partridge and pomegranates*,
Roman fresco from Herculaneum;
NATIONAL ARCHEOLOGICAL MUSEUM, NAPLES
Partridge was a popular food in imperial
Roman times as were birds of all kinds,
including guinea fowl, duck, chicken,
goose and pigeon.

cockerels to be either caged or castrated. Thus, the culinary pleasures of the bird were discovered. The sixteenth-century cookery writer Cristoforo di Messisbugo gives a recipe for cooking *cappone* in sweet white wine with a sweet and sour sauce, adding "a pinch of saffron to give it color." Boiled capon is still a traditional Christmas Eve meal in many families in Italy.

Italians are famous, infamous even, for eating every kind of bird, from the tiniest *uccellini* (thrushes and larks) to plump *fagiani* (pheasants). During the Renaissance the important landed families of the North-central regions created private game reserves on their estates, where they also built hunting lodges often just a few miles from the main

134

house. Only the lord of the manor and his friends were allowed to hunt, so game was a delicacy reserved for the rich and occasionally enjoyed by the family of a poor poacher. In later times *corridoi* (corridors) through one estate to another were established, where everyone could hunt. Now relatively little wildlife survives, with the result that local game remains an occasional pleasure of the table.

*Uccellini* are usually skewered and roasted and eaten whole, bones and all, while pheasant and *faraona* (guinea hen) are pot-roasted with herbs. Today, as in the past, *piccioni* (wild pigeons) are one of the most popular game birds for hunting and serving at the table. Bartolomeo Scappi dedicates a chapter to them in his *Opera*, written at a time (the sixteenth century) when flocks of them flew over Rome. He gives advice on how to tell young birds from old ones. The former, whose meat is tender and flavorful, have dark flesh and white feet; the ones to avoid have white flesh and red feet. One recipe calls for roasting them on a spit until they are nearly cooked and then baking them in a crust made from flour, seasoned with fennel, sugar, salt, and breadcrumbs. Scappi writes that the pigeon should be plucked and cooked immediately. The modern method is also to serve pigeon fresh, without hanging it.

*Mallards*, Cesare Dandini (1596–1668); CORRIDOIO VASARIANO, FLORENCE
In traditional Italian recipes for duck, mute ducks were used as the meat was thought to be tastier.

*Bollito* with *vegetables*

# BOLLITO WITH VEGETABLES

*Bollito con verdure*

The *bollito* is a typical dish generally offered every Thursday in restaurants in northern Italy. In northern Italian homes it is served frequently, because it is simple to make and full of flavor. It is usually accompanied by *salsa verde* (green sauce – see p. 242), or by pickled vegetables or horseradish sauce, according to the region. The earliest recipe for *salsa verde* appears in the *Liber de Coquina* (*Book of Cooking*) by an anonymous fifteenth-century writer of the Angevin court, and suggests chopping up herbs such as mint, parsley and cardamom, and adding nutmeg and ginger as well. Often *bollito* is eaten with a bowl of vegetables with a little of the cooking liquid added.

*3 lb (1.5 kg) beef suitable for boiling*
*8 cups (2 qt/2 l) water*
*3 pieces of marrow bone, 1 lb (500 g)*
*6 young carrots, scraped and chopped*
*6 leeks, trimmed and washed well*
*6 white celery stalks, chopped*
*6 baby onions, peeled*
*10 oz (300 g) Savoy cabbage*
*1 boneless chicken breast, cut into thin strips*

Cut up the beef into slices and put it in a saucepan. Cover with the water, and add the bones. Cover and bring the water to a boil. Cook the meat over gentle heat for about 2 hours.

Add the carrots, leeks, celery, onions and cabbage and cook for a further 30 minutes.

Remove the meat and vegetables from the stock. Discard the bones and transfer the meat and vegetables to a large plate.

Degrease the stock. Add the chicken breast and return the stock to a boil. Cook for 10 minutes. Add the meat and vegetables and bring back to a boil. Serve.

# FRANKFURTERS AND PANCETTA

*Wurstel alla pancetta*

This is one of the very simple dishes made at home when something is needed for unexpected guests. It was a special tradition in the Trentino region, which offers a wide variety of particularly tasty frankfurters.

Now that communication is so much easier, frankfurters, which unfortunately are no longer made at home, are to be found all over Italy and are popular everywhere. Sliced and sautéed in a little butter, frankfurters also make a quick sauce for spaghetti or *tagliatelle*.

*6 frankfurters*
*6 very thin slices* fontina *cheese*
*6 fresh sage leaves*
*6 slices smoked* pancetta

Wrap each frankfurter in a slice of cheese, put a sage leaf on top and then enclose all this in a slice of the *pancetta*, rolling it tightly around the frankfurter. Secure each roll with a toothpick.

Arrange the rolls in a row in a baking dish. Bake in a preheated 400°F (200°C) oven for 15 minutes, turning from time to time.

*Frankfurters and* pancetta

# COTECHINO AND CABBAGE

*Cotechino con le verze*

In the old days, recipes always included lessons in making different types of sausage, *cotechini, cervellate* and so on, using the gut of the pig. This is still done in many families, especially in Tuscany and Umbria in the autumn, when a pig is killed and provisions are made for the winter. Now we find very good quality sausages of all kinds in the shops. *Cotechino* and *salsiccia* are never spicy.

*1 cotechino sausage, about 1¾ lb (800 g)*
*1 cabbage, about 2 lb (1 kg)*
*1 onion, finely chopped*
*2 oz (60 g) pancetta, finely chopped*
*1½ tablespoons (¾ oz/20 g) butter*
*2 tablespoons extra virgin olive oil*
*salt and freshly ground pepper*
*½ cup (4 fl oz/120 ml) dry white wine*
*1 cup (8 fl oz/250 ml) clear meat stock, boiling*
*3 tablespoons white vinegar*

Prick the sausage with a needle. Wrap tightly in cheesecloth and put it in a saucepan of cold water. Bring slowly to a boil. Reduce the heat and simmer gently for about 2 hours. Set aside to cool in the cooking liquid. Remove from the cheesecloth and slice.

Separate the cabbage leaves, discarding the tough outer leaves and core. Wash the leaves thoroughly; drain well. Cut into thin strips.

Put the onion and *pancetta* in a saucepan with the butter and oil; cook over low heat for 5 minutes, stirring often until softened. Add the cabbage strips, some salt and a little pepper and cook until the cabbage wilts. Add the wine. Cover the saucepan, lower the heat and cook the cabbage for about 2 hours, adding some of the boiling stock from time to time.

Ten minutes before taking the cabbage off the heat, sprinkle with the vinegar and add the slices of *cotechino*. Continue cooking, covered, over low heat.

Arrange the *cotechino* on a serving dish and surround it with the cabbage. Serve at once.

Cotechino *and cabbage*

# FOR A GOODLY DISH OF TRIPE

*Per un buon piatto di trippa*

Ippolito Cavalcanti, Duke of Buonvicino, born in 1787, wrote a book called *La Cucina Teorico-Pratica* (*Cooking Theory and Practice*), retitled in its second edition *Cucina Casareccia in Dialetto Napoletano* (*Home Cooking in the Neapolitan Dialect*). The recipes are interspersed with witty advice, anecdotes and observations about friends, all of which make the book a pleasure to read. One example of his jokes is in the recipe for *fritto di pesce* (fried fish), where he remarks that it seems futile to give the recipe because everybody knows how to make it. The book is written in the Neapolitan dialect, and most of the dishes are from that region. There is some amusing advice on how to buy tripe, and the reader is even told which butcher to buy from. The modern recipe is typical of the cuisine of Naples today.

*Preparation of the meat and other food, a scene from the story of the Prodigal Son* (1562), Philipp Galle (1537–1612), etching;
PRINT COLLECTION, MILAN

This is a good main course, as long as you know how to shop for it. You should go to Pennino, where there are a number of merchants, including one who is particularly conscientious, the one who is there with an old lady: he always has good tripe and do not fear if he has some with excrement on it. Get your tripe, the one from the fat belly (thicker), wash it so that it is thoroughly clean and when the water begins to boil you put it in, then when it is half-cooked, change the water and put in more water, but it must be boiling. When it is cooked you can do it in two ways; The first: cut it into small pieces, put with it grated cheese with beaten eggs, chopped parsley, salt and pepper and a little bit of rendered pork fat and cook it like a stew. The second is the way the Capuchin friars do it: cook the sauce until it is reduced and you put it in a pan with a handful of grated cheese underneath and on top and toast it in the oven, or with a lid, and covered with embers. Do it like that and then tell me what you've eaten.

*For a goodly dish of tripe — modern recipe*

2 lb (1 kg) tripe
salt
2 garlic cloves, chopped
1 onion, chopped
2 oz (60 g) prosciutto, chopped
1 handful parsley, chopped
2 tablespoons extra virgin olive oil
1 lb (500 g) canned peeled tomatoes

Cut the tripe into strips. Put it into cold water with a little salt, bring to a boil and cook on low heat for about 5 hours. Drain.

In a saucepan, add the garlic, onion, prosciutto and parsley to the oil and brown lightly over low heat. Add the tomatoes and tripe and cook for 30 minutes, until the sauce is reduced. Transfer to a serving dish and serve.

*Lamb cutlets with sage*

# LAMB CUTLETS WITH SAGE

*Costolette di agnello alla salvia*

In old recipes for lamb cutlets, they were stuffed with many flavorings, including sweet ones, whereas today, cooking has been greatly simplified. These cutlets are taken from small lambs no more than a couple of months old, and the meat is naturally tender and succulent and is much sought after. The cutlets do not have a strong taste, and so they must not be combined with other strong flavors in cooking. The best way of preparing them to produce a traditional and very delicate dish is either broiling (grilling) (*a scottadito* as the Romans call it — "until they burn the fingers") or marinating with sage before cooking them briefly in butter.

*3 lb (1.5 kg) lamb cutlets, each ½ inch (1 cm) thick*
*2 tablespoons extra virgin olive oil*
*salt and freshly ground pepper*
*1 handful fresh sage leaves*
*¼ cup (2 oz/60 g) butter*
*⅓ cup (3 fl oz/90 ml) dry white wine*

Prepare the cutlets by removing all fat, the cartilage around the bone and the end of the bone that protrudes from the meat. Pound lightly with a meat mallet; brush the cutlets with the oil. Sprinkle with salt and grind plenty of pepper over them. Press the sage into the meat and oil. Set aside to marinate in the oil and sage for 2 hours.

Heat the butter in a skillet. Add the cutlets and sage and brown over high heat for about 5 minutes on each side. When the meat is well browned, add the wine and boil for 2 minutes. Transfer to a serving platter and serve.

139

# SLICED BEEF IN BELL PEPPER SAUCE

*Fettine in salsa di peperoni*

The method used for these steaks — a lengthy braising — can also be used for a single large piece of beef, but in that case it needs to remain in the oven for at least 4 hours if it is to become tender. Sliced meat is often used nowadays in place of whole pieces, because slices cook more quickly, but at one time it was customary to cook mainly whole animals. Cut up meat was used in particular for baked dishes (such as pies), which were covered in saffron and spices and sometimes even filled with gold. In this case the *Liber de Coquina* (*Book of Cooking*), by an anonymous fifteenth-century writer, advised that the filling should take place in secret, so that the baker whose oven was used for the cooking could not remove the gold and substitute something else.

*2 onions, finely sliced*
*1 celery stalk, cut into thin strips*
*1¾ lb (800 g) beef slices, ¼ inch (0.5 cm) thick*
*salt and freshly ground pepper*
*1 bay leaf*
*juice of ½ lemon*
*1 thyme sprig*
*1 cup (8 fl oz/250 ml) dry red wine*
*1 tablespoon all purpose (plain) flour*

*Sliced beef in bell pepper sauce*

*3 tablespoons extra virgin olive oil*
*1 red bell pepper (capsicum), chopped*
*1 green bell pepper (capsicum), chopped*

Scatter the onions and celery over the bottom of a baking dish. Lay the meat slices on top and season with salt and pepper. Add the bay leaf, lemon juice, and thyme leaves, and sprinkle on the wine.

Cover the dish and marinate in the refrigerator for at least 2 hours.

Drain the meat thoroughly and pat it dry; strain the marinade reserving the solids and the liquid. Dredge the slices in the flour. Heat the oil in a large skillet, add the beef and brown on both sides for about 5 minutes. Add the marinade liquid and let it evaporate a little before adding all the other marinade ingredients. Cook for a few minutes. Add the bell peppers, cover and cook very slowly, on the lowest possible heat or in a 275°F (140°C) oven, for about 2 hours, stirring from time to time.

When the meat is well cooked, carefully remove the slices from the sauce and arrange them on a serving dish. Strain the sauce, pour it over the meat and serve.

*Rosemary* (1534), from the *Herbal* of Leonhart Fuchs

# STUFFED BREAST OF VEAL

*Petto di vitello ripieno*

One of the best ways of preparing rolled meat is to use a breast or "*tasca*" (pocket) of veal which is easy to fill and roll up. The slightly fatty meat gives this dish a special soft quality. The filling is a mixture of eggs, prosciutto and spinach. Other ingredients such as bacon (*pancetta*), a mixture of almonds and sausage, chicken livers or pâté with truffles may be substituted.

*Stuffed breast of veal*

*1 lb (500 g) spinach, trimmed*
*1 cup (4 oz/120 g) freshly grated Parmesan cheese*
*3 eggs*
*salt and freshly ground pepper*
*1 large slice of veal breast, about 2 lb (1 kg)*
*3 oz (90 g) thinly sliced prosciutto*
*1½ tablespoons (¾ oz/20 g) butter*
*2 tablespoons extra virgin olive oil*
*2 fresh sage sprigs*
*2 fresh rosemary sprigs*
*½ cup (4 fl oz/120 ml) dry white wine*
*½ cup (4 fl oz/120 ml) clear beef stock*

Cook the spinach in a very small amount of boiling salted water. Drain and set aside to cool. Squeeze as dry as possible. Place in a bowl and add the Parmesan and eggs; mix well. Add salt and pepper to taste.

Pound the meat well to flatten it. Salt it lightly. Spread the spinach mixture over the meat. Cover with the prosciutto slices and roll up the meat, closing it well around the filling. Tie tightly with string.

In an oval casserole gently melt the butter with the oil. Add the sage and rosemary and sauté over moderate heat. Add the meat and brown on all sides, turning often, for about 15 minutes. Add a little salt and the wine. Cover and cook in a preheated 350°F (180°C) oven for 1 hour, turning the meat often and moistening from time to time with a tablespoon or two of the stock.

Remove the lid and increase the heat to 400°F (200°C). Cook for 10 minutes more. Take out of oven, remove the string, slice the meat and serve.

*Escalopes of veal with spinach*

# ESCALOPES OF VEAL WITH SPINACH

*Scaloppine agli spinaci*

Veal escalopes are one of the classic dishes of northern Italian cuisine. Traditionally they are cooked fairly quickly over high heat so they take on a good color, and then a dessert wine such as Marsala is added to enhance their flavor. At one time it was the custom to enrich them further with spices, or with "*salsa cammellina*," a brown sauce used with meats. They are often served as a garnish for *risotto alla Milanese*. This recipe using spinach makes a perfect single-dish meal if served with the risotto.

2 lb (1 kg) spinach
⅓ cup (3 oz/90 g) butter
1¾ lb (800 g) veal escalopes
salt and freshly ground pepper

Clean and trim the spinach. Cook in a saucepan with a small amount of boiling salted water. Drain and chop.

Put half the butter in a skillet. Add the escalopes and brown on both sides over high heat for 10 minutes, turning often. Add the spinach, the remaining butter and a little salt. Cover, reduce the heat and cook for 5 minutes.

When the spinach is cooked, season with pepper and arrange on a serving dish. Arrange the veal on top and serve.

*Lunch in the country* (eighteenth century), plate by the Rubati pottery company, Milan; PRIVATE COLLECTION, MILAN

# VEAL BAKED IN RED WINE

*Arrosto di vitello al vino rosso*

**B**artolomeo Platina, a cookery writer from the fifteenth century, often recommended the use of wine in cooking, "the better to dilute and digest what we have eaten." The best cut of meat for this roast is the piece closest to the tail, which is known as *arrosto di codino* (literally, "pigtail roast"). The veins of fat running through it give it a softer texture than meat from other parts of the animal. When the meat is almost cooked it is given a flavor boost by the addition of vegetables, and these with their juices make it even more tender.

*1¾ lb (800 g) roasting veal*
*¼ cup (2 oz/60 g) butter*
*3 tablespoons extra virgin olive oil*
*2 leeks, trimmed, washed well and chopped*
*2 onions, chopped*
*2 carrots, scraped and chopped*
*1 celery stalk, chopped*
*4 potatoes, chopped*
*1 handful mixed fresh herbs: thyme, parsley and
    a bay leaf*
*salt and freshly ground pepper*
*2 cups (16 fl oz/500 ml) dry red wine*
*1 tablespoon all purpose (plain) flour*
*1 cup (8 fl oz/250 ml) clear beef or veal stock*
*2 tablespoons tomato purée*

Tie the meat securely with fine string so it will keep its shape during cooking. In a large casserole, heat the butter with the oil. Add the roast and brown gently for about 20 minutes, turning from time to time. Add the vegetables and the bunch of herbs. Season with salt and pepper. Pour on the red wine and simmer for about 1½ hours.

In a bowl, stir the flour into the stock, a little at a time so no lumps form. Stir in the tomato purée. Pour the mixture into the casserole with the meat and blend thoroughly into the cooking liquid. Stir the sauce carefully as it thickens for about 30 minutes. Turn off the heat. Take out the meat and remove the string. Slice the veal and arrange it on a heated serving plate. Surround it with the vegetables, spoon the hot sauce over both meat and vegetables and serve.

*Veal baked in red wine*

# STUFFED VEAL ROLLS WITH FRUIT MUSTARD

*Involtini alla mostarda di Cremona*

Over the centuries there have been many variations of *involtini* (stuffed meat rolls), and families still have their own particular recipes. This one has its roots in the cuisine of Lombardy, where Cremona mustard is made. *La mostarda di Cremona* is made from preserved fruit in a mustard sauce. It is served as an accompaniment to boiled meats and is excellent with roasts. (See recipe for *mostarda di Cremona*, p.249)

*6 oz (180 g) mild sausage, skinned*
*2 tablespoons bread soaked in milk*
*2 egg yolks*
*2 tablespoons freshly grated Parmesan cheese*
*salt and freshly ground pepper*
*1¾ lb (800 g) veal escalopes, cut very thin and regular in shape*

*6 oz (180 g) mostarda di Cremona (Cremona mustard)*
*¼ cup (2 oz/60 g) butter*
*¼ cup (2 fl oz/60 ml) dry white wine*

Make the stuffing: mix together the sausage meat, soaked bread (after squeezing it as dry as possible), egg yolks and Parmesan. Season with salt and pepper and mix thoroughly.

Pound the veal slices lightly with a meat mallet and divide the prepared stuffing among them. Put a dab of Cremona mustard on top and roll up. Tie each roll with kitchen string. Heat the butter in a skillet over moderate heat. Cook the rolls for 15 minutes, turning often to brown on all sides.

Add the wine and deglaze the pan. Add a few tablespoons of water and finish cooking, covered, on low heat for another 10 minutes, adding more water if necessary to keep the bottom of the pan moist.

*Stuffed veal rolls with fruit mustard*

*Escalopes of veal with artichokes*

# ESCALOPES OF VEAL WITH ARTICHOKES

*Scaloppine di vitello con carciofi*

At one time lamb was used for this dish, but gradually the recipe became more refined and now, particularly in the North, escalopes with artichokes are prepared from milk-fed veal. The same method is sometimes used with breast of chicken or slices of turkey. The meat may be served accompanied by some freshly-made buttered *tagliatelle* or a risotto.

*6 large artichokes*
*juice of 1 lemon*
*2 tablespoons extra virgin olive oil*
*1 tablespoon (½ oz/15 g) butter*
*1¾ lb (800 g) veal escalopes*
*salt and freshly ground pepper*
*¼ cup (2 fl oz/60 ml) dry white wine*
*1 tablespoon chopped parsley*
*¼ cup (2 fl oz/60 ml) heavy (double) cream*

Trim the artichokes, removing the tough leaves and the spiky tips. Cut them into segments, dropping them into a bowl of water acidulated with the lemon juice as you go, to prevent them from darkening.

Heat the oil and butter in a large skillet. Add the veal and brown gently over moderate heat for about 10 minutes. Add the artichokes, season with salt and pepper and sprinkle the wine over all. As soon as all the wine has evaporated, stir in the parsley and cream. Cover and reduce the heat to low. Continue cooking for about 15 minutes.

Transfer the escalopes to a serving dish. Arrange the artichokes on the dish and coat with the sauce. Serve immediately.

145

## TO STUFF A PEACOCK

*A riempire un pavone*

Originally by an anonymous fourteenth-century Tuscan author, this recipe was later taken up by Maestro Martino and also by Bartolomeo Platina, who gives detailed instructions on how to kill the bird before cooking it. He finishes up with a warning that peacock meat makes the bile turn black, is not very nourishing and is harmful to anyone with liver or spleen problems. However that may be, the recipe demonstrates the magnificent presentation of meat dishes, which at that time were evidently the major component of the meal. Platina also tells us how to stuff a whole calf with ducks, hens and capons. The modern recipe substitutes a guinea fowl.

---

Skin the peacock, keeping the head and the feathers, then take some pork meat, not too fat, and pound the flesh of the said peacock and mince the two together. Pound spices, cinnamon and nutmeg, whatever you wish, and mix them with the whites of egg and then mix in the meat and keep the yolks for yourself. Then stuff the said peacock with the said minced meat and wrap the said peacock in a pig's caul and fasten it with wooden skewers and put it into a boiler of tepid water and let it boil softly. And when it has been reduced by boiling, roast it on the spit or over the grill and color it with the beaten yolks of egg which you have reserved. But do not use all of them: with the rest you are to make balls, as I shall explain, that is you take some raw pork loin and chop it very finely with a knife and mix the said meat with the said reserved eggs and aforementioned spices and make them thick enough so that with the palm of your hand you can make little balls, and color them and set them to boil in boiling water. And so when they are cooked you can roast them and color them with feathers dipped in egg yolk. You can put these balls inside and outside the peacock, under the caul. This done, dress the peacock once more in its skin and feathers which you had put aside, and take it to the table, and when the skin has been removed, pass it around to be eaten.

---

*10 oz (300 g) sausage, skinned*
*3 oz (90 g) pitted (stoned) green olives, chopped*
*1 peacock (or guinea fowl), about 4 lb (2 kg)*
*1 celery stalk, chopped*
*1 carrot, scraped and chopped*
*1 small onion, chopped*
*3 tablespoons extra virgin olive oil*
*salt and freshly ground pepper*
*1 tablespoon (½ oz/15 g) butter*
*¼ cup (2 fl oz/60 ml) dry Marsala*

Mix the sausage meat with the olives. Stuff the peacock with this mixture and sew up the opening with thread so the filling will not escape.

Put the celery, carrot and onion in a casserole with the oil. Place the bird on top, and season with salt and pepper. Thickly butter a piece of parchment (baking) paper, the size of the casserole, and place it over the bird, buttered-side down. Cover with a lid. Roast in a preheated 350°F (180°C) oven for about 2 hours. Turn the peacock and stir the vegetables a couple of times during cooking.

Transfer the peacock to a serving dish and keep warm. Pour the Marsala into the casserole and stir to incorporate the browned bits from the bottom. Strain the sauce. Reheat and pour over the bird, then serve.

*Kitchen scene*, print; BERTARELLI PRINT COLLECTION , MILAN

## STUFFED CALVES' EARS

*Orecchi di vitella pieni*

An unknown writer from Reggio Emilia was responsible for an eighteenth-century collection of recipes entitled *Libro Contenente la Maniera di Cucinare e Vari Segreti e Rimedi per Malattie e Altro (Book Containing the Manner of Cooking and Various Secrets and Remedies for Illness and Other Matters)*, written for the household of Count Cassoli. The recipes represent the day-to-day cooking for a relatively unpretentious family of the nobility. There are directions for making liqueurs and for preserving vegetables and making herb vinegars. The ingredients specified are those that were popular locally, and it is no surprise to find among them calves' ears, which today are still considered a delicacy in Lombardy and Emilia-Romagna and are usually served boiled, as a salad dressed with oil, lemon and parsley. The modern recipe explains how to stuff chops, rather than calves' ears.

*To stuff a peacock — modern recipe (left)   Stuffed calves' ears — modern recipe (right)*

Take 6 ears and put them to cook with a glass of white wine and consommé, salt, pepper, greens, small onions, garlic, 2 cloves, half a bay leaf, thyme, basil and a little butter and when they are cooked stir in a handful of grated bread and the same of cheese, cook with some milk until thick, and then leave to cool. Add to the mixture 3 egg yolks and a small amount of butter, fill the ears with the mixture and grease them with butter and cover them with breadcrumbs and cheese and put them in a saucepan with a little butter and a lid on, let them color over the heat and serve them without sauce.

¾ cup (3 oz/90 g) freshly grated Parmesan cheese

1½ cups (6 oz/180 g) dry breadcrumbs

3 egg yolks

6 veal chops

1½ tablespoons (¾ oz/20 g) butter

1 tablespoon mixed chopped fresh herbs
   (rosemary, thyme, sage)

salt

½ cup (4 fl oz/120 ml) dry white wine

In a bowl, thoroughly combine the Parmesan, ¾ cup (3 oz/90 g) of the breadcrumbs and the egg yolks.

Butterfly the veal chops to the bone. Stuff the chops with the cheese mixture and close the meat over the filling. Heat the butter with the herbs in a saucepan.

Butter 6 small sheets of greaseproof paper. Place 1 chop on each and sprinkle with a little salt and the butter and herbs. Pour on a little of the wine. Fold and seal the packages. Bake the parcels in a preheated 400°F (200°C) oven for about 20 minutes.

Remove the chops from the paper cases. Place on a broiling (grilling) pan and broil for 2 minutes on each side until browned. Transfer to a serving dish, pour the cooking juices over and serve.

*Still life with birds*, school of Caravaggio (seventeenth century);
BORGHESE GALLERY, ROME

## PIE WITH LIVE BIRDS

*Pasticcio di uccelli vivi*

The *Liber de Coquina* (*Book of Cooking*), by an anonymous fifteenth-century writer who worked at the Angevin court, is perhaps the oldest book on Italian cooking. Dedicated to Charles II of Anjou, it is an extremely varied volume with a cosmopolitan collection of recipes from France, the court of England, Rome, Campania, Genoa and Parma. It is written in Latin, though the influence of Italian is conspicuous (Latin was giving way to written Italian at this period), and reflects the fact that the recipes were intended for very aristocratic families, largely families of the court. This *pasticcio di uccelli vivi* was taken up by other more or less contemporary authors. For the modern recipe, naturally, dead birds are to be used, and must be well cooked to boot!

You can make a pie with live birds in the following manner. First, make a pastry casing and fill it with bran, and after you have covered it put it on to cook. When it has cooked and thoroughly cooled, make a small hole in the bottom to take out the bran, and put in a few live small birds and plenty of leaves from a tree. Then put the piece of pastry you took out to make the hole back in exactly the same position. And be sure to make several tiny holes on top so that the little birds will not suffocate for want of air. Then you set the abovementioned pie before some gentlemen and ladies, if you wish to have a little fun, and when they open the pie the above-mentioned birds will fly away.

3¼ cups (13 oz/400 g) all purpose (plain) flour
¾ cup (6 oz/180 g) butter
2 tablespoons water
12 quails
1 tablespoon fresh juniper berries
12 very thin slices pancetta
½ cup (4 fl oz/120 ml) dry white wine
1 celery stalk, sliced
1 carrot, scraped and sliced
3 potatoes, peeled and diced
salt and freshly ground pepper

Heap the flour in a mound on a work surface. Make a well in the center and put in (almost all) the butter cut into small pieces. Work with your fingertips until the flour is absorbed by the butter. Add water and mix well. Shape the mixture into a ball. Wrap it in a sheet of plastic film and refrigerate for about 30 minutes.

Meanwhile, stuff the quails with the juniper berries and wrap them in the *pancetta* slices. In a skillet, melt the remaining butter over moderate heat. Brown the quails until they are golden all over. Add the wine, celery, carrot and potatoes. Season with salt and pepper. Cover and cook for about 20 minutes.

Butter and flour a pie dish. Roll out ⅔ of the pastry; line the pie dish with it. Add the quails and vegetables. If desired, roll out the remaining dough and cover. Seal and flute the edges. Prick the surface with a fork and bake the pie in the oven at 350°F (180°C) for about 40 minutes until the pastry begins to brown. Turn out the pie and serve.

*Still life with bird*, from the tomb of Clodius Hermes, fresco;
CATACOMBS OF SAN SEBASTIANO, ROME

*Pie with live birds — modern recipe*

# RABBIT AND POTATO STEW

*Coniglio in umido con patate*

Stewed meat was always one of the main dishes served at Italian banquets of the old days. It used to be offered after the roast meat, because it was richer and more strongly flavored. In family cooking, stewing is often preferred to roasting, in spite of the longer cooking time. This is because less expensive meats can be used in stewing, and they become tender and tasty with the long cooking time. Potatoes cooked with the meat are especially tasty, because they absorb the flavors of the meat.

*3 tablespoons all purpose (plain) flour*
*salt and freshly ground pepper*
*1 rabbit, about 2 lb (1 kg), cut into serving pieces*
*3 tablespoons extra virgin olive oil*
*1 onion, finely chopped*
*1 garlic clove, chopped*
*2 tablespoons chopped parsley*
*2 cups (16 fl oz/500 ml) clear beef stock, boiling*

*2 lb (1 kg) potatoes, sliced*
*1 tablespoon (½ oz/15 g) butter*

In a wide, deep platter mix the flour with a few pinches of salt and plenty of pepper and dredge the pieces of rabbit in it.

Pour the oil into a large casserole. Add the rabbit pieces and onion and brown over moderate heat, stirring from time to time, for about 15 minutes, until the rabbit pieces are golden. Sprinkle with the garlic and half of the parsley.

Pour in the hot stock. Cover the pan and cook in a preheated 350°F (180°C) oven for about 20 minutes. Add the potatoes and cook, covered, for 1 hour. Ten minutes before serving, remove the lid, scatter knobs of butter over the potatoes and turn the heat up to 425°F (220°C) to brown them.

Arrange the rabbit and potatoes on a serving dish. Sprinkle the remaining parsley over them and serve.

*Rabbit and potato stew*

*Pigeon and olives*

# PIGEON AND OLIVES

*Piccioni alle olive*

The tastiest pigeons are the wild variety, but these days pigeons are bred specially for eating. Because their flesh is rather dry, they are usually wrapped in slices of bacon. As the bacon cooks it melts and provides the fat that is lacking in the pigeon.

This recipe with olives comes from the Neapolitan cook of a well-known family, and is written in a small exercise book with the date 1905. Such notebooks were kept secret, and were handed over to the cooks' successors only when they had shown themselves worthy of receiving them.

*3 pigeons*
*1 thick slice of prosciutto, about 5 oz (150 g)*
*2 spring onions, chopped*
*2 bay leaves*
*1 tablespoon fresh juniper berries*
*¼ cup (2 fl oz/60 ml) extra virgin olive oil*
*1 cup (8 fl oz/250 ml) clear beef stock*
*¼ cup (2 fl oz/60 ml) dry Marsala*
*salt and freshly ground pepper*

*3 slices pancetta*
*6 oz (180 g) pitted (stoned) green olives*

Clean the pigeons and reserve the livers.

Cut the prosciutto into small pieces. In a saucepan, combine the prosciutto, pigeon livers, spring onions, bay leaves, juniper berries and 2 tablespoons of the oil. Cook for a few minutes over high heat. Add ½ cup (4 fl oz/120 ml) of the stock and the Marsala. Reduce the heat, season with salt and pepper and cover the pan. Cook for about 30 minutes, until the liquid evaporates.

Finely chop the stuffing mixture. Stuff the pigeons with it. Wrap the *pancetta* slices around the birds and tie them. Brush with 1 tablespoon of the oil and season with salt and pepper. Bake in a preheated 350°F (180°C) oven (brushing them with the remaining oil), for about 1 hour. Add the remaining stock and the olives. Cook for 5 minutes, stirring to incorporate the browned bits on the bottom of the pan.

Arrange the pigeons on a serving dish, surround with the olives and serve.

151

*Duck in white wine with vegetables and herbs*

# DUCK IN WHITE WINE WITH VEGETABLES AND HERBS

*Anatra alle verdure*

It used to be traditional in dishes such as this one to use "mute" ducks, because their flesh was considered superior. Nowadays it is no longer possible to find these, but certainly if you can obtain a wild duck rather than a battery one it will be tastier.

*1 duck, about 4 lb (2 kg)*
*¼ cup (2 oz/60 g) butter*
*3 oz (90 g) pancetta, diced*
*½ bottle dry white wine*
*1 handful parsley*
*1 fresh rosemary sprig*
*1 handful fresh sage*
*2 bay leaves*
*salt and freshly ground pepper*
*1 lb (500 g) onions*
*2 carrots, scraped and sliced*

Prepare and clean the duck. Cut it into medium-sized serving pieces. In a large skillet or casserole, combine the butter with the *pancetta* over moderate heat. Add the duck pieces and brown for about 20 minutes. Pour in the wine, add the herbs and salt and pepper. Cover the pan and cook on low heat for about 1 hour.

In another pan, gently fry the onions with the remaining butter. Add the carrots and season with salt and pepper. Cover and cook gently for about 40 minutes over low heat.

When ready to serve, remove and discard the herbs. Stir the vegetables in with the duck and cook together for 5 minutes. Transfer to a serving platter and serve.

# ROLLED BREAST OF TURKEY WITH HAM STUFFING

*Petto di tacchino al prosciutto*

The rolled roast is one of the most typical dishes in Italian cuisine, and there are thousands of versions of it. In my own home I cannot remember having eaten the same version of the rolled roast more than twice! Apart from turkey, veal or beef may be used, and of course minced meat can equally well be made into a roll around the filling.

One of the earliest recipes for rolled roast is to be found in the fourteenth-century work by an anonymous Venetian author, where the description of what is to be used for the filling (pork, fresh and salted, spices, spleen, etc.) takes up a full closely-written page.

*1¾ lb (800 g) turkey breast*
*4 eggs*
*1 rosemary sprig, chopped*
*salt and freshly ground pepper*
*2 tablespoons (1 oz/30 g) butter*
*6 oz (180 g) sliced cooked ham*
*2 tablespoons extra virgin olive oil*
*½ cup (4 fl oz/120 ml) dry white wine*

Pound the turkey breast with a meat mallet until it is rectangular.

Meanwhile, prepare the *frittata* filling. Beat the eggs in a bowl. Add the rosemary and a pinch each of salt and pepper and mix well. Melt half the butter in a skillet. Pour in the eggs and let them set into a *frittata*, or omelet, ½ inch (1 cm) thick. Turn over and cook the other side.

Lay the ham slices on the turkey meat. Set the *frittata* on top. Roll up the meat and tie it with string.

In an oval casserole heat the remaining butter with the oil. Season the turkey roll with salt and pepper and lay it in the casserole. Cook over moderate heat for about 15 minutes, turning often. As soon as it is uniformly browned, transfer it to a preheated 350°F (180°C) oven and bake for about 1 hour.

Remove the turkey roll from the sauce and let it rest for a short time. Untie the string, slice the meat and arrange the slices slightly overlapping on a serving platter. Pour the wine into the casserole, stir in the browned bits from the bottom, heat and strain the sauce over the meat before serving.

152

*Rolled breast of turkey with ham stuffing*

*Chicken and Swiss chard*

# CHICKEN AND SWISS CHARD

*Pollo con le bietole*

It is still possible sometimes to find free-range corn-fed chickens whose meat is firm and tasty. Once, every family kept chickens for its own use, both for the goodness of the meat and in order to have fresh eggs. Many families still do so today, because chickens raised in cages, although they are never over-fattened, give very loose-textured meat. In Italy, chicken that is too fat is considered bad and there is no demand for it.

*1 chicken, about 3 lb (1.5 kg)*
*2 carrots*
*1 celery stalk, chopped*
*salt*
*6 oz (180 g) onions, finely sliced*
*¼ cup (2 fl oz/60 ml) extra virgin olive oil*
*2 lb (1 kg) Swiss chard, trimmed and chopped*
*freshly ground pepper*
*¾ cup (6 fl oz/180 ml) heavy (double) cream*

Pluck the chicken and wash it carefully. Put aside the neck, feet and wings and cut the rest into smallish pieces. Put the neck, feet and wings in a ceramic pan, cover with cold water and add one of the carrots and the celery for flavoring. Season with salt and boil for 1 hour. Strain the stock and set aside.

Chop the remaining carrot. In a casserole, combine the carrot, onion and oil. Sauté, stirring constantly for 10 minutes over low heat. Before the vegetables begin to color, add the remaining chicken pieces and brown, stirring frequently, over moderate heat for about 15 minutes.

Pour ½ cup (4 fl oz/120 ml) of the reserved stock over the chicken. Bring to a boil. Add the Swiss chard and some pepper and cook for about 1 hour. If necessary, add more boiling stock to keep the bottom of the pan moist. Adjust the seasonings.

Pour in the cream and heat through for about 2 minutes. Serve from the casserole at the table.

154

# CHICKEN STEWED WITH BELL PEPPERS

*Pollo ai peperoni*

I n the old days chickens would first be boiled and then fried with salt pork, onions and other vegetables such as bell peppers (capsicums) or eggplants (aubergines). Sometimes golden raisins (sultanas), dried prunes, almonds or dates would be added to these chicken and vegetable dishes.

The *spezzatino*, a light stew, is one of the most popular dishes in Italy, whether it be made with chicken, veal or beef. Every cook has a secret recipe, or else takes over someone else's recipe and makes it into his or her own specialty, and one rarely eats a *spezzatino* that is the same as any other. This version with the *peperoni* is full of flavor and very colorful: a delight to the eye as well as the palate.

*1 chicken, about 3 lb (1.5 kg)*
*1 tablespoon all purpose (plain) flour*
*¼ cup (2 fl oz/60 ml) extra virgin olive oil*
*2 tablespoons (1 oz/30 g) butter*
*salt and freshly ground pepper*
*¼ cup (2 fl oz/60 ml) dry white wine*
*½ cup (4 fl oz/120 ml) clear beef stock*
*3 red bell peppers (capsicums)*
*1 garlic clove, chopped*
*1 small piece of chile pepper, chopped*
*1 tablespoon chopped basil*

Wash and dry the chicken; cut it into medium-sized serving pieces. Flour them lightly.

Heat the oil and butter in a large skillet. Add the chicken pieces and brown over moderate heat for 20 minutes. When they are well browned, season with salt and pepper and pour on the wine. Cook until the wine evaporates almost completely. Continue cooking until well done, moistening the meat from time to time with a little of the stock. Meanwhile, roast the peppers directly in a flame or under the broiler (griller). Remove the charred skin. Cut the peppers into small pieces.

When the chicken is half-cooked, add the peppers, garlic and chile pepper. Finish cooking over low heat, sprinkling on a little of the stock from time to time and stirring so that the meat does not stick to the bottom of the pan.

Remove from the heat, sprinkle with the basil and serve hot.

*Chicken stewed with bell peppers*

# VEGETABLES AND SALADS

In Italy vegetables are treated with respect! For centuries fragrant herbs and fresh vegetables in season have been the foundation of Italian cooking. The Italian passion for vegetables can be most poignantly seen in the tiny verdant garden plots flourishing bravely on the outskirts of major cities. On warm summer evenings families can be seen happily picnicking on their miniature oases amidst the grime and appalling urban sprawl. Each green space will have a little potting shed and is symbolic of the great tradition of growing and preparing fresh green vegetables. These parcels of land are usually leased by the city, free of charge, to the numerous "displaced" farmers among its citizens. Many are second-generation farmers, who have reluctantly left the land and taken up residence in city apartments, but still feel compelled by tradition to toil the earth for the satisfaction of the inimitable taste of home-grown vegetables. During the summer months many Italians live almost exclusively on vegetables.

The distinction of Italian food is given an extra dimension by the time-honored usage of a bewildering variety of herbs. In days gone by, entire hillsides in some regions would be covered with the pungent smell of basil wafting for miles around. Many an old recipe begins with: "take a handful of the usual *aromi*." The *aromi* is the cook's special blend of herbs and spices which he or she uses in many recipes. Italian shoppers today will often ask their greengrocer (usually after they have paid their bill), to put *"un po' di aromi"* in their bags in order to make their *soffritto*. There is no real English equivalent for *soffritto* which is derived from the Italian *soffriggere*, meaning to "under-fry." The *soffritto* normally consists of a little onion, celery, carrot and the *aromi*, and is used to add its aromas to meat, fish or vegetables. The vegetables are chopped using a *mezzaluna* — a cutting utensil with a halfmoon-shaped blade — which, when used with a kind of rocking motion by the experienced cook, achieves a particular fineness. The vegetables are then gently sautéed (under-fried) in olive oil or butter or a mixture of both until they just begin to take on color.

In ancient times aromatic herbs graced the kitchen mostly to disguise the flavor of (and disinfect) tainted meat and fish. Grown in monastery and villa gardens, and gathered from the hillsides by peasants, they were also thought to aid digestion as well as sharpen a dull dish. Today the cooks of Italy make judicious use of many traditional herbs, the variety depending on the location and the dish.

Usage and attitude to different herbs varies widely from region to region! Liguria is a region famous for the herbs that literally fill the air with their wonderful perfume as well as enhance the cooking. A familiar sight is women chatting in the fields as they take their children to pick wild *borragine* (borage) for their *preboggion*. In her book, *Italian Food,*

*Country life*, Ruggero Focardi (1864–1934); GALLERY OF MODERN ART, FLORENCE
For centuries Italian peasant women have scoured the hills for edible plants to go into their *misticanza* (mixture of wild greens). *Misticanza* is still a specialty of Rome today.

*Market scene with shopkeepers and customers* (detail), (late fifteenth century), fresco; CASTELLO DI ISSOGNE, VAL D'AOSTA

Elizabeth David notes that "Borage has always been said to have exhilarating properties, and to give courage, which no doubt accounts for its traditional use in wine cups." *Preboggion* is a bouquet that combines the somewhat bitter dandelion, chervil and chicory, and is used for stuffing *pansoti* (the Ligurian ravioli). When making *frittata* (an Italian omelet), the Ligurians will season it delightfully with *maggiorana* (sweet marjoram), another popular Ligurian herb. On their city window-sills or in their country gardens Ligurians grow *basilico* (basil), whose fragrant spicy scent fills the house or the garden and whose sweet leaves are pounded with a pestle to make *pesto* sauce (a paste of basil, pine nuts, olive oil and garlic).

Tuscans favor *salvia* (sage), which they reverently call "the sacred herb" (its name comes from the Latin *salvare*, meaning "to heal"). There is a legend that says it was given this power when, during the flight of the Christ Child into Egypt, the plant laid down its branches every time Christ needed a place to rest. Appropriately, the devoted Tuscans use this herb assiduously, even composing four-course meals around it. As an *antipasto* they lightly coat its large leaves in a batter of flour and egg and deep-fry them in olive oil. *Tortelli* (pasta) is sautéed in melted butter and sage. Veal is wrapped in sage and stuffed in the dish *involtini* (meat rolls). Sage is also used to flavor the bean dish *fagioli all'uccelletto*. It even appears as a background to a regional dessert, *salviata*, a baked custard pudding flavored with fresh, young sage. Siena asserts its uniqueness with its own herb, *dragoncello* (tarragon), whose distinctive and subtle flavor is added to local pasta sauces and meat dishes. Siena is the only town in Italy with the tradition of using tarragon.

There are cooks who claim chile pepper improves practically any dish. They have probably visited Abruzzo and Basilicata, where it is very popular! First brought to Europe from South America by Spanish explorers, chile pepper is often referred to affectionately as *diavolillo* (the little devil). It is featured in one of the easiest and tastiest pasta dishes of all — *spaghetti aglio, olio e peperoncino* (spaghetti dressed in olive oil flavored with garlic and chile pepper).

*The month of September* (detail), (fifteenth century), fresco;
CASTELLO DEL BUONCONSIGLIO, TRENTO
During the Renaissance, vegetables were not served with the main course as they are today. They were served by themselves, perhaps in a salad at the beginning or end of a meal, in sweet pies or in a sauce.

161

*The asparagus harvest* (fifteenth century), illumination from the Theatrum Sanitatis, code 4182; CASANATENSE LIBRARY, ROME
Asparagus is as popular today in Italy as it was in Roman times. The earliest recipe for asparagus is from an anonymous Tuscan from the fourteenth century who recommended cooking it with saffron.

In Italy salad is almost a religion, and it is the home of what many gourmets consider the ultimate salad. An astonishing variety of herbs, wild greens and edible weeds come together for the incomparable *misticanza* (a mixture of wild greens), whose origins go beyond recorded time. For centuries, peasant women have scoured neighboring hills for anything edible to feed their families. As with so many Italian recipes, the triumph over poverty has created a legacy, handed down over generations and still is delighting diners today. *Misticanza* is a specialty of Rome, where all the ingredients can still be gathered in the Castelli Romani, the hills surrounding the Eternal City. In the vibrant neighborhood markets, elderly women clean and cut the greens to sell by the bushel. The list of greens that make up the salad is endless and many of them can only be found locally. In the fifteenth century Platina listed thirteen wild plants, and modern Roman gastronomes list numerous others. An authentic *misticanza* usually includes *rughetta* (rocket lettuce), various kinds of wild *cicoria* (chicory) such as *barba di frate* (friar's beard), dandelion, borage and mint, which is considered good for the digestion. It is seasoned with the classic dressing of salt, vinegar, and olive oil, but Platina notes that this particular salad requires more oil than vinegar. He also gently reminds his readers that wild greens should be well-chewed.

Italians, it would seem, have always taken the subject of salad seasoning very seriously. In the sixteenth century the botanist, Salvatore Massonio, wrote a treatise on the subject containing many observations that were before their time. He drew on the Greek and Latin classics to explain the considerable medical and gastronomic benefits of eating greens and herbs as well as the reasons for using salt, vinegar and olive oil to season them. At family meals today the mistress of the house performs the ritual of dressing the salad moments before serving, in order to keep the delicate leaves flavorsome, fresh and crisp. The lady of the house will first put the salt into a large spoon, into which she will add the vinegar, stirring it to dissolve the salt. She then blends it into the greens which are tossed well. Olive oil, added last, seals the leaves. The ratio of each condiment is determined by the type of salad. All the wholesome greens should be well coated with dressing without soaking them or leaving a puddle at the bottom of the bowl. A soggy salad in Italy would be a veritable crime!

*The vegetable market*, Achille Beltrame (1871–1945); MILAN

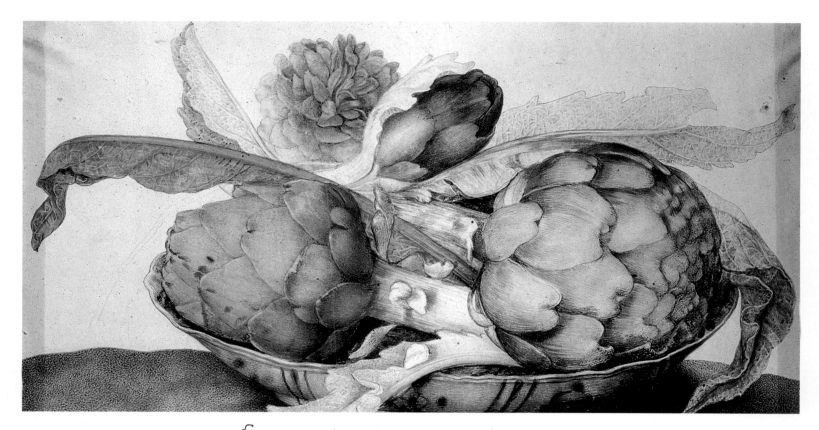

Costanzo Felici, a doctor and naturalist from the sixteenth century, wrote several treatises on herbs and greens, which contained much gastronomic advice on how to eat them, both raw and cooked. Radishes, he also observed, are a stimulant to the appetite and should be eaten raw; sound advice that is being rediscovered 400 years later.

Felici's treatment of the popular bulbous plant, *finocchio* (wild and domestic fennel), remains the custom today. Bundles of fennel stems are dried and used as a herb to season chicken and pork dishes, especially in Tuscany and Umbria. The seeds flavor the Tuscan sausage, *finocchiona*, and the celebrated dried figs of Puglia. Its aniseed fragrance and taste are particularly refreshing when eaten raw, dressed with lemon and olive oil. After Renaissance banquets, when the dessert had been eaten and the guests had washed their hands, raw fennel would be used as an effective way to recover the palate.

It is a telling indication of the justifiable Italian passion for food that the word "gluttony" (*la gola*) does not have the negative connotations of its English equivalent — despite its being one of the seven deadly sins. The *carciofi* (artichoke) originally grew wild in Sicily. Felici attributes its rapid domestication to sheer gluttony. In his day it was already "most common and highly esteemed by the rich and powerful." During the Renaissance this highly-prized flower was considered a powerful aphrodisiac. In modern Italian markets great bouquets of different kinds of artichokes, with lavish, leafy stalks, are strung through the marketplaces in wintertime.

One of the staple dishes of Italy, the bright-green globe-shaped variety of artichoke, *mammole*, is used in a dish that can be traced back to medieval times — *carciofi alla Giudea* (Jewish artichokes). This dish originated in the ancient Jewish ghetto of Rome, which is the oldest in Europe, and restaurants in this area surrounding the synagogue still specialize in this time-honored method of preparing artichokes. The *mammole* are trimmed back to their tenderest leaves, flattened and gently fried in olive oil until they are crisp and golden-brown on the outside and moist and tender at the heart.

*Tray with artichokes*, Giovanna Garzoni (1660–70); PALATINA GALLERY, FLORENCE
A traditional dish of Italy which dates back to medieval times is Jewish artichokes. The *mammole* variety of artichoke is used in this dish which is still served in restaurants in Rome today.

*Still life with pumpkin*, Giacomo Ceruti
(1700–1768); BRERA GALLERY, MILAN
Early Italian cookbook writers did not
differentiate between *zucche* (pumpkin)
and *zucchine* (zucchini or courgettes).
Pumpkin is served in a variety of different
ways in the regions of Italy, including a
soup in Milan, and a risotto in Lombardy.

The small narrow variety of artichoke, with tapered, violet-colored, thorn-tipped leaves, is finely sliced, sautéed in olive oil, and served with many meat and pasta dishes. An elaborate vegetable pie from Liguria called *torta pasqualina* (Easter pie) uses only the tenderest leaves and hearts of this type of artichoke. This dish celebrates Easter, as its name suggests, when the vegetable is at its most succulent and tender. The pie-filling consists of artichokes, cooked in olive oil, and garlic, borage, and marjoram, mixed with a rich sauce of fresh cheese. This delicious savory sauce is baked between two multiple layers of transparently thin pastry. Tradition holds that there should be twelve layers on top and twelve on the bottom to honor the Apostles, who were the guests at the first paschal supper.

It is now almost impossible to imagine Italian cooking without the tomato. Yet it only reached Italy in the sixteenth century, after Cortez had conquered Mexico. Felici, writing at that time, dismissed the *pomo d'oro* ("golden apple" or "apple of Peru") as *"piu presto bello che buono"* ("more good-looking than good"). What is now Italy's most popular salad ingredient Felici scoffed at, as being altogether too showy and favored by those "eager for novelties." It was not until the eighteenth century that the tomato achieved culinary respectability, particularly in the South, in Naples and Campania. There, over two centuries, its cultivation was perfected. By 1773, in his book *Il Cuoco Galante (The Gallant*

*Cook)*, the Neapolitan chef, Vincenzo Corrado, granted the tomato the status it enjoys today and included it in numerous recipes. As an *antipasto*, fresh tomatoes are served with alternating slices of fresh mozzarella cheese. More elegantly and deliciously, the tomato can be stuffed with beans or rice. A popular recipe today, and similar to one given by Corrado, is *pomodori gratinati alla Napoletana*, in which tomatoes are halved and stuffed with parsley, garlic and oregano, sprinkled with breadcrumbs and baked in the oven. Another dish, that is humble in origin but makes an unusual summer luncheon, is a tomato and bread salad flavored with a few vegetables and extra virgin olive oil. The juicy, ripe Italian tomato is, however, at its best on its own, lightly dressed with olive oil and decorated, perhaps, with a few sprigs of fresh basil. It is not unusual for visitors to Italy to exclaim with joy that they have tasted a tomato for the very first time!

*The market of Florence*, Giuseppe Moricci (1806–79); GALLERY OF MODERN ART, FLORENCE

165

*Eggplant*
Eggplants, or aubergines, have been
popular in the South of Italy since the
eleventh century. However, they became
widely popular only in recent times as
early cooks considered them unhealthy,
and they were even thought to induce
madness.

Italians have invented many different methods for cooking their cornucopia of invigorating fresh greens and vegetables. *Spinaci* (spinach) is mostly prepared *saltati*, or "leaping" in the pan: first parboiled, it is then quickly sautéed in a little olive oil and garlic. *Melanzane* (eggplant or aubergine) is often served *trifolati*: thinly sliced and sautéed in olive oil, garlic and parsley. Small, young spring zucchini (courgettes) are unparalleled *lessi*: lightly boiled, cut in half and served sprinkled with lemon juice and olive oil. Fennel is baked *gratinato*: briefly parboiled, sautéed in butter, sprinkled with grated Parmesan, and cooked for a few minutes in the oven. *Peperoni* (large green, yellow and red bell peppers or capsicums) are at their most inviting when roasted whole on the grill, peeled and served with olive oil, salt and crushed pepper corns. Renaissance recipes had *carote* (carrots) immersed in a sweet and sour sauce, a treatment which has understandably withstood the test of time. *Porri brasati* (braised leeks) are a perfect accompaniment to braised meats.

There are many charming traditional regional recipes which combine the natural flavors of several vegetables into all sorts of surprises. To make *caponata* (a mixed vegetable dish), Sicilians mix fried eggplant, onions, celery, tomatoes, olives, capers, and an abundant handful of fresh basil leaves all seasoned with a traditional sauce of olive oil, vinegar and sugar. For family meals a robust and nourishing dish is vegetable casserole — in the North with combinations of cabbage and potatoes and in the South, peppers and eggplant — with the vegetables layered for an inviting formal presentation. Perhaps the finest Italian cooking method for vegetables is the *fritto misto* (mixed fry), which is also a popular method for cooking meat. This classic dish has been developed by the chefs of Naples into high art! They fry zucchini flowers, asparagus tips, tomatoes, peppers, onions and fennel, all coated in a very light batter, which are brought to the table as soon as they are cooked so the diner can fully savor this hot, crisp and delectable dish.

*Still life with asparagus*, Giovanni Martinelli (1610–1659); PITTI PALACE, FLORENCE

Towards the close of the sixteenth century Annibale Carracci painted a picture entitled *Il Mangiafagioli (The Bean Eater)*. Painted in earthy tones, it depicts a peasant eating a bowl of white legumes with some raw spring onions, brown country bread, and a glass of wine. This painting captures the Italian enjoyment and sense of this popular food more than any recipe by the contemporary Bartolomeo Scappi could. Legumes were traditionally a peasant food and, as a result of characteristic peasant ingenuity, many clever and delicious ways of preparing them have evolved over the centuries. There is the Venetian *pasta e fagioli* (bean soup); the Tuscan *fagioli all'uccelletto* (boiled *cannellini* beans seasoned with sage and tomato sauce), and the Roman *fagioli con le cotiche* (beans with rinds of pork).

In Lazio another popular legume, *fava* (broad bean), is eaten raw with a piece of the delicious local cheese, *pecorino Romano*, served with carafes of chilled, white Frascati wine. A well-known sight in Rome on May Day is groups of people sitting outside taverns in the old neighborhood of Trastevere, shelling *fava* beans while celebrating the traditional workers' holiday — a rustic scene worthy of Carracci's skill. A more sophisticated version of this tasty dish is to serve raw *fava* beans with fine shavings of Parmesan cheese, and a light dressing of olive oil and lemon juice.

Well before the game-hunting season, the Sila mountains of Calabria come alive with thousands of men, women and children intent on a hunt of their own. They are searching

*The bean-eater*, Annibale Carracci (1560–1609); COLONNA GALLERY, ROME
The Bolognese painter Annibale Carracci was a brilliant draughtsman who firmly believed in drawing directly from nature. He is famous for his frank and realistic genre paintings and is considered the inventor of the caricature.

167

*The mushroom harvest* (fifteenth century), illumination from the Theatrum Sanitatis, code 4182; CASANATENSE LIBRARY, ROME
Mushroom-gathering has been a popular pastime in Italy for centuries.

for the elusive and highly prized wild mushrooms that begin to surface after the late summer rains in hot and humid July and August. Everyone has his or her own closely guarded secret spot where, in seasons past, they had the good fortune to have gathered a basket full of huge *porcini* (the boletus), or orange-capped *ovoli* (Caesar's mushroom), or *cantarelli* (apricot-colored chanterelles).

Formerly the mushroom was held in some suspicion. Popular tradition abounded with stories about famous people who had died from eating poisonous mushrooms. The Roman Emperor, Claudius, was thought to have been fed them by his wife Agrippina, with fatal results, and it was said that Lucrezia Borgia was fond of serving them to further her sinister purposes. The fact that mushrooms thrived in dark and humid places also cast a shadow on their reputation. The Archbishop of Milan, Saint Carlo Borromeo, as well as the de'Medici Pope, Clemente VII, counseled the faithful against eating the dubious fungi. One of the first to provide a detailed list of mushrooms was Pierandrea Cesalpino, in 1583. His *De Plantis (Concerning Plants)* painstakingly describes some fifty families of mushrooms. Mushrooms then began to lose their bad reputation and started appearing in recipes. Bartolomeo Scappi, cook to Pope Pius V, began a banquet in honor of Charles V with a *prugnoli* soup (St George's mushrooms) and concluded the banquet with *prugnoli* tarts.

*Still life with fruit and landscape*, anonymous Florentine painter (seventeenth century); PITTI PALACE, FLORENCE

Today the flavorsome first mushrooms of the season are a cause for celebration for family and friends, and a risotto or *pasta ai funghi porcini* (pasta with boletus mushrooms) is often prepared. The prized *ovoli* are best enjoyed raw in a salad sprinkled with lemon juice and extra virgin olive oil. The large cap of an Apennine *porcino* is superb simply seasoned with a little olive oil, garlic and salt, and then broiled (grilled). In many regions the entire mushroom is used when the chopped mushroom stems are stuffed into the caps and then baked in the oven. When the season for fresh *funghi* is over for another year, their perfectly delicious flavor lives on in a wide variety of sauces for pasta and meats made from dried mushrooms, especially *porcini*.

Perhaps Italy's most remarkable and highly regarded delicacy is the truffle (*tartufo*). Before winter sets in, Mother Nature, who has been so generous to Italians all year long, yields this exquisite treasure from its underground hiding place. The truffle is a superior mushroom which bears its "fruit" beneath the soil of such venerable trees as the hazelnut, beech, poplar, willow and oak. The cherished *tartufo bianco* (white truffle) is mainly found in Piedmont, where it is usually associated with the city of Alba and is hunted for with specially trained dogs. Its pungent scent and magnificent flavor are quite delicious. Less fragrant but still characteristically piquant is the black truffle, associated with Norcia, a town in Umbria. Even in the fifteenth century the truffle excited Platina, who mentioned the "marvelous snouts of the sows from Norcia" that could sniff out this buried treasure. He also recommends washing the soil off in wine, cooking the truffles in hot embers and bringing them to the table while still warm, dusted with a little pepper.

Truffles are so rare and costly (around US$100 per ounce — 30 grams) that Italians eat them sparingly and reverently, "shaving" them over other dishes such as risotto, pasta, fried eggs in butter, and sliced raw fillet of beef dressed in olive oil and lemon juice. Their ancestors, on the other hand, could afford to indulge. On his menu for a Renaissance banquet, Bartolomeo Scappi included two truffle dishes: besides several platters of raw truffles seasoned with salt and pepper, he also served them stewed divinely in a sauce of olive oil and oranges.

*The olive grove*, Giovanni Colacicchi (twentieth century);
GALLERY OF MODERN ART, FLORENCE
There are many varieties of olive in Italy and many ways of preserving them. The earliest recipe for preserving olives is from the first century AD, by a botanist named Columella. He advises scalding and draining them, then covering them in layers of amphora, salt and herbs.

169

# "REINFORCED" TURNIPS

*Rape "armate"*

**M**aestro Martino da Como, author of the *Libro de Arte Coquinaria* (*Book of Culinary Art*), which is now kept in the Library of Congress in Washington, lived in Rome in the second half of the fifteenth century and worked for a long time as personal cook to the Patriarch of Aquileia. His recipes are the first to be structured and precise with ingredients, and like almost all the recipes of that time, they often mix sweet with savory.

The modern version of this recipe, much lighter than the original, takes its inspiration from the Trentino region, where the turnips are particularly good, since turnips grow best in cold climates.

> Cook the turnips under the embers, or alternatively boil them whole when they are young and smooth and cut them into slices as thick as the blade of a knife; and you will have some good fat cheese cut into slices as large as the turnip slices, but thinner, and some sugar, some pepper and some sweet spices mixed together; put all this into a cake pan, set out in order on the bottom, first some slices of cheese to make the bottom crust, and on top of this you will put a layer of turnip, scattering over it the abovementioned spices, and plenty of good fresh butter; in this way you will gradually use up the turnips and the cheese until the pan is full; letting them cook for a quarter of an hour or more, like a cake. And this dish should be served after the others.

*2 lb (1 kg) turnips*
*¼ cup (2 oz/60 g) butter*
*salt and pepper*
*1 cup (8 fl oz/250 ml) milk*
*1 cup (8 fl oz/250 ml) heavy (double) cream*
*¾ cup (3 oz/90 g) freshly grated Parmesan cheese*
*2 tablespoons chopped parsley*

*Greengrocers from Veneto* (late eighteenth century)

Peel the turnips. Wash them and slice them thinly. Heat the butter in a saucepan and add the turnips, salt and pepper. Pour in the milk and cook on low heat, stirring gently from time to time. After 10 minutes add the cream and the Parmesan and cook for a few minutes more until the cooking liquid thickens slightly. Sprinkle with the chopped parsley and serve.

# ARTICHOKES WITH PULLETS

*Carciofi a pollastri*

**L**a *Cuciniera Piemontese* (*The Piedmontese Cook*), which gives simple instructions for the best ways of presenting meat and vegetarian dishes suitable to modern tastes was published in Turin in 1798. This cook addresses herself to the upper middle class more than aristocratic families, with an eye to the neighboring European countries (and particularly France) as well as the other Italian regions. She presents a great variety of recipes, and as she says herself, the book is very modern, with many of the names having a French flavor, as is the custom in Piedmont. Even today the speech of educated Piedmontese is laced with a mixture of French and typical dialect words. The old recipe is for a very rich artichoke dish, which is greatly simplified in the modern version.

> You will have some artichokes which you will cut in quarters. Clean them and blanch them and then put them into cold water, drain them and put them to cook with salt pork, ham and veal and lemon slices, and when they are cooked to your good taste, transfer them to their plate. To make the sauce take two pullets [young chickens] which you will cut as for a fricassée of chicken, some mushrooms, a bunch of herbs, a slice of ham, blanch as usual moistening with some stock; when they are cooked, put the sauce through a sieve and mix with egg yolks, finish to your taste with lemon juice and pour over the artichokes and serve.

*1 handful dried mushrooms*
*6 large artichokes*
*juice of 2 lemons*
*2 oz (60 g)* pancetta, *chopped*
*3 oz (90 g)* prosciutto, *chopped*
*3 tablespoons extra virgin olive oil*
*½ cup (4 fl oz/120 ml) dry white wine*
*salt and freshly ground pepper*
*1 egg yolk*
*½ teaspoon all purpose (plain) flour*

*"Reinforced" turnips — modern recipe (left) Artichokes with pullets — modern recipe (right)*

Soak the mushrooms in cold water for 30 minutes.

Trim and slice the artichokes, discarding the tough leaves and the stalks. As each one is prepared drop it into a basin of water acidulated with half of the lemon juice.

Gently fry the *pancetta* and prosciutto in the oil in a saucepan until the fat becomes crisp. Drain and dry the artichokes. Add to the pan and cook for about 2 minutes over low heat. Pour in ¼ cup

(2 fl oz/60 ml) of the wine. Squeeze the moisture from the mushrooms and chop. Add to the artichokes. Season with salt and pepper. Cover and cook for about 10 minutes.

Mix the egg yolk with the flour, a pinch of salt, the remaining lemon juice and the remaining wine. Pour over the artichokes and stir constantly over very low heat until the sauce thickens.

Transfer the artichokes and sauce to a serving dish and serve.

*Artichokes stuffed with ham and parsley*

slightly. As each one is prepared, drop it into a bowl of water acidulated with the lemon juice to prevent it from darkening. Blanch the artichokes in boiling salted water for 2 minutes; drain. Mix together the ham, onion and parsley. Fill the artichokes with this mixture and arrange them in an oiled baking dish. Push the tomatoes through a sieve over the artichokes. Season with salt and pepper.

Cover the artichokes and bake in a preheated 350°F (180°C) oven for about 30 minutes, basting often with the cooking liquid. Serve.

# ARTICHOKES STUFFED WITH HAM AND PARSLEY

*Carciofi al prosciutto*

**A**rtichokes, raw or cooked, are one of the most commonly used vegetables in Italian cooking. They may be cooked simply, sliced and sautéed in a small amount of oil, or filled with any one of a multitude of stuffings. The best-known artichoke dishes are the traditional Roman ones — *carciofi alla giudea* (Jewish artichokes), fried whole, and *carciofi alla Romana*, with herb stuffing. This recipe is a rich and tasty variation of the latter.

*6 large artichokes*
*juice of 1 lemon*
*6 oz (180 g) cooked ham, chopped*
*1 small onion, chopped*
*2 tablespoons chopped parsley*
*2 tablespoons extra virgin olive oil*
*1 can (8 oz/250 g) peeled tomatoes*
*salt and freshly ground pepper*

Remove the stalks, outer leaves and spiky tips from the artichokes and hollow out the centers

# BROAD BEANS IN LEMON SAUCE

*Fave in salsa di limone*

**W**hen broad beans are fresh only the pods need be removed, otherwise it is better to take off the skin surrounding the seed as well, since it becomes slightly bitter. In spring, when broad beans are young and freshly picked, they are eaten raw with a pecorino-type cheese, especially in Tuscany.

*4 lb (2 kg) young, tender broad beans*
*¼ cup (2 oz/60 g) butter*
*1 tablespoon all purpose (plain) flour*
*juice of 1 lemon*
*2 egg yolks*
*freshly ground black peppercorns*
*salt*
*1 tablespoon chopped parsley*

*Broad beans in lemon sauce*

Shell the beans and cook them in salted boiling water for 5 minutes. Drain them, reserving a cup of the cooking liquid, and set aside.

Melt 2 tablespoons (1 oz/30 g) of the butter with the flour in a double boiler over simmering water. Stir in the reserved cooking liquid, followed by the lemon juice, the remaining butter and the egg yolks.

Stir briskly, and as soon as the sauce begins to thicken remove it from the heat. Season with pepper and salt.

Arrange the beans in a serving dish. Pour the sauce over them, sprinkle with chopped parsley and serve.

# ASPARAGUS WITH SWEET AND SOUR SAUCE

*Asparagi in salsa al miele*

In his cookery book published in the fifteenth century, Platina wrote of the many curative properties of asparagus: that it was diuretic and thus would remove the swelling in hands and legs, and, rather curiously, that it would make the eyes shine (which at the time was one of the few means of expression permitted for girls to demonstrate their love for the young man of their choice).

*4 lb (2 kg) asparagus*
*1 tablespoon acacia honey*
*1 hardboiled egg*
*⅓ cup (3 fl oz/90 ml) extra virgin olive oil*
*2 tablespoons vinegar*
*2 tablespoons chopped parsley*
*freshly ground pepper and salt*

Trim and wash the asparagus. Tie in bundles and cook, standing up, in a small amount of boiling salted water, so that the tips remain above the level of the water.

Make a sweet and sour sauce by whisking together the honey, egg, oil, vinegar and parsley with a little pepper and salt.

Drain the asparagus. Arrange them on a serving platter radiating out from the center. Cover them with the sauce and serve.

*Asparagus with sweet and sour sauce*

*Chicory with garlic sauce*

# CHICORY WITH GARLIC SAUCE

*Cicoria all'aglio*

This typical Neapolitan dish was mentioned by the eighteenth-century cookery writer Vincenzo Corrado in his book *Il Cuoco Galante* (*The Gallant Cook*). It represents an excellent way of cooking chicory (curly endive), because it tones down the slightly bitter taste. This type of chicory, known as asparagus chicory, is particularly suitable for eating cooked. It grows plentifully in kitchen gardens, sprouting again within a few days of being cut.

*1 head chicory, about 2 lb (1 kg)*
*1 handful fresh basil*
*¼ teaspoon paprika*
*⅓ cup (3 fl oz/90 ml) vinegar*
*3 garlic cloves, chopped*
*salt and freshly ground pepper*
*¼ cup (2 fl oz/60 ml) extra virgin olive oil*

Wash the chicory and cut it into small pieces, discarding any wilted or bruised leaves. Cook in plenty of boiling salted water for 5 minutes. Drain.

Transfer the chicory to a plate. Cover with small basil leaves and sprinkle with paprika. Keep warm.

In a small saucepan, bring the vinegar, garlic and a little salt and pepper slowly to a boil. Boil gently until the liquid is reduced by a ¼. Pour over the chicory. Add the oil and mix thoroughly before serving.

# BABY ONIONS BRAISED WITH BAY LEAVES

*Cipolline all'alloro*

**B**ay leaves add a special flavor to little onions. The bay leaf is one of the few herbs that retains its flavor and fragrance when dried. Bay trees, both wild and cultivated, are found all over Italy. They withstand the cold admirably and do not need attention. Along with rosemary and sage, bay is one of the most commonly used ingredients in Italian cooking.

*2 oz (60 g)* pancetta, *chopped*
*6 small sage leaves, chopped*
*1 tablespoon chopped parsley*
*2 tablespoons extra virgin olive oil*
*1½ lb (750 g) small new onions*
*¼ cup (2 fl oz/60 ml) dry white wine*
*salt and freshly ground pepper*
*3 tablespoons home-made tomato sauce*
*1 handful bay leaves*
*⅓ cup (3 fl oz/90 ml) clear chicken stock*

Fry the *pancetta*, sage and parsley gently in the oil. When the *pancetta* is a light golden color, add the onions and cook, turning often, over low heat for 10 minutes.

Sprinkle with the wine and let it evaporate completely. Season with salt and pepper. Stir the tomato sauce and bay leaves into the stock. Add to the onions and continue cooking until the liquid is absorbed. Serve.

*Baby onions braised with bay leaves*

175

*Lettuce au gratin (left) Baked fennel Parmigiana (right)*

# LETTUCE AU GRATIN

*Lattuga gratinata*

One of the most widely and easily grown vegetables in every region of Italy, lettuce is mostly used raw in salads with a simple dressing of oil and vinegar. But at one time it was also often eaten cooked, wrapped around a filling, in soups such as barley soup or stuffed whole. In this modern recipe, the lettuce is covered with béchamel sauce and baked in the oven. This gratin may also be used for broccoli, fennel or cauliflower.

*6 lettuces*

*¼ cup (2 oz/60 g) butter*

*2 tablespoons all purpose (plain) flour*

*2 cups (16 fl oz/500 ml) milk, at room temperature*

*salt and freshly ground pepper*

*a little freshly grated nutmeg*

*¾ cup (3 oz/90 g) freshly grated Parmesan cheese*

*1 egg yolk*

Parboil the lettuces in a small amount of salted water. Drain. Melt 2 tablespoons (1 oz/30 g) of the butter in a saucepan over low heat. Add the lettuces and cook, turning them once only.

In another pan melt the remaining butter, stir in the flour; then stir in the milk a little at a time and season with salt and pepper and flavor with the nutmeg. Remove this béchamel sauce from the heat as soon as it begins to boil. Add half the Parmesan, and then the egg yolk, stirring briskly to blend thoroughly.

Preheat the oven to 400°F (200°C). Arrange the lettuces in a buttered ovenproof dish. Cover with the bechamel and sprinkle on the remaining Parmesan. Brown in the oven for about 20 minutes before serving.

# BAKED FENNEL PARMIGIANA

*Finocchi alla Parmigiana*

In the South, this very fragrant and rather sweet vegetable is traditionally sliced thinly and eaten raw as a salad. Northerners, on the other hand, eat it cooked in any number of ways. The most suitable dressing for raw fennel is oil and lemon juice, because the lemon juice brings out its unique flavor more delicately. Vincenzo Agnoletti, cook to the Duchess of Parma, gives a recipe similar to this one in his book *La Nuovissima Cucina Economica* (*The New Economical Cuisine*), published in 1814.

*6 fennel bulbs*
*1 small white onion, chopped*
*¼ cup (2 oz/60 g) butter*
*salt*
*a little vegetable stock*
*½ cup (2 oz/60 g) freshly grated Parmesan cheese*

Trim the fennel bulbs and cut them into thick segments. In a shallow casserole or gratin dish, soften the onion in the butter. Add the fennel, season with salt and pour in the stock. Cook over low heat for 10 minutes.

Sprinkle the Parmesan over the fennel. Finish cooking in a preheated 425°F (220°C) oven for about 10 minutes more, or until the top of the fennel and sauce are lightly browned. Serve.

*Braised leeks*

# BRAISED LEEKS

*Porri brasati*

The delicious, delicate-tasting leek, a vegetable somewhere between onion and garlic, is grown all over Italy. In early cookery books we find instructions for cooking leeks with spices, golden raisins (sultanas) and pine nuts, whereas today, the traditional method of serving them in many areas is as a separate dish, *alla Parmigiana*, sprinkled with melted butter and grated Parmesan cheese. For serving as an accompaniment, however, braising offers a more suitable method of cooking.

*2 lb (1 kg) leeks*
*3 tablespoons extra virgin olive oil*
*½ cup (4 fl oz/120 ml) dry white wine*
*1 stock cube*
*salt and freshly ground pepper*

Cut the leeks in half lengthwise and remove most of the dark green leaves. Trim the root ends and wash well in several changes of water.

Heat the oil in a wide skillet. Add the leeks and cook on low heat for a few minutes. Pour in the wine, add the crumbled stock cube, cover and lower the heat. Cook for 20 minutes.

One minute before the end of the cooking time adjust the seasonings. Drain the leeks, arrange them on a serving plate and keep warm. Thicken the cooking liquid by reducing over high heat. Pour the sauce over the leeks and serve.

*Onion field* (fifteenth century), illumination from the Theatrum Sanitatis, code 4182; CASANATENSE LIBRARY, ROME

177

*Honeyed carrots*

# CASSEROLE OF VEGETABLES

*Verdure in casseruola*

Vegetable casseroles in the recipes of Bartolomeo Scappi or Maestro Martino da Como were called *pastelli*. Today they go under a variety of names and there are many different recipes for them. They are among the most typical of dishes found in the cuisine of every Italian region. In the South, the most used varieties tend to be bell peppers (capsicum) and eggplant (aubergine), whereas northerners use more potatoes, artichokes and various types of cabbage. Classic dishes include *caponata*, *peperonata*, *cianfotta* and the Friulan dish *zastoch*.

*⅓ cup (3 fl oz/90 ml) extra virgin olive oil*
*2 potatoes, sliced*
*2 onions, sliced*
*2 carrots, scraped and sliced*
*1 eggplant (aubergine), sliced*
*1 bell pepper (capsicum), sliced*
*1 celery stalk, sliced*
*2 tablespoons shelled peas*
*4 ripe tomatoes, sliced*
*salt and freshly ground pepper*
*½ cup (4 fl oz/120 ml) clear chicken stock*
*2 garlic cloves, finely chopped*
*1 tablespoon chopped parsley*

Coat a casserole with 1 tablespoon of the oil. Add the potatoes, onions, carrots, eggplant, bell pepper, celery, peas, and tomatoes in alternating layers, seasoning each layer with salt and pepper.

Mix the remaining oil with the stock and garlic. Pour over the vegetables. Cover the casserole and cook over very low heat for about 1 hour.

Arrange the vegetables on a serving platter or on individual plates. Scatter the parsley over them and serve.

# HONEYED CARROTS

*Carote al miele*

A typical element in the cuisine of Renaissance Florence was the sweet and sour sauce made from vinegar and sugar or — as in this recipe — honey, with many added spices. The vinegar would sometimes be replaced by lemon juice, especially in the cooking of vegetables, which are generally not strongly flavored.

*2 lb (1 kg) carrots, very thinly sliced*
*1 tablespoon (½ oz/15 g) butter*
*2 tablespoons water*
*salt*
*1 tablespoon lemon juice*
*¼ cup (2 fl oz/60 ml) honey*
*a pinch of ground cinnamon*

In a saucepan, combine the carrots, butter and water. Add salt, cover and cook for about 10 minutes over low heat.

Stir in the lemon juice and honey and cook for about 2 minutes, stirring with a wooden spoon. Sprinkle with the cinnamon and remove from the heat. Serve.

*Chile pepper*
In Italy this is often referred to as *diavolillo* (the little devil).

*Casserole of vegetables*

*Brussels sprouts and sausage*

# BRUSSELS SPROUTS AND SAUSAGE

*Cavolini alla salsiccia*

The intense flavor of this dish comes from the marriage of cabbage with sausage — a union very popular in Venetian cooking, and also often mentioned as a choice dish in Florentine recipe books from the Renaissance.

*1¾ lb (800 g) Brussels sprouts, trimmed*
*2 oz (60 g) pancetta, thinly sliced*
*10 oz (300 g) salsiccia (mild sausage), cut into*
*small pieces*
*2 tablespoons white wine vinegar*
*1 tablespoon all purpose (plain) flour*
*1 cup (8 fl oz/250 ml) clear beef stock*
*salt and freshly ground pepper*
*freshly grated nutmeg*
*1 tablespoon chopped parsley*

Cook the sprouts in plenty of boiling salted water for 5 minutes. Drain.

In a skillet over moderate heat, gently fry the *pancetta* and the *salsiccia* until well browned. Sprinkle the vinegar over. Cook until evaporated. Stir the flour into the fat on the bottom of the pan until it turns golden. Stir in the stock. Stir everything thoroughly, add the Brussels sprouts and adjust the salt to taste. Season with pepper and nutmeg. Add the parsley, heat for 1 minute and transfer to a serving dish.

# POTATOES WITH OREGANO

*Patate all'origano*

Oregano is a fragrant herb that grows naturally all along Italy's dry, sunny Mediterranean coast. It has always been used in sauces for spaghetti, on pizzas, and sprinkled on vegetables to add to their flavor. When the cook was unable to buy oregano fresh from the market, he or she would always have a ready supply that had been gathered in autumn and hung in bunches in the kitchen to dry so it would be available during winter.

*2 lb (1 kg) potatoes, peeled and cut into small dice*
*2 garlic cloves, chopped*
*1 lb (500 g) ripe tomatoes, peeled and chopped*
*⅓ cup (3 fl oz/90 ml) extra virgin olive oil*
*salt and freshly ground pepper*
*1 tablespoon oregano*
*1 handful basil leaves*

Put the potatoes, garlic and tomatoes into a bowl. Add the oil and salt and pepper; mix well.

Turn the mixture into a baking dish. Bake in a preheated 350°F (180°C) oven for 45 minutes. Two minutes before the end of cooking, sprinkle on the oregano. Garnish with a few leaves of basil and serve.

*Oregano* (1534), from the *Herbal* of Leonhart Fuchs
Oregano is a herb widely used in Italian cooking, especially in the South.

180

# CELERY AND ANCHOVY SALAD

*Insalata di sedano alle acciughe*

As well as being a wonderfully fresh and crisp accompaniment for summer dishes, this salad is also suitable for serving as an antipasto. In the old days the normally green stalks and leaves of the celery were covered with soil to obtain the delicate white stalks, which are better for eating raw. These days, the growers cover the stalks with tar-paper well before picking time so they are protected from the light and remain white and tender.

*3 anchovy fillets packed in oil, mashed*
*1 tablespoon lemon juice*
*salt and freshly ground pepper*
*¼ cup (2 fl oz/60 ml) extra virgin olive oil*
*6 tender white celery hearts, sliced*

In a bowl mix the anchovy fillets with the lemon juice, a pinch of salt and a pinch of pepper. Whisk in the oil. Pour over the celery, mix well and serve.

*Potatoes with oregano (left) Celery and anchovy salad (right)*

181

*Salad of bread and tomatoes*

# SALAD OF BREAD AND TOMATOES

*Insalata di pane e pomodori*

Bread is looked upon almost as a sacred food in Italy. It is never thrown out when it gets stale, but is used in soups, main dishes, or even mixed with raw vegetables in salads. This recipe is a specialty of the South, and is enriched with anchovy fillets and capers. It is important that the bread be several days old, and its texture be coarse, otherwise the salad will be mushy.

*6 plum (egg) tomatoes*
*salt and freshly ground pepper*
*3 slices stale Italian country bread*
*1 yellow bell pepper (capsicum)*
*2 hardboiled eggs*
*2 anchovy fillets packed in oil*
*1 celery stalk*
*2 onions*
*1 tablespoon capers*
*handful fresh basil leaves*
*2 tablespoons chopped parsley*
*¼ cup (2 fl oz/60 ml) extra virgin olive oil*
*2 tablespoons vinegar*

Wash and dry the tomatoes and cut them into thickish rounds. Place in a salad bowl and sprinkle with salt. Cut the bread into small pieces, add to the tomatoes and leave for at least 10 minutes to absorb the juice from the tomatoes.

Wash and dry the bell pepper, remove the seeds and ribs and cut it into small squares. Slice and chop the eggs; cut up the anchovy fillets into small pieces; slice the celery and finely slice the onion. Add all these ingredients to the bread and

tomatoes, along with the capers, the chopped basil and the parsley. Add salt, plenty of pepper, and the oil and vinegar. Mix in well and leave to rest, covered, for about an hour before serving.

# MIXED SALAD WITH OLIVES

*Insalata mista alle olive*

This is a classic summer salad encompassing all the flavors of Mediterranean cooking. It goes particularly well with fish, and is enriched by the addition of balsamic vinegar. This vinegar is a product of Modena that has become fashionable all over the world, and was at one time used as a medicine, believed to cure a multitude of ills.

*2 tomatoes, sliced*
*2 uncooked artichoke hearts, sliced*
*2 anchovy fillets, chopped*
*2 oz (60 g) pitted (stoned) black olives*
*⅓ cup (3 fl oz/90 ml) extra virgin olive oil*
*2 tablespoons balsamic vinegar*
*1 handful fresh basil leaves, torn into pieces*
*1 escarole lettuce, cut in pieces*

Combine the tomatoes, artichoke hearts, anchovies and olives in a salad bowl.

Pour on the oil and vinegar. Add the basil and the *escarole*, and mix together for a moment before serving.

*Mixed salad with olives*

*Tomato and cucumber salad with herbs*

# TOMATO AND CUCUMBER SALAD WITH HERBS

*Insalata di pomodori e cetrioli alle erbe*

In general, salads are dressed with oil and vinegar, although some salads lend themselves to a dressing of lemon juice rather than vinegar. Vinegar was already known in ancient times, and Pliny wrote that the Roman soldiers drank it diluted with water to quench their thirst during long marches. Tomatoes, since their introduction from Peru in the sixteenth century, have become a major ingredient in Italian cooking.

3 firm tomatoes
3 cucumbers
salt
1 tablespoon chopped red onion
1 tablespoon chopped fresh parsley
1 tablespoon chopped fresh basil
2 tablespoons capers in vinegar, drained
1 tablespoon chopped fresh oregano leaves
2 tablespoons vinegar
1 tablespoon extra virgin olive oil

Slice the tomatoes and cucumbers, sprinkle them with salt and spread them on a plate set at an angle, or in a strainer, to drain.

Arrange the tomatoes in the center of a serving plate with the cucumbers around them. Over the tomatoes scatter a mixture of the chopped onion, parsley and basil, and over the cucumbers sprinkle the capers and the oregano.

Mix together the salt, vinegar and oil, and pour this dressing over the salad before serving at room temperature.

*Breakfast in the garden*, Giuseppe de Nittis (1846–84); CIVIC MUSEUM, BARLETTA  Cakes are rarely made at home in Italy.  Almost every town has a *pasticceria* (cake shop) where

both the restaurateur and family cook will purchase a few choice desserts.

# DESSERTS

There are few more satisfying or civilized ways to conclude a fine meal than with fresh, ripe fruit and cheese. Italians appreciate their bounty of good fruit and have, over the centuries, devised numerous wonderfully simple ways of using it to cleanse the palate and stimulate digestive juices after the daily meal. The famous, seductive Italian desserts are usually reserved for special occasions, holidays and feast days. But, as the calendar is gratifyingly replete with religious feast days and Italians love to celebrate with exuberant meals, the national heritage of desserts has thankfully remained intact.

Italian pastry-cooks have deservedly acquired a great reputation. Many of the simple but delicious home-made desserts come from recipes written in little notebooks and effectively kept within the family by being handed down from mother to daughter over generations. Nevertheless, the pastry shop is an important part of Italian life: every neighborhood in a large town or each small village will have one or two. Both the restaurateur and the family cook wisely purchase those elaborate desserts and small sophisticated sweets for which Italy is famous from the professional pastry cooks at their *pasticcerie* (pastry shops).

In the regions the pastry shop will double as the local cafe and is a hub of social life and gossip. In large cities the pastry shops, which have existed since the late eighteenth century, are the height of elegance with crystal chandeliers and marble-topped tables and counters. In these sensuous surroundings, frothy capuccinos are accompanied at any time of the day by either a pastry or a couple of small, individual cakes chosen from the countless varieties available — jam and fruit tartlets, almond and custard pastries, chocolate and cream *bigné*. In winter *cioccolato con panna* (hot chocolate with fresh whipped cream) warms the body and gladdens the soul.

The first writer to collect and publish the traditional home-made desserts was Pellegrino Artusi in his nineteenth-century bestseller *La Scienza in Cucina e l'Arte di Mangiar Bene (The Science of Cooking and the Art of Eating Well)*. This "practical manual for families" has over 150 recipes for desserts, pies, cakes, cookies, sweets ("to be eaten with a spoon"), puddings, creams and soufflés. Most have remained in the repertoire of home-made desserts, although some require rather a high degree of skill and dedication.

Sugar cane, which came from the East some time in the eleventh century, remained a luxury until the Renaissance, when sugar and spices were sprinkled in the sweet and savory sauces that accompanied every course of a meal. One favorite sweet was marzipan (pounded almonds and sugar baked to make little *dolcetti*, predecessors to *petit fours*). Another was *frutti di pasta reale*, a Sicilian specialty made with *pasta di mandorle* (a

*The birth of John the Baptist* (detail), *Ginevra de'Benci and Lucrezia Tornabuoni*, Domenico Bigondi, known as Ghirlandaio; SANTA MARIA NOVELLA, FLORENCE
Until the sixteenth century, Italians always ate fruit before a meal rather than at the end, which is the custom today.

mixture of almonds, sugar and eggs, shaped and colored to represent various fruits). The white blossoms of the almond trees in southern Italy in February are a truly beautiful sight. Especially in the South, cloistered nuns, carrying on a venerable tradition that dates at least from the seventeenth century, use much the same ingredients to fashion almond cakes in the form of "holy lambs" for Easter and *pesce di Natale* (Christmas fish), an early Christian symbol of Christ. The sisters sell their sweets from the convents and, sadly, the recipes are kept behind the walls. Some startling Renaissance recipes for extravagant pies and desserts have survived — like the one recorded by Cristoforo di Messisbugo for *cinquanta pani di latte e zuccaro* ("fifty breads of milk and sugar"), each bread weighing 9 ounces (255 g); the whole recipe called for 35 pounds (16 kg) of flour, 6 pounds (2.7 kg) of sugar, 3 pounds (1.35 kg) of rosewater, 6 pounds (2.7 kg) of fresh milk and 75 egg yolks!

Recipes of more manageable proportions began to appear in cookbooks by the eighteenth century. Vincenzo Corrado dedicates a section of *Il Cuoco Galante (The Gallant Cook)* to *croccanti*, which are sweets made with sugar, almonds and eggwhites. Cinnamon, nutmeg, lemon and other spices enliven the dish, which is then baked in the oven and served cold, with jam spread on top. Similar "crunchy" confections give pleasure in many Italian regions today. The sensuous *torta di fragole alla Napoletana* (a strawberry tart made with a sweet pastry dough) features, along with lady's fingers, among dessert recipes given by Leonardi in the late eighteenth century.

*Still life with fruit*, Roman fresco;
NATIONAL ARCHEOLOGICAL MUSEUM, NAPLES
The Romans were particularly fond of fruit. The apple was one of their favorites as were the apricot, peach, cherry, fig and melon.

Italy's rich variety of fruits gives enormous pleasure to its people. It is not surprising then, that there is an abundance of fruity desserts. One dessert that blends many fruits into a lively and enchanting dish is as popular in restaurants as it is at the family table. *Macedonia di frutta* (Macedonian fresh fruit salad) requires fruit to be cut into small pieces, sprinkled with sugar and lemon juice and left to macerate in the refrigerator for several hours. Apples, bananas, oranges and pears are the basic components. Apricots, melon, peaches and berries are added according to the season. (Macedonia is said to have been given its name from the mixture of different peoples that Alexander the Great united to form the ancient country.) It is sometimes flavored with spumante, maraschino and other liqueurs. An elegant way to serve it is in a sparkling glass goblet. Artusi suggests pouring it in a mold and freezing it. This, he promises (rightly), will delight the dinner guests with its colorful marbled form.

One of the most charming and perfect ways to cap a convivial meal is with wild berries, *frutta di bosco* ("from the woods"). Tiny strawberries, raspberries, blackberries and currants make a tantalizing fruit cup on their own, as do large, fresh strawberries cut in half and served with a splash of fine, red wine vinegar. Peaches are a delicious family favorite and are prepared at the table. They are peeled, cut into small slices, put in a glass and covered with white wine. *Magnifico!*

Perhaps the most characteristic summer fruit is *anguria* (watermelon), known as *cocomero*. On hot and balmy evenings in July and August, people line up at roadside stalls,

*Blue bowl with strawberries and pears*, Giovanna Garzoni (1600–70);
PALATINA GALLERY, FLORENCE
A popular dish of the Renaissance to conclude a meal was fresh strawberries steeped in balsamic vinegar.

A nineteenth-century chocolate-maker's sign; MUSEUM OF MILAN
Italian cuisine does not use chocolate as much as other cuisines of the world. Surprisingly, however, it is sometimes used in savory dishes, and in the recipe for "black rice" where boiled rice is mixed with chocolate and flavored with cinnamon and sugar.

especially in central and southern Italy, to savor a slice of freshly cut melon chilled in a bucket of ice. At the table a hollowed-out melon is an effective serving bowl for a fruit salad. A surprising and different combination is the pulp combined with another traditional sweet ingredient — ricotta cheese.

Sheep's ricotta, made by cooking the residual whey from cheesemaking, has a well-defined but delicate taste that does not intrude on sweet flavors. A seventeenth-century Tuscan, Antonio Frugoli, in his voluminous treatise on stewardship, was one of the first to write about the use of cheese in cooking. In his chapter on ricotta he recommends it as an ingredient for tarts and fritters or else just by itself, with sugar sprinkled on top. In Sicily it is mixed with vanilla, chocolate and candied peel and used as the filling for the region's two most famous desserts — the exquisite *cassata* and the little tubes of fried pastry known as *cannoli*. The traditional Easter tart of Naples, the *pastiera*, is made with ricotta, candied fruit and spices, baked in a shell of *pasta frolla* (shortcrust pastry), with strips of dough laid in a pattern over the filling. Tuscany enlivens its fine ricotta with a couple of spoons of freshly ground coffee and a shot of brandy mixed together (sometimes, impressively, right at the table in restaurants) to form a quick creamy dessert. Artusi provides recipes for a ricotta pudding — *budino alla ricotta*, made with sugar, eggs, almonds and lemon — as well as a ricotta tart using the same ingredients, which was, he notes, the preferred wedding cake of the peasants of Emilia-Romagna (his native region). A simple and elegant ricotta dessert is *crespelle alla ricotta*: crêpes filled with ricotta mixed with cream and a few raisins. An unforgettable combination is ricotta and chocolate. A few shavings or drops of chocolate can be added to these desserts with a most happy effect.

Rice is called upon to perform many functions in Italian cooking. In the North it often begins a meal; in the South it is frequently served as a sweet at the end of a meal. The ancient Sicilian dish of *riso nero* (black rice) is not, as you might imagine, cooked in the ink of cuttlefish but is boiled rice mixed with melted chocolate until it is uniformly "black," then sprinkled with sugar and cinnamon. A simple Sicilian recipe exists for a pudding that combines rice with chestnut purée. From the North a traditional sweet is *torta di riso e pane* (rice and bread cake); rice and fresh breadcrumbs mixed with raisins, nuts, butter, eggs, sugar and cream, some orange zest (rind) and a dash of cognac, all baked in the oven into a delicious tart.

*Still life with fruit*, Cristoforo Munari (1667–1720); UFFIZI GALLERY, FLORENCE
Melons were known to the ancient Egyptians and later to the Romans. The canteloupe (rockmelon) variety reached Italy in the fifteenth century from Armenia and was first cultivated in the garden of the papal residence.

Neapolitan customs, the ice-cream-seller, Pelliccia (nineteenth century), watercolor; NATIONAL MUSEUM OF SAN MARTINO, NAPLES The Arabs originally introduced ices to Italy, in the form of drinks. By the sixteenth century the technique of freezing liquids was developed and the sorbet was created. Today in Italy every town has at least one *gelateria* (ice-cream shop).

Italians are renowned and envied for their superb ice-cream. Canny ice-cream vendors in other parts of Europe will sell their produce as "Italian," such is the craving for genuine ice-cream made with real cream and sugar and only natural flavors. For the same reason Americans often call ice-cream by its Italian name, *gelato* — a fitting tribute to the Italians, who invented it.

It was the Arabs who actually introduced delightful refreshments of iced drinks made with milk and fruit juices and sweetened with honey, which the Sicilians adopted in the Middle Ages. By the Renaissance these sustaining sherbets had been developed into *sorbetti* (sorbets), thanks to an invention for freezing liquids by the sixteenth-century architect, Bernardo Buontalenti. Credit is usually given to one of the Medici family (either Caterina or Maria), for introducing this dish, no longer a drink, into France. *Sorbetti* originated in the Florentine neighborhood of Santa Maria Novella, near the present train station, where sharp, local citrus juices were frozen in an underground *ghiacciaia* ("icehouse"). In the age of opulent banquets sorbets were served between courses to rest and refresh the palate before the next onslaught of elaborate dishes. In the late nineteenth century, Artusi listed many recipes using lemons, strawberries, raspberries, peaches and apricots to aid digestion and as a cooling influence in hot weather.

We are beholden to another Sicilian for the first real ice-cream. It is thought to be Procopio de'Coltelli, owner of the Cafe Procope in Paris in the late seventeenth century, who added sugar and eggs to his sorbets, thus producing a dish that went on to conquer the world.

Like pasta, ices are nowhere better than in their native land. Sicily has marvelous *sorbetti* of unusual flavors made from fruits of its uncommon plants: *fichi d'India* (prickly pear), *gelsomino* (jasmine), *melagrana* (pomegranate) and pistachios. Artusi noted that, to deepen the green color of pistachio, a little puréed Swiss chard was sometimes added.

*Cupids and fruit* (detail), Rinaldo Bolti (seventeenth-eighteenth century); ceiling fresco; ROOM II, PALAZZO CORSINI, FLORENCE

Another delicious treat is to serve *gelato di crema* — a custard cream made with eggs and milk — with hot honey poured over the top or *affogato* ("crowned") in fresh, hot espresso coffee or *grappa*. The famous and wonderful *cassata* is of relatively recent origin. This uses a pound cake soaked in rum, layered with vanilla and pistachio ice-cream, covered with whipped cream and candied peel and fruits, a creation inspired by the traditional Sicilian recipe.

Every Italian town and major street in large cities has at least one *gelateria* (ice-cream shop). Outside each one a sign proudly proclaims *"produzione propria"* (made on the premises); within, the refrigerated case displays a myriad of mouth-watering flavors, from tangy fresh fruits to rich creams and chocolates. At its best Italian ice-cream is characterized by a fine balance between the proportion of fruit juice or other natural flavorings to cream, which is frozen to a perfect consistency so that it melts in the mouth.

Now, with the advent of the portable automatic ice-cream machine, ice-cream can be made much more easily in the home and it has become a popular inclusion in the traditional family meal. Nevertheless, Italians most often like to relish their national sweet at a convivial outdoor cafe in the late afternoon heat or during a romantic after-dinner stroll in the cool of a summer's evening.

*Flowers and fruit*, Pietro Navarra (seventeenth–eighteenth century); VATICAN GALLERY, ROME
Italy has a rich variety of fruits so it is not surprising that there is an abundance of fruit desserts, including the popular Macedonian fresh fruit salad. The basic components of this dessert are apples, bananas, oranges and pears, with whatever fruits are in season.

*Chocolate cake — modern recipe (left)  Tendril pie — modern recipe (right)*

# CHOCOLATE CAKE

*Torta di cioccolata*

This recipe comes from a book called *L'Arte Della Cucina — Ricette di Cibi e Dolci* ('*The Art of Cooking — Recipes of Foods and Sweets*') by Don Felice Libera. The writer was a priest born in Avio, a small village near Trento, in 1734, and it is likely that only the last years of his life were devoted to compiling this recipe collection, which is also filled with notes about what the finished dishes should look like. In addition to its importance as a recipe book, it also demonstrates the richness of the cuisine of the Trentino region at the time, which was mistakenly considered to be rather poor and uninteresting. The modern recipe has only minor variations, providing more specific detail and reducing the quantities.

> With a knife crush twenty ounces of almonds without their skins and then put them through a perforated iron ladle. Stir into them ten ounces of fine sugar, ten ounces of finely grated chocolate, nine eggs, and mix all these things together, always stirring in the same direction for the space of a quarter of an hour, then beat nine eggwhites with a wooden spatula so they will be nice and fluffy and then put them into the abovementioned concoction and then mix everything together once more for a quarter of an hour, then add a little grated bread and some lemon rinds cut up very fine or orange rinds cut as above and give them a stir or two, no more, and then put this preparation into a mold that you have first greased with fresh butter and put on top some grated bread and then put it into the oven to cook. This cake can be mixed to a stiff batter with four eggs only and baked on an oven tray.

*6 eggs, separated*
*¾ cup (6 oz/180 g) sugar*
*6 oz (180 g) bitter chocolate, finely grated*
*1½ cups (6 oz/180 g) dry breadcrumbs*
*grated zest (rind) of 1 lemon*
*6 oz (180 g) shelled almonds, blanched and finely ground*
*1 tablespoon (½ oz/15 g) butter*

Whisk the egg yolks and sugar together. Gradually whisk in the chocolate, breadcrumbs, lemon zest and almonds. Beat the eggwhites until very stiff and gently fold into the mixture. Butter a 9 inch (23 cm) cake pan. Pour the batter into it and level the top. Bake in a preheated 350°F (180°C) oven for 1 hour or until a skewer inserted in the center comes out dry.

*Adriana Giustinian Barbarigo with her son Gerolamo Ascanio Giustinian having a cup of chocolate* (*circa* 1780), Pietro Longhi (1702–85); CORRER MUSEUM, VENICE

*Plums, jasmine, wainuts and convolvulus*, Giovanna Garzoni
(1600–70); PITTI GALLERY, FLORENCE

# TENDRIL PIE

*Torta di viticci*

**M**aestro Martino da Como, one of the earliest cookery
writers from the fifteenth century, was also Bartolomeo
Platina's teacher. Many of his sweet dishes were made with
flowers, roses or even sometimes the tendrils of plants, which were
boiled and then mixed with fresh cheese, probably ricotta. As well
as cheese, his desserts feature grains such as rice or spelt, and
often different kinds of fruit. He advises using milk fresh from the
cow, which is sufficiently smooth and fat, in place of butter. In the
modern recipe the tendrils are replaced by slightly tart fruit that
has more or less the same taste.

> Take some tendrils that grow on the vine and boil
> them. Beat them and crush them thoroughly with a
> knife, and do the same with the pink roses; and you
> will have some good fresh cheese and some milk fresh
> from the cow, that has been well boiled; and beat
> everything well. And, if you prefer, instead of cow's
> milk you can use pork fat or butter and put into it
> ginger and cinnamon and sugar to your taste.
>
> Put this mixture in the pan with a crust underneath
> and one on top, and when it is nearly cooked you make
> holes in the upper crust, lots and lots of little holes in
> many places, almost all over. And when it has finished
> cooking you put on top of it some sugar and some
> rosewater of good quality, as much as necessary.

*3¼ cups (13 oz/400 g) all purpose (plain) flour*

*2 egg yolks*

*¾ cup (6 oz/180 g) sugar*

*¾ cup (6 oz/180 g) butter, cut into small pieces
 and softened*

*1 lb (500 g) pitted (stoned) plums*

*a little grated ginger*

*pinch of ground cinnamon*

*6 oz (180 g) ricotta*

Heap the flour in a mound on a work surface.
Make a well in the center and put into it the egg
yolks, ⅔ cup (5 oz/150 g) of the sugar and the
butter. Work the mixture into a smooth, soft
dough. Shape into a ball, wrap in plastic and set
aside for about 30 minutes. Roll out ⅔ of the
dough and use it to line a buttered 9 inch (23 cm)
pie dish.

Cook the plums with the remaining sugar until
most of the liquid evaporates. Remove from the
heat and add the ginger and the cinnamon; mix
well. Stir in the ricotta and spread the plum and
ricotta mixture over the pie dough. Roll out the
remaining dough and cover the pie. Seal the
edges and prick the surface. Bake in a preheated
350°F (180°C) oven for about 45 minutes, or until
the top of the pie is lightly browned. Serve.

Sign of a chocolate-making company showing woman eating a
biscuit dipped in chocolate; MUSEUM OF MILAN

197

*Marzipan — modern recipe (marzipan fruit)*

# MARZIPAN CAKE

*Torta detta marzapane*

Like most of Bartolomeo Platina's recipes, this one ends with some advice on health, as Platina was concerned as much with diet and the science of nutrition as with culinary art. His book represents the most comprehensive account of the state of gastronomic art in the second half of the fifteenth century. Platina, who was born Bartolomeo Sacchi in Cremona, was interested in philosophy as well as cooking. He traveled from Mantua to Florence, and then from Florence to Rome, where he died on 21 September 1481. This recipe is from volume 8 of his book *De Honesta Voluptate ac Valetudine* (*Concerning Honest Pleasure and Well-being*). The modern recipe gives instructions for making marzipan.

---

The cake known as "marzipan" is made as follows. For a night and a day leave in cold water some almonds which have been peeled with as much care as possible. Then pound them, continuing to add a little water so they will not give out oil. If you wish the cake to turn out excellent, add an amount of sugar equal to the almonds. When you have pounded everything well, dilute it with rosewater, and put it into a pan lined with a thin sheet of pastry, moistening again with rosewater, and then put it in the oven and once more moisten it continually with rosewater so it will not become too dry. It may be cooked over the fire if you follow the cooking with care so that the cake does not end up burnt rather than cooked. This cake must be flat, not too thick, if it is to be good. I do not recall ever having eaten anything more delicious with my friend Patrizio the elder. Indeed, it is very nourishing, quite digestible, is good for the chest, the kidneys and the liver, and it makes the sperm grow, stimulates one to the pleasures of Venus and refreshes the urine.

---

*1 lb (500 g) blanched almonds*
*2 cups (1 lb/500 g) granulated sugar*
*8 cups (2 lb/1 kg) powdered (icing) sugar*

Scatter the almonds on a baking sheet in a preheated 275°F (140°C) oven. Toast and dry them out for about 20 minutes, stirring from time to time, without letting them color.

Pound the nuts in a mortar with a pestle, adding the granulated sugar a little at a time, until all of the sugar is absorbed. Lay the mixture on a board and gradually knead in the powdered sugar until a soft, smooth texture is obtained.

# POACHED PEARS WITH CHOCOLATE COATING

*Pere cotte al cioccolato*

In the second volume of *De Honesta Voluptate ac Valetudine* (*Concerning Honest Pleasure and Well-being*), Bartolomeo Platina discusses pears, recommending them as astringent and adding that they are more nourishing than other fruits and can be kept for long periods placed on a beam that has been put in a room facing South, and covered with straw. Because they keep well over part of the winter, they are widely used for desserts, and even sometimes as an *antipasto* with strong cheeses such as Parmesan or gorgonzola. A well-known Italian saying is, *"al villan non far sapere quant'è buono il formaggio con le pere"*. ("Don't tell the peasants how good cheese is with pears".)

*6 pears*
*⅓ cup (3 oz/90 g) butter*
*¼ cup (2 fl oz/60 ml) dry white wine*
*¾ cup (6 oz/180 g) superfine (caster) sugar*
*11 oz (330 g) semisweet dark chocolate, grated*
*zest (rind) of 1 lemon, cut into strips*

Peel the pears and remove the cores with a corer, leaving the stems attached. Melt the butter in a saucepan and add the pears. Cook for 5 minutes. Pour on the wine and sprinkle with the sugar and continue cooking, spooning the wine over the pears, until tender. Drain and set aside to dry.

Melt the chocolate over simmering water on low heat. As soon as it has melted, pour over the pears and leave to set. Garnish the pears with the lemon zest and serve.

*Pear*
A popular way to eat pears is with a strongly flavored cheese — an ancient Italian custom.

*Poached pears with chocolate coating*

*Bread and rice cake*

# BREAD AND RICE CAKE

*Torta di riso e pane*

One of the most traditional cakes in the North of Italy mixes bread with rice. This version, with walnuts and golden raisins (sultanas) added, was often prepared in vast quantities by my grandmother's cook on a Sunday night, so that some would be left over for us to eat for breakfast or take to school for lunch the next day.

*¾ cup (6 oz/180 g) Arborio rice*
*6 oz (180 g) crustless fresh bread, crumbled*
*1 cup (8 fl oz/250 ml) heavy (double) cream*
*3 oz (90 g) golden raisins (sultanas)*
*¼ cup (2 oz/60 g) butter, melted*
*3 oz (90 g) chopped walnuts*
*3 whole eggs*
*¾ cup (6 oz/180 g) superfine (caster) sugar*
*¼ cup (2 fl oz/60 ml) cognac*
*grated zest (rind) of 1 orange*
*1 egg yolk, beaten*

Boil the rice in plenty of water without salt for 10 minutes. Drain and set aside to cool.

Meanwhile, soak the crumbled bread in the cream. Soak the raisins in lukewarm water.

Add the rice to the soaked bread and then stir in the melted butter, walnuts, whole eggs, sugar, raisins, cognac and orange zest. Stir carefully until well blended.

Butter a 9 inch (23 cm) cake pan. Spread the mixture in the pan, and level the surface with the blade of a knife dipped in water. Brush the top with the egg yolk.

Bake the cake in a preheated 350°F (180°C) oven for about 1 hour. Turn out and allow to cool.

# PUMPKIN CAKE

*Torta di zucca*

Pumpkin was often used in desserts in ancient times, because it was easy to grow and would last throughout the winter without problems. This simple dessert from the Emilia region may also be enriched with crumbled *amaretti* biscuits, which complement it perfectly, in keeping with the most authentic ancient tradition.

*1 lb (500 g) pumpkin flesh, skin and seeds removed*
*¼ cup (2 oz/60 g) butter*
*¾ cup (3 oz/90 g) all purpose (plain) flour*
*3 eggs, separated*
*1 sachet dry yeast*
*grated zest (rind) of 1 lemon*
*¾ cup (6 oz/180 g) sugar*
*3 oz (90 g) blanched almonds, very finely chopped*
*2 oz (60 g) golden raisins (sultanas), soaked*

In a saucepan, cook the pumpkin pulp and 2 tablespoons (1 oz/30 g) of the butter over low heat, stirring all the while. Remove the pan from the heat. Scrape the pumpkin into a blender and add the flour, egg yolks, yeast, lemon zest, sugar and almonds. Blend thoroughly. Beat the eggwhites until stiff. Add the raisins (sultanas) and the eggwhites. Butter a 9 inch (23 cm) cake pan and sprinkle with flour. Spoon the batter into the pan and smooth the top.

Bake in a preheated 350°F (180°C) oven for about 45 minutes, until a wooden skewer inserted in the center comes out dry. Turn out, leave to cool and serve.

*Pumpkin*
In olden times pumpkin was often used in sweet dishes.

# PINE NUT CAKE

*Torta di pinoli*

One of the most traditional of all ingredients in Italian cooking is the pine nut. Pine nuts are mainly gathered in Tuscany, along the sea shore where there are whole forests of pines. One of the most beautiful is the Migliarino forest near Pisa.

Pine nuts are used in sweet dishes, often with raisins or candied fruits, in savory dishes, and even with fish and meat. Normally they are used raw, but occasionally as in this recipe, they are first toasted in the oven.

*4 eggs, separated*
*¾ cup (6 oz/180 g) superfine (caster) sugar*
*⅓ cup (3 oz/90 g) butter*
*2½ cups (10 oz/300 g) all purpose (plain) flour*
*6 oz (180 g) pine nuts*
*1 tablespoon (¼ oz/8 g) powdered (icing) sugar*

In a bowl, beat the egg yolks with half the sugar. In another bowl, beat the remaining sugar with the butter. Gently stir the two mixtures together. Gradually add this to the flour, mixing in a little at a time to avoid lumps forming. Beat the eggwhites until stiff and gently fold them into the mixture, taking care to retain as much air as possible.

Scatter the pine nuts over a baking sheet. Toast in a preheated 350°F (180°C) oven until they begin to color. Grind 5 oz (155 g) of them in a blender and reserve the remainder. Fold the ground nuts into the batter. Butter and flour a 9 inch (23 cm) springform pan and fill it with the batter. Bake at 350°F (180°C) for about 45 minutes, or until a skewer inserted in the center comes out dry.

Turn the cake out onto a serving plate. Decorate the top with the remaining pine nuts, sprinkle with the powdered (icing) sugar and serve.

*Pumpkin cake (left) Pine nut cake (right)*

# PRUNE PUFFS

*Sfogliatine di prugne*

This dessert used to be fried in very hot oil or melted pork fat, which produces a very light, crisp result. These days the prevailing rules of nutrition suggest that it be baked in a hot oven. Puff pastry can be bought already prepared, even frozen, or else fillo pastry (sold in Italy in "Eastern" shops) may be used.

6 oz (180 g) prunes
½ bottle white dessert wine
1 small piece of lemon zest (rind)
3 tablespoons superfine (caster) sugar
10 oz (300 g) puff pastry
1 tablespoon (½ oz/15 g) butter

In a bowl, soak the prunes in the wine for several hours. Drain, reserving the wine. Place the prunes in a saucepan. Add the lemon zest, sugar, and ½ cup (4 fl oz/120 ml) of the reserved wine. Cook, covered, over low heat for about 15 minutes. Drain the prunes and pit (stone) them. Set aside.

Roll out the pastry to a fairly thin sheet. Cut into 4 inch (10 cm) circles. Place a prune on each pastry disk, fold the dough over it and press the edges of the dough to seal.

Butter a baking sheet and place the prune puffs on it. Bake for 20 minutes in a preheated 350°F (180°C) oven, until golden. Transfer to a serving dish and serve.

*Prune puffs*

# BREAD PUDDING

*Dolce di pane*

*Il Cuciniere Moderno Ossia la Vera Maniera di Ben Cucinare* (*The Modern Cook, or the True Method of Cooking Well*), by Pietro Santi Puppo, was published in Lucca in 1849 with the sub-title *colla maggiore economia possibile utile non solo a quelli che si dilettano del mestiere della cucina, ma ad ogni famiglia bene ordinata* (*with the greatest possible economy useful not only to those who go in for the cooking trade, but to every well organised family*). The introduction specifies that to be able to please whoever he or she shall have the honor to serve, the cook must work in absolutely clean conditions. In keeping with the promise of the title to give economical recipes, the author lists a good number of desserts based on bread, including stuffed eggs in which the hardboiled yolks are mixed with milk-soaked bread and used to fill the whites; these are served with a *zabaglione* (a dessert made from eggs, sugar and Marsala). The modern recipe is for a dessert from the Lombardy region which is quite popular during the winter months.

> Take a large chunk of bread without crust, which has been soaked in milk, and put into it some lemon rind and cinnamon and then break some egg yolks into it, and put in also a little candied fruit and some sugar: the sugar you will measure according to the volume of the bread, so that it will be sweet; then you grease a casserole with butter and line it all over with paper and put it in a moderate oven to bake, and it will be an excellent pudding.

1 lb (500 g) crustless bread
2 cups (16 fl oz/500 ml) milk
⅔ cup (5 oz/150 g) sugar
4 egg yolks
grated zest (rind) of 1 lemon
pinch of ground cinnamon
2 oz (60 g) candied (crystallized) fruit, diced
1 tablespoon (½ oz/15 g) butter

Tear the bread into pieces. Submerge it in the milk and let soak for about 1 hour.

Squeeze out the bread. In a bowl, combine the bread with the sugar, egg yolks and lemon zest. Add the cinnamon and candied fruit and mix well.

Line a shallow loaf pan with parchment (baking paper). Butter the paper. Fill the pan with the bread mixture, smoothing the surface.

Bake in a preheated 350°F (180°C) oven for about 1 hour. Cool briefly before turning out onto a serving plate. Cut into thick slices and serve warm.

*Bread pudding — modern recipe*

*Apple and potato pie (left) Orange meringue puddings (top right) Ricotta pancakes (bottom right)*

# APPLE AND POTATO PIE

*Torta di mele e patate*

In the northern regions in particular, where the fruit ripens only during the summer season, Italian desserts often feature a mixture of vegetables and fruit.

Vegetables such as potatoes, carrots and sometimes zucchini (courgettes) take the place of flour, making the dessert not only lighter and more digestible but also more crumbly in texture. Another common combination in desserts is fruit with cooked rice or with bread which has been soaked in milk.

*1 lb (500 g) potatoes, peeled and sliced*
*salt*
*⅓ cup (1½ oz/45 g) all purpose (plain) flour*
*⅓ cup (3 oz/90 g) superfine (caster) sugar*
*¼ cup (2 oz/60 g) butter*

*3 egg yolks*
*1 lb (500 g) golden delicious apples, peeled, cored and very thinly sliced*

Put the potato slices in a saucepan and barely cover them with lightly salted water. Bring to a boil. Reduce the heat and cook until tender. Drain. Push the potatoes through a sieve into a saucepan.

Place the pan over low heat and add 1 tablespoon of the flour, 3 tablespoons of the sugar and 2 tablespoons (1 oz/30 g) of the butter. Mix well. Stir over low heat to dry the mixture. Remove from the heat and let cool to lukewarm. Stir in the egg yolks. Little by little, add the remaining flour. Turn the mixture out onto a board and knead until soft and smooth. Roll out the dough a few millimeters thick, and place over a 9 inch (23 cm) buttered pie pan.

204

Arrange the apple slices in concentric circles on the pastry shell, reserving a few slices for decoration. Sprinkle with 1 tablespoon of the sugar.

Roll out the remaining dough on a floured board. Cover the apples with the pastry and flute the edges.

Decorate the top of the pie with the reserved apple slices. Bake in a preheated 350°F (180°C) oven for 40 minutes. Meanwhile, combine the remaining sugar and butter in a small saucepan and melt over moderate heat.

After 40 minutes remove the pie from the pan and brush the top with the sugar and butter mixture. Return it to the oven and bake for 5 minutes. Allow to cool before serving.

# ORANGE MERINGUE PUDDINGS

*Coppe meringate*

It is very common in Italian homes to serve desserts made with *savoiardi* or sponge cake soaked in a liqueur and mixed with various other ingredients. One very rich variation on this theme is the *zuppa Inglese* ("English soup") or *tiramisu* as it has recently been christened. *Zuppa Inglese* was created in Siena for the Grand Duke Cosimo III de' Medici; it was first called *Zuppa del Duca.*

*1¼ cups (10 oz/300 g) superfine (caster) sugar*
*3 eggwhites*
*½ cup (4 fl oz/120 ml) sweet white dessert wine*
*½ cup (4 fl oz/120 ml) orange juice*
*6 oz (180 g) savoiardi (lady fingers or sponge fingers)*
*grated zest (rind) 1 orange*
*1 tablespoon powdered (icing) sugar*

To make the meringue: Pour 5 fl oz (150 ml) water in a small saucepan and dissolve the superfine sugar in it over moderate heat. Bring to boil and continue cooking until the syrup reaches 100°F (39°C). Mix the eggwhites into the syrup, and transfer it to an icing bag.

Mix the wine and orange juice together. Steep the *savoiardi* in this and put them into individual ramekins. Strew the grated orange zest over them and pipe the meringue on top in a layer about 1 inch (2.5 cm) thick. Sprinkle with powdered sugar, and bake in a preheated 425°F (220°C) oven for 2 minutes. They should be taken out as soon as the surface of the meringue is lightly browned.

# RICOTTA PANCAKES

*Crespelle alla ricotta*

At one time these pancakes used to be filled with a creamy cheese much fatter than ricotta called *mascarpone.* Small pieces of chocolate are often used instead of the raisins, perhaps mixed with candied fruit or candied orange peel. Ricotta pancakes are a northern version of the Sicilian *cannoli.*

*2 oz (60 g) golden raisins (sultanas)*
*3 eggs*
*3 tablespoons all purpose (plain) flour*
*salt*
*⅓ cup (3 fl oz/90 ml) milk*
*8 oz (250 g) ricotta*
*1 tablespoon superfine (caster) sugar*
*3 tablespoons cream*
*1½ tablespoons (¾ oz/20 g) butter*

In a bowl, soak the raisins (sultanas). Beat the eggs in a bowl. Add the flour and whisk until smooth. Add the salt. Slowly add the milk and whisk well. Set aside to rest for a few minutes. Drain the raisins and pat dry.

Push the ricotta through a sieve into a bowl. Stir in the sugar, raisins and the cream.

Melt the butter in a small nonstick skillet. Pour in a small amount of the batter and tilt the pan until the bottom is evenly coated with the batter. Cook the pancake on one side; turn carefully and cook on the other side. Continue making the pancakes in this manner until all of the batter is used.

Fill the pancakes with the ricotta cream, rolling them around it. Arrange on a serving dish and serve.

*Still life with peaches and glass vase,* Roman fresco;
NATIONAL MUSEUM, NAPLES

*Fruit kebabs in a parcel*

# FRUIT KEBABS IN A PARCEL

*Spiedini di frutta al cartoccio*

Caramelized fruit or fruit cooked in a packet used to be served to guests at the end of the evening meal with a glass of spumante. Little plates of small fruits such as winter cherries, or ordinary cherries coated in chocolate were served with them. The tendency today is to serve this type of fruit in place of the traditional desserts which are seen as too heavy and too rich.

*2 firm bananas, cut into 1 inch (2.5 cm) chunks*
*6 oz (180 g) cherries, pitted (stoned)*
*6 firm apricots, cut into wedges*
*6 oz (180 g) green grapes*
*6 oz (180 g) strawberries*
*1 tablespoon (½ oz/15 g) butter*
*⅓ cup (3 oz/90 g) superfine (caster) sugar*
*1 tablespoon vanilla powder*
*3 oz (90 g) slivered almonds*

Thread the fruit onto long wooden skewers, alternating colors and flavors.

Spread out a large sheet of foil. Grease with a little butter and sprinkle with a small amount of the sugar mixed with the vanillin. Lay the skewers on top, sprinkle the fruit with the remaining sugar and the almonds. Dot with butter here and there. Close the foil and seal it well. Bake the parcel in a preheated 350°F (180°C) oven for 15 minutes. Open the foil at the table and serve.

# SPUMANTE FRUIT SALAD

*Macedonia di frutta allo spumante*

The city of Asti in Piedmont is famous for its spumantes, the best known being Moscato which can be either slightly sweet ("*abboccato*", sweetish) or very sweet and better suited to the end of a meal. Any spumante will do for this dish, as long as it is not too dry. The fruit is marinated in the spumante for a couple of hours before serving. Naturally, it is best to use seasonal fruits, because they will have more flavor.

*½ canteloupe*
*4 pineapple slices, diced*
*2 peaches, peeled, pitted (stoned) and cubed*
*3 oz (90 g) strawberries, hulled*
*3 oz (90 g) blueberries, trimmed*
*8 oz (250 g) grapes, peeled*
*⅓ cup (3 oz/90 g) superfine (caster) sugar*
*2 tablespoons rum*
*¼ cup (2 fl oz/60 ml) cognac*
*½ bottle sweet spumante*

Remove rind, seeds and center filaments from the melon; scoop the flesh into balls with a melon baller. Put all the fruits into a bowl and add the sugar, rum and cognac. Pour the spumante over. Refrigerate for at least 2 hours before serving.

*Autumn, gathering and crushing the grapes* (fifteenth century), illumination from the Theatrum Sanitatis, code 4182;
CASANATENSE LIBRARY, ROME

*Spumante fruit salad*

*Apple cream with almond praline (left) Orange mousse (right)*

# APPLE CREAM WITH ALMOND PRALINE

*Crema di mele al croccante*

Fruit creams are always given some added decoration, especially if they are to be served to guests. At one time this apple cream was served at family dinners with chopped nougat. The Italian nougat, known as *torrone* and made with honey and almonds, is a specialty of the city of Cremona in Lombardy, but is very popular all over Italy, particularly in the South. At village festivals, and especially at Christmas, both adults and children receive gifts of *torrone*, and often it is hung on the Christmas tree for decoration.

*1 cup (8 oz/250 g) superfine (caster) sugar*
*1 tablespoon lemon juice*
*6 oz (180 g) chopped blanched almonds*
*1 tablespoon almond oil*
*7 golden delicious apples*
*1 tablespoon (½ oz/15 g) butter*
*1 handful mint leaves*
*1 cup (8 fl oz/250 ml) whipped cream*

Put ¾ cup (6 oz/180 g) of the sugar in a saucepan with the lemon juice and almonds. Cook over moderate heat until the sugar caramelizes and becomes quite dark in color. Coat a plate with the almond oil. Pour the praline over the plate and let cool completely.

Peel and slice 6 of the apples. Cook with the butter and mint in a wide skillet over moderate heat. When quite soft, push through a sieve held over a saucepan. Add the remaining sugar and stir to let the mixture dry out a little over moderate heat. Remove from the heat; set aside to cool. Mix in the whipped cream. Spoon into a serving bowl.

Pound or chop the almond praline and scatter over the apple cream. Refrigerate for about 2 hours. Garnish with slices of the remaining apple.

# ORANGE MOUSSE

*Spuma all'arancia*

Dessert creams have always had a place in Italian cuisine, even in the most ancient recipes. In the early days, however, the cream base was often fried.

For a more elegant presentation of this simple, wonderfully flavored cream, a little gelatin is often added. In this case it should be refrigerated for a few hours until set; and then turned out of its mold and decorated as desired. It is then often accompanied by a very dark chocolate sauce, preferably hot.

*4 eggs, separated*
*⅔ cup (5 oz/150 g) superfine (caster) sugar*
*2 tablespoons potato flour*
*2 tablespoons Grand Marnier*
*2 cups (16 fl oz/500 ml) fresh orange juice*
*grated zest (rind) of 1 orange*

In the top of a double boiler, whisk the egg yolks with the sugar until the mixture falls from the whisk in a flat ribbon shape, onto the rest of the batter.

Set the pan over simmering water and continue beating as you gradually add the other ingredients: the potato flour, Grand Marnier, orange juice and zest. Continue cooking, without boiling, until you have a thick cream. Remove from the heat; let cool slightly.

Beat 2 of the eggwhites until stiff. Fold into the cream. Pour the mousse into a glass dish or goblet and refrigerate until ready to serve.

# STUFFED PEACHES

*Pesche farcite*

The peach has always been a favorite dessert in Italy. Its generous and succulent flesh and round shape make it ideal for stuffing. It is often served simply cooked and accompanied by pouring cream or sometimes a chocolate cream. Generally however, it is filled with one of a variety of stuffings. This one based on rice which has been cooked in milk and flavored with *amaretti* biscuits is a classic. A recipe similar to this one is to be found in a Piedmontese cookbook of the nineteenth century, where the stuffed peaches are first enclosed in sweet pastry and then fried in boiling oil.

*¾ cup (6 oz/180 g) Arborio rice*
*a pinch of salt*
*1¼ cups (10 fl oz/300 ml) milk*
*grated zest (rind) of 1 lemon*
*6 yellow peaches*
*⅔ cup (5 oz/150 g) superfine (caster) sugar*
*6 amaretti biscuits, crushed*
*2 egg yolks*
*¼ cup (2 oz/60 g) butter*
*2 oz (60 g) blanched almonds, chopped*

Boil the rice with the salt, milk and lemon zest until all of the milk is absorbed. Allow to cool.

Peel the peaches, halve them and discard the stones. With a teaspoon, scoop out a little of the flesh around the center and put it in a bowl; mix in ¼ cup (2 oz/60 g) of the sugar, the *amaretti* biscuits, egg yolks and cold rice.

Generously butter a baking dish. Fill the cavities of the peaches with the rice mixture, forming a little dome in the center of each peach half. Arrange the halves in the baking dish; sprinkle the remaining sugar over them, and strew the almonds on top. Bake in a preheated 350°F (180°C) oven for 15 minutes. Serve hot or cold.

*Stuffed peaches*

# WATERMELON AND RICOTTA

*Anguria alla ricotta*

Traditionally watermelon has always been used in desserts and ices in Sicily, one of the most famous being "*gelu u muluni*," a watermelon ice served on a bed of almond paste. In the rest of Italy however, it simply represents a classic, easy way to end a meal with a dessert that is quick and light. The ricotta can be mixed with chocolate broken into tiny pieces, or with mint-flavored sweets very finely chopped, which will give it a distinctive fresh taste.

*1 completely ripe watermelon, about 4 lb (2 kg)*
*juice of ½ lemon*
*⅓ cup (3 oz/90 g) superfine (caster) sugar*
*6 oz (180 g) ricotta*
*1 cup (8 fl oz/250 ml) heavy (double) cream*
*pinch of ground cinnamon*

Cut a slice from the top of the watermelon and discard; scoop out the flesh and discard the seeds. Refrigerate the empty shell.

Cut the flesh into cubes and put them in a bowl with the lemon juice and half the sugar. Refrigerate for 2 hours, stirring the mixture from time to time, so that the flavors blend. After half an hour drain off the liquid that will have formed, and stir into it the ricotta. Add the remaining sugar and the cream. Add the cubes of watermelon. Mix thoroughly and fill the watermelon shell with the mixture. Sprinkle the cinnamon over and serve.

# MELON CREAM

*Melone alla crema*

This exquisite dish with its intense summer fragrance is easy to prepare and is a perennial favorite because it is so light. Often the melon flesh is also mixed with ricotta, especially in the South where the marriage of fruit with ricotta is common. Melon cream also used to be flavored with ground cinnamon, as spices had become very fashionable after the time of the Crusades.

*1 ripe melon (honeydew or canteloupe), about 3 lb (1.5 kg)*
*⅓ cup (3 oz/90 g) superfine (caster) sugar*

*Watermelon and ricotta (left) Melon cream (right)*

*Still life with cherries*, Giovanna Garzoni (1600–70);
PITTI GALLERY, FLORENCE

*1 cup (8 fl oz/250 ml) whipped cream*
*10 glacéed cherries*

Cut a slice from the stalk end of the melon and discard, together with the seeds and filaments from the center. Scoop the flesh out carefully and put it in a saucepan; set aside the melon shell. Add the sugar to the flesh and cook, stirring constantly, over low heat until all of the liquid evaporates. Set aside to cool.

Push the melon flesh through a sieve into a bowl. Add the cream and mix gently. Spoon the mixture into the melon shell.

Refrigerate for about 2 hours. Garnish with the glacéed cherries just before serving.

# ICE-CREAM WITH BLACK CHERRY SAUCE

*Gelato alle amarene*

**B**lack cherries were once very common, but they are now becoming difficult to find. Because they have a slight tartness about them they need to be cooked with plenty of sugar. But they are among the tastiest of all cherries and are perfect for cooking; served over ice-cream they are absolutely delicious. In a few *gelaterie* (ice-cream shops) in Italy you can still find vanilla ice-cream served with stewed black cherries and a dash of soda water or *selz* as the Italians used to call it.

*10 oz (300 g) pitted (stoned) morello cherries,*
  *stones reserved*
*¾ cup (6 oz/180 g) sugar*
*½ lemon*

*1 vanilla bean*
*4 egg yolks*
*2 cups (16 fl oz/500 ml) milk*

Tie the cherry stones in a piece of cheesecloth.

Put the cherries in a saucepan and add half the sugar, the cherry stones, the zest and juice of the lemon, vanilla bean and sufficient water to barely cover the cherries. Simmer for 30 minutes. Set aside to cool. Discard the cherry stones. Push the sauce through a sieve into a bowl.

In the top of a double boiler, beat the egg yolks with the remaining sugar until the mixture falls from the beater in a ribbon. Add the milk. Place over simmering water and cook, without boiling, until the custard thickens enough to coat a spoon. Remove from the heat and set aside to cool. Freeze the mixture in an ice-cream machine and churn until set.

Transfer the ice-cream to a shallow serving bowl. Pour the morello cherry sauce over it and serve.

*Ice-cream with black cherry sauce*

211

# BREADS

Italians say that bread is like *il campanile* (the bell tower) — every town has its own and boasts that it is more beautiful (and better) than the one in the neighboring town. The late nineteenth-century cookery writer, Artusi, observed that the study of Italian food is like entering a Tower of Babel. This is especially true in regard to the breads of Italy. In two regions the same bread can have completely different names, or the same name refers to totally different recipes! It has been calculated that Italians eat half a pound (275 grams) of bread a day — an extremely high consumption rate. Bread is placed on the table as an accompaniment to every meal, and is always eaten plain without butter.

Today in Italy it is estimated that there are some 35 000 bakers producing Italy's daily bread, 90 per cent of them artisans, turning out their rich variety of loaves with consummate skill and dedication; and almost every street in the large cities has its *panetteria* (bread shop), specializing in the regional favorites. Well over a thousand different shapes of bread are baked in Italy in the *panetterie*: rolls, rounds and loaves, many of them flavored with the same distinctive ingredients that have been used for centuries.

However, there was a period, in the 1950s and 1960s, when industrially prepared bread threatened to force the regional *panetterie* out of business, but eventually popular tradition prevailed, together with a renewed interest in regional baking.

However, in olden times and even until as recently as the Second World War, it was customary for tenant farmers living on large estates and in small isolated hamlets to bring their dough to a communal oven once a week to be baked. These ovens were large and beehive-shaped with a terracotta interior. Each family's loaves were identified with little marks embossed in the dough. Today the little carved wooden stamps used for this purpose have become collector's items.

Strangely enough, in early Italian cookbooks it was more usual to find recipes which used bread as an ingredient rather than to find recipes for bread itself. Domenico Romoli, the sixteenth-century Florentine writer on cooking and household management, described in detail how the bread cupboard should be kept and even dedicated an entire chapter to the dietary qualities of bread, beginning the chapter: "bread is the foundation of all other foods," which illustrates that Italians thought very highly of bread from early times. In his nineteenth-century *La Scienza in Cucina e l'Arte di Mangiar Bene (The Science of Cooking and the Art of Eating Well)*, Artusi does not include even one recipe for bread.

Italians first learned the art of breadmaking from the Greeks, who, in turn, had been taught by the Egyptians. According to the historian Pliny, bakers from Macedonia were among the prisoners brought back to Rome with the legions in 168 BC. Soon they were

*The harvesters*, Silvestro Lega (1825–95); GALLERY OF MODERN ART, MILAN
Lega was a leading exponent of the *Macchiaioli* group of painters who painted *plein-air* landscapes using *macchie* or "patches" of light and dark colors to render immediate impressions of light and landscape.

*A Christian banquet* (detail), sarcophagus cover; NATIONAL MUSEUM, ROME
Bakers first appeared in ancient Rome in about 170 BC. However, bread was to remain a luxury for the rich until the Christian era.

at work tending the ovens of the Empire as freed slaves. The bakers spread across the country and eventually each region developed its own characteristic style of bread.

The best way to approach the study of Italy's rich heritage of breadmaking is by region. One could generalize that the breads of the North of Italy are rolls rather than loaves — although there are a few notable exceptions. *Biovette* are the classic rolls of Piedmont, highly leavened to come out of the oven plump, crusty and practically hollow. Sometimes the same dough is baked into a large, round pointed loaf called *biova*. A similar roll peculiar to Lombardy is *la michetta*, shaped like a rosette. *La Francesina* ("the French"), a roll which originally came from the lake district of Como, is so called owing to its long, narrow form similar to a French *baguette*. It also has a crunchy crust but is hollow and chewy inside. In the same region they bake rolls or small loaves with a thin crust called *chiabatte* which are deliciously light and delicate, with a satin-like texture on the inside. *La ciopa* is a bread with a firm, thick crust and porous interior that is made into rolls in the Trentino and into loaves in the Veneto. Italians often eat these breads for breakfast with jam, or use them for *panini* (sandwich rolls), or serve them at supper.

Emilia-Romagna, which has produced so many gastronomic specialties, can also boast of baking one of the world's oldest types of bread — *pasta dura*. The Egyptians and Romans kneaded this (literally) "tough dough" with their feet. Today, however, the bakers of Bologna create the region's traditional *pasta dura* rolls with slightly more modern machinery! The most famous of these rolls is the *manina Ferrarese* ("little hand of Ferrara"), which looks, as its name suggests, like a small hand; it is also called *coppietta*

*Ferrarese* ("couple from Ferrara") as it is formed by knotting together a "couple" of croissant-shaped pieces of dough. *Pasta dura* rolls are characterized by their hard, smooth crust and dense cotton-like interior and are often considered Italy's most delicious bread.

The traditional bread of Tuscany is saltless — probably to counteract the extreme saltiness of the other Tuscan regional dishes. The large round Tuscan loaves of *pane sciocco* (tasteless bread) or *pane azimo* (bland bread) complement the salty prosciutto, salami and cheese. The bread is also used for the favorite Tuscan snack *fettunta* — a slice of grilled bread rubbed with garlic, salted and drizzled with extra virgin olive oil. *Pane sciocco* lasts a long time owing to the absence of salt and there is always plenty left over in the cupboard. This probably explains the origin of the wealth of Tuscan bread soups and salads! Bread never goes to waste in Italy as it is thought sacrilegious to waste even a crumb of the "staff of life."

*Bread* (1926), Editta Broglio (1886–1977); EDITTA BROGLIO COLLECTION, SAN MICHELE OF MORIANO Well over a thousand different shapes of bread are baked in Italy today, and it is thought that 35 000 bakers are employed in producing Italy's rich variety of regional breads.

Shovel of Francesco Ridolfi, called "The Flourishing One," (seventeenth century); ACCADEMIA DELLA CRUSCA, FLORENCE
It is possible to generalize when discussing the regional variations of Italian bread and say that the breads of the North are rolls rather than loaves, while bakers of the South create huge "wheels" of bread.

The tradition of breadmaking in the South is quite different. Here large crusty "wheels" of bread are prevalent. Traditionally, these can weigh up to four pounds (1.8 kilograms) and are made to last a week. The bread of Puglia, now popular throughout Italy, originated right at the "heel" of Italy in the town of Altamura. This bread is made from durum wheat, which has been grown on the nearby Tavoliere plain since the time of the Romans. (Puglia was an important granary of the Roman Empire.) It is the same hard grain that is milled into semolina and used to make the region's celebrated pasta. The Puglian bread is baked to a golden brown and is chewy inside; sometimes a handful of Puglia's plump juicy olives are also kneaded into the dough for that little extra something.

In the ninth century the island of Sicily was occupied by the Saracens. Traces of the effect this had on the local populace can still be seen today in local customs and also in the Sicilian bread with its exotic shapes and the custom of sprinkling on sesame seeds. One variety, *mafalda*, is made from specially milled semolina flour and then shaped into crosses, crowns, ladders, snakes and even a pair of eyes in honor of Santa Lucia (the Christian martyr who had her eyes put out by the Romans because she would not surrender her virginity and deny her faith). *Mafalda* is sprinkled with sesame seeds and baked to a deep gold.

*The bakery*, Roman fresco; NATIONAL ARCHEOLOGICAL MUSEUM, NAPLES
The Romans first learned the art of breadmaking from the Greeks who had been taught by the Egyptians.

*Still life*, Antonio de Pereda (*circa* 1599–1668); HERMITAGE MUSEUM, LENINGRAD
The regions of Italy all have their own special recipes for *biscotti* (cookies/biscuits). *Biscotti* are usually sweet but a savory recipe from the Chianti area for *biscotti salati* (salt crackers) is particularly delicious.

Perhaps the most unusual Italian bread of all comes from Sardinia. It is called *carta da musica* (music-paper bread) because it is as thin as parchment, and also because it is so brittle that the crunching sound one makes while eating it has been likened to "singing"! This bread is made with unleavened dough, rolled out into large wafer-thin disks and baked until golden and crunchy. It lasts for quite a while and in olden times shepherds took this bread with them into the hills to eat while watching their flocks. Today this simple bread is considered quite sophisticated and is served at smart northern restaurants.

Curiously, whole-wheat bread is not popular in Italy, possibly because in the past its "unrefined" texture was looked down upon by the well-to-do. It was even thought to be less nutritious than white bread and bad for the digestion! The sixteenth-century writer, Romoli, is emphatic about its negative qualities, even saying that it causes melancholy! The poor, who confused prosperity with well-being, thought white bread the finest and ate it whenever they could — as sustenance for the sick or at special occasions such as weddings. Today this prejudice has been largely overcome and whole-grain bread, or *pane integrale*, is widely available. *Pan bigio* (dark bread) is one classic peasant bread made from unrefined flour. Because of the modern predilection for refined flour, it has become scarce.

*A Neapolitan tavern* (1831)
*Biscotti salati* (salt crackers) have always
been a popular snack to eat with a glass
of chilled white wine.

Another quite different kind of Italian bread is "sweet" bread enriched with sugar, spices or herbs. Many sweet breads are *pani festivi* (feast-day breads) originally created to celebrate significant religious or family events, and are kneaded into appropriate symbolic shapes. *Pampepato* is a sweet bread which dates back to the Middle Ages. In Ferrara it is made in a ring-shape, with almonds and pine nuts and is sometimes coated in chocolate. It is the local Christmas cake and bakers presented it to their customers as a goodwill gesture at Christmas. This tradition dates back to the Renaissance, when cooks gave the cake to the mistress of the house. In central Italy, however, *pampepato* is shaped into small rolls filled with nuts, chocolate and dried fruit.

The *pandoro* of Verona is star-shaped and covered with powdered (icing) sugar. It is called *pandoro* (golden bread) because generous amounts of egg and butter are kneaded into the dough. At Easter the *colomba pasquale* (Easter dove) appears in pastry shops all over the country. It is a light, sweet bread, dotted with almonds and sprinkled with sugar, similar to the Milanese Christmas bread, *panettone*, with its raisins and candied peel. Legend has it that *panettone* was named after a fifteenth-century Milanese baker called Toni. The story goes that a rich young man fell in love with Toni's beautiful daughter. The young man provided Toni with enough money to buy more butter, eggs and candied fruit than the rival bakers could afford. Therefore, Toni's bread became celebrated as the most delicious in the city and was called *pan di Toni* (Toni's bread), which eventually became "*panettone*." For the feast days of All Saints and All Souls at the end of October, the delightful nut and raisin *pan coi santi* (bread of the saints) tumbles out of bakers' ovens all over the country. The Milanese bake *pan di miglio* (millet bread) to celebrate St George's Day. It is a flat, round bread made with millet flour sprinkled with sugar. It is often served with fresh cream.

Some Italian sweet breads are available only when their special ingredients are in season. The supreme bread in this category is *panforte* ("strong" bread), which is not really a bread but a traditional fruitcake of Siena. It is rich with cinnamon, coriander, cloves, nutmeg, and white pepper. *Panforte* is filled with the rare spices that were brought to Italy on the spice route from the East in medieval times. The spices were then stored for distribution in the cool vaulted cellars of Siena's gothic *palazzi* (palaces). *Panforte* was reputed to have many extraordinary and beneficial effects and was actually made and sold by the city's apothecaries. Today it is simply considered a very good sweet and is shipped all over the world.

Trying to discover whether bread, *focaccia* or pizza came first in the sequence of Italian culinary history is rather like the riddle of the "chicken and the egg." Today one person's pizza is often another person's *focaccia*, depending on the region. Basically *focaccia* and pizza are both flat breads with various savory ingredients spread on top. In their primitive forms they were probably unleavened disks of dough cooked on a hot stone in the fire ("*focaccia*" is derived from the Latin word for "hearth"). The Roman writers Cato and Virgil both mention rounds of dough dressed with herbs, cheese, and honey. These types of bread were invented by peasants as a cheap but filling meal, made from simple ingredients.

However, *focaccia* is usually more simply seasoned on top than pizza, and is traditionally eaten as a snack. Although the name varies from region to region, *focaccia* (which means "cake" or "bun") is found throughout Italy. Liguria is probably the home of the most famous *focaccia*. Here there are *focaccerie* that bake these flat breads simply drizzled with olive oil and sprinkled with salt or topped with sweet onions or black olives. In Tuscany they are called *schiacciata* (meaning "crushed" or "flattened") and are flavored with herbs. Domenico Romoli advises the steward of the house to keep several fresh *schiacciate* on hand for the master. He says the well-supplied bread cupboard should always include *schiacciate* seasoned with *fiori di sambuco* (elderberry flowers), sugar and butter, as well

*Panettone "Cova"*
The story goes that *panettone* was named after a fifteenth-century Milanese baker called Toni — hence *pan di Toni* (Toni's bread) which became shortened to *panettone*.

*Peasant working in the country* (fifteenth century), illumination from Plinius' manuscript *Naturalis Historia*
Durum wheat has been grown on the Tavoliere plain since Roman times. The grain is milled into semolina to make the famous bread of Puglia.

as other varieties similar to the popular *schiacciata con l'uva* ("with grapes") traditionally made at harvest time with red grapes and raisins soaked in sweet *vin santo*. *Fugazza* is the Venetian dialect word for *focaccia*, and the Venetian recipe includes sugar, eggs, and a splash of sweet spirit such as rum.

Although pizza does share a similar ancestry to *focaccia*, it was truly born and bred in Naples. Nineteenth-century travelers in Italy described the street vendors who walked the city's narrow streets calling to the citizens to come and buy their tasty pizzas. Customers would purchase a piece (at a discount if it were cold), fold it in half and eat these *libretti* ("little books") while they took their stroll.

Pizza achieved its immense popularity when the Neapolitan *pizzaioli* (pizza-makers) were inspired to top it with two of the region's best products: tomatoes and mozzarella cheese, made from buffalo milk. These two ingredients (as well as a little oregano and some anchovy fillets) are all that is needed to create the classic *pizza Napoletana*. The dough base is kneaded and thrown into the air to shape and flatten it, and then baked in the wood fires of a brick-lined oven. It should be well cooked but remain tender and fragrant with a soft raised rim or edge called *il cornicione* (large frame).

The *pizza margherita* and *la marinara* are probably the two other best-known varieties. The *pizza margherita* was named after Queen Margherita of Savoie, who tasted this variety of pizza during a visit to Naples in 1889 and declared it was her favorite. It is made without anchovies or oregano but with a handful of basil leaves instead, creating a pizza of the three colors of the Italian flag — red, white and green. *La marinara* is the simplest pizza of all, but is considered the most challenging test of a *pizzaiolo*'s talent. It is topped with tomato, garlic, clams, mussels and a generous seasoning of oregano.

*Saint Facio giving alms* (detail), Andrea Mainardi, known as Il Chiaveghino (1550–1613); GENERAL HOSPITAL, CHIESA DELLE ESEQUIE, CREMONA

A Neapolitan variation of pizza is the *calzone*. Originally it was a long tube of pizza dough that resembled the *calzone* (pants) that the Neapolitans wore in the nineteenth century. Today the dough is simply folded over to a halfmoon-shape and filled with a combination of ingredients such as tomatoes, mozzarella, ricotta, and salami. For family meals it is also common to make many mini *calzone* or "*calzoncini*" and fry them in oil. Sometimes just small plain pieces of pizza dough are dropped into boiling oil and fried. These tiny "*pizzelle*" are brought to the table hot, and are delicious topped with fresh tomato sauce and grated Parmesan cheese.

The Romans, on the other hand, make pizza in large, rectangular pans; it is cut into various lengths and sold according to weight. It comes in a myriad of colors and one particularly delicious topping is thinly sliced potato. At the southernmost part of Italy in Palermo, Sicily, pizza is known as *sfinciuni*. It is rolled out thicker than the Neapolitan variety and baked in a rectangle like its Roman counterpart. In place of mozzarella, the topping used is the regional *caciocavallo* cheese, which is made from cow's milk and has a slightly smoky flavor. One recipe for *sfinciuni*, which is said to have been created by the nuns of San Vito in Palermo, uses ground meat, sausage, ricotta and sometimes greens, all between two fine sheets of pizza dough.

Towards the end of the nineteenth century, pizza emigrated to Little Italy in New York where, in 1895, the Neapolitan, Gennaro Lombardi, opened the first pizzeria. It continued to follow in the path of Italian emigration to the New World and later to other parts of Europe. However, unfortunately, the pizza lost much of its authentic flavor along the way. But in its home town, if you are lucky enough to find a traditional pizzeria with an expert *pizzaiolo*, pizza is still the original, humble yet delicious dish with lively, direct flavors.

*Preparation for a banquet* (detail), fresco from the Golini Tomb; ARCHEOLOGICAL MUSEUM, FLORENCE
The Greek bakers, employed by the Romans, baked their bread in huge ovens — a tradition which has continued to modern-day Italy.

*Tuscan white bread (left) Bread with olives (right)*

# TUSCAN WHITE BREAD

*Pane Toscano bianco*

Tuscan bread is perhaps one of the simplest breads to make. It is completely lacking in salt which means it lasts for at least a week. It used to be made on the farms on a Saturday, not only for the family but also for the peasants who came from a distance to do a day's labour.

In Tuscany, bread was made in the home until very recently: every home had a wood stove built specially for the purpose. After the bread had been baked on feast days, it was customary to put the meat into the oven to cook, because the heat would have reduced by this time to just the right temperature, and then when the meat was taken out and the heat of the oven was still lower, in would go the *Africani*, delicate, rich little biscuits made with sugar and egg yolks.

*2 tablespoons (⅓ oz/10 g) fresh yeast*
*⅔ cup (5 fl oz/150 ml) lukewarm water*
*3 cups (12 oz/350 g) all purpose (plain) flour*

Dissolve the yeast in the water.

Mound the flour onto a board. Make a well in the center and add the yeast mixture. Add more water if necessary, and knead the dough until smooth. Shape into a ball, place in a floured bowl and set aside to rise until doubled in volume.

Punch down the dough again. Form into 2 oval loaves and set aside to rise for 30 minutes, until the surface is slightly cracked.

Bake in a preheated 400°F (200°C) oven for 10 minutes. Reduce the temperature to 390°F (195°C) and finish baking until slightly golden for about 10 minutes.

# BREAD WITH OLIVES

*Pane alle olive*

It appears that there are more than 7000 varieties of bread in Italy. So writes Carol Field in her book, *The Italian Baker*. In fact I think there are probably many more, if we consider that nobody really makes exactly the same bread as is suggested in recipes or by tradition. The custom of making not only breads of different shapes and different types and proportions of flour, but also with a variety of other ingredients mixed in, is very ancient, and each region has its particular specialties based on the traditional local ingredients. Like *focaccia*, olive bread is a Genoese speciality.

*2 tablespoons (⅓ oz/10 g) fresh yeast*
*¾ cup (6 fl oz/180 ml) lukewarm milk*
*3 cups (12 oz/350 g) all purpose (plain) flour*
*1 teaspoon salt*
*¼ cup (2 fl oz/60 ml) extra virgin olive oil*
*4 oz (120 g) pitted (stoned) black olives, chopped*

Dissolve the yeast in the milk.

Heap the flour and salt in a mound on a board. Make a well in the center and pour in the oil. Mix while adding the yeast and milk. Knead the dough for 5 minutes then shape it into a ball. Put the dough in a floured bowl, cover, and set aside to rise until doubled in volume.

Punch down the dough. Add the olives and mix well. Divide the dough in half and shape into 2 rounds. Set aside to rise again until doubled in volume.

Bake in a preheated 400°F (200°C) oven for 20 minutes, until golden.

# A WONDERFUL AND NUTRITIOUS WALNUT LOAF

*Pane di noci meraviglioso e buono*

The anonymous Venetian author who wrote this recipe in the fourteenth century wrote in the Venetian dialect, and in a rather unsophisticated style. But his recipe book is useful to us for many dishes, and especially for regional recipes which teach us about the Veneto region in particular, through its food and its cooking. Here for the first time we find recipes using cuttlefish ink, and not merely using it, but also explaining how to extract the sac full of ink from the cuttlefish.

This walnut loaf is really a type of *focaccia* or flat bread; made to a modern recipe it is very good and light, particularly because the flour is kneaded with milk. By adding a few tablespoons of sugar it can also be made into an excellent dessert (in that case naturally leaving out the onion).

If you want to make walnut bread, take the walnuts and shell them and pound them and take some good herbs and a little grated onion and spices both hot and sweet, and a small amount of sugar, and put all these into a mortar and make a paste with them. Then take pure wheaten flour and make a sheet of dough like a large lasagna, thin and wide, and put the mixture on this and knead everything together and shape it like a loaf and then punch it down so it becomes as thin as a *focaccia* and put it into the oven to bake and when it is cooked, take it out and let it cool.

*1 oz (30 g) fresh brewer's yeast*
*¾ cup (6 fl oz/180 ml) lukewarm milk*
*3 cups (12 oz/350 g) all purpose (plain) flour*
*1 tablespoon chopped fresh rosemary*
*salt*
*3 tablespoons extra virgin olive oil*
*6 oz (180 g) shelled walnuts, very finely chopped*
*1 onion*

Dissolve the yeast in the milk.

Heap the flour in a mound on a board. Make a well in the center and add the rosemary, milk and yeast, a little salt and 2 tablespoons of the oil. Knead into a soft, smooth dough. When the kneading is almost finished, add the walnuts and knead for a few more minutes to mix thoroughly. Shape the mixture into a ball and then set aside to rise in a warm place until the dough has doubled in volume.

Meanwhile, in a skillet, fry the onion in the remaining oil over low heat until translucent.

Punch down the ball of dough. Roll it into a circle of 8 inch (20 cm) diameter, ½ inch (1 cm) thick on a floured working surface. Leave it to rise in a floured tart pan for about 30 minutes.

Cover the dough with the onion. Bake in a preheated 400°F (200°C) oven for about 25 minutes. Allow to cool before serving.

*A wonderful and nutritious walnut loaf — modern recipe*

*Kitchen* (fifteenth century), illumination from the Theatrum
Sanitatis, code 4182; CASANATENSE LIBRARY, ROME

# BRESCIA SPICED BREAD

*Pane speziale alla bresciana*

This recipe by the early nineteenth-century Milanese
gastronome, Giovan Felice Luraschi, is for a very rich sweet
bread which is perhaps more suitable for serving with morning
coffee or as a snack than for lunch or dinner. In Italy the bread
traditionally eaten with meals is plain bread served alone, without
butter or any other accompaniment. It is placed to the left of the
diner's plate, on a small plate, possibly made of silver.

Bread always used to be made with fresh yeast, and in sufficient
quantity to ensure there was enough fresh dough left over to serve
as a starter for the next batch of bread when required. To prevent
the dough from drying out, it was kept soaking in water. That way
it remained soft enough to mix with the flour (there were of course
no refrigerators to keep it fresh!).

Take one pound of pure wheaten flour, one pound of
sugar, half a pound of butter, a little warm water, and
form these into a dough that is just a little softer than
short pastry; shape it into a cake, then fill it with the
following stuffing. Take one pound of blanched
almonds and pound them in a mortar with the white
of an egg, then put them into a dish and add one pound
of whole pine nuts, mixing in also one pound of powdered sugar, two ounces of sweet spices, nine ounces
of raisins, some chopped citron peel. Knead all this
with a little must from the bottom of the wine cask and
fill the cake with a little of this, then cover it with the
dough, making some ornamentation or amusing decor-
ations with the tip of a knife. Put it into the oven, and
when it is baked place it on a serviette, dust the surface
with sugar and serve.

*3 oz (90 g) raisins*
*1 oz (30 g) fresh yeast*
*¾ cup (6 fl oz/180 ml) lukewarm milk*
*3½ cups (14 oz/420 g) all purpose (plain) flour*
*salt*
*⅓ cup (3 oz/90 g) sugar*
*½ teaspoon ground cinnamon*

Soak the raisins in warm water for about 30 minutes. Drain and pat dry. Dissolve the yeast in the
milk.

Heap 3 cups (12 oz/350 g) of the flour into a
mound on a board. Make a well in the center, and
pour in the milk and yeast. Add a little salt and
the sugar and knead into a smooth, soft dough.
Set aside to rest in a warm place, covered with a
towel, until doubled in volume.

Mix the cinnamon with the remaining flour.
Sprinkle over the raisins.

Punch down the dough. Add the flour-coated
raisins and shape the dough into an oval loaf
about 2 inches (5 cm) high. Set aside to rise again
for about 30 minutes.

Bake the loaf in a preheated 400°F (200°C)
oven for 20 minutes or until lightly browned.
Allow to cool before cutting and serving.

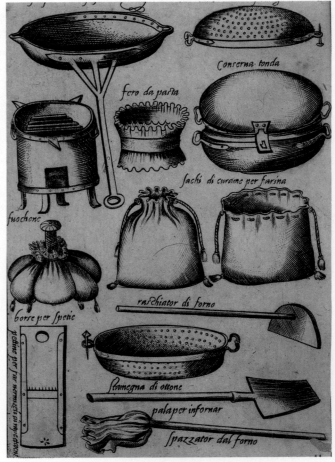

*Various instruments*, from Bartolomeo Scappi's book *Of the Art
of Cooking with the Master of the House and Carver*, from
Scappi's *Opera* (1570); LEVY PISETZKY COLLECTION, MILAN

226

*Brescia spiced bread — modern recipe*

*The Neapolitan Pizza (left) The* calzone *(right)*

# THE NEAPOLITAN PIZZA

*La pizza Napoletana*

There are by now an infinite number of variations on the pizza theme. Indeed the pizza, like spaghetti or rice, has become a foundation on which both home cooks and restaurants indulge their fancies. At one time the pizza was a staple dish for poor families, being made with flour and a little tomato, almost always without cheese. It has become fashionable in the homes of the upper middle class relatively recently, and is most often served in a very small individual size with cocktails or at buffets.

*⅔ cup (5 fl oz/150 ml) lukewarm water*
*2 tablespoons (⅓ oz/10 g) fresh brewer's yeast*

*1 lb (500 g) all purpose (plain) flour*
*1 tablespoon salt*
*¼ cup (2 fl oz/60 ml) extra virgin olive oil*
*1 lb (500 g) plum (egg) tomatoes, peeled and cut in half lengthwise*
*10 oz (300 g) mozzarella, sliced*
*2 tablespoons capers, drained*
*6 anchovy fillets*

Put the warm water in a small bowl and dissolve the yeast in it.

Heap the flour in a mound on a board. Make a well in the center and pour in the water and yeast; add the salt. Work the mixture into a smooth, elastic dough. Knead vigorously, rolling the dough out and gathering it up again several times. Shape it into a ball, put it into a floured bowl and set aside to rise, covered with a cloth, for about 2 hours or until doubled in volume.

Punch down the dough and knead it for several minutes, pummeling it a number of times. Roll out into a circle of 10 inch (25 cm) diameter, ¼ inch (0.5 cm) thick with slightly thicker edges. Transfer it to an oiled pizza pan.

Arrange the tomatoes, mozzarella, capers and anchovies on top. Add some salt and the rest of the oil. Bake in the center of a preheated 400°F (200°C) oven for about 25 minutes, or until it begins to brown.

# THE CALZONE

*Il calzone*

**A** *calzone* is an envelope made from the same dough as that used for pizzas, inside which the cook puts whatever filling takes his or her fancy. One of the most traditional fillings is ham with *scamorza*, a firm cheese with a delicate flavor somewhat similar to mozzarella. A small and very popular restaurant in Milan called Paper Moon makes a particularly simple version which is highly acclaimed for that very reason. There is no filling in their *calzone*, but it is puffed up quite high and covered with a slice of prosciutto which is placed on top at the very last moment, after the *calzone* is cooked. The recipe was discovered in a very old book belonging to a Neapolitan family.

*10 oz (300 g) onions, thinly sliced*
*⅓ cup (3 fl oz/90 ml) extra virgin olive oil*
*1 lb (500 g) bread dough (see recipe for Tuscan white bread, page 224)*
*6 oz (180 g) sliced cooked ham*
*6 oz (180 g) ricotta*

In a skillet, fry the onions in 3 tablespoons of the oil over moderate heat. Do not let them color.

Roll out the dough to about ⅛ inch (2 mm) thick. Using a pastry wheel, cut it into 4 inch (10 cm) squares.

Divide the onion among the squares of dough. Add to each a slice of ham, 1 tablespoon of ricotta and a dribble of oil. Fold one corner of each square diagonally over the filling to form a triangle; press the edges down well to seal them.

Flour a baking sheet and place the *calzoni* on this. Brush them with oil and bake in a preheated 400°F (200°C) oven for about 15 minutes.

*The harvest* (1877), Federico Pastoris, woodcut from *L'Illustrazione Italiana*; SORMANI LIBRARY, MILAN
The Campania region of southern Italy grows abundant crops due to the fertile volcanic soil.

229

# TO MAKE A PIE WITH VARIOUS INGREDIENTS, WHICH THE NEAPOLITANS CALL PIZZA

*Per fare torta con diverse materie, dai Napoletani detta pizza*

**B**artolomeo Scappi, a sixteenth-century cook who was probably originally from Bologna, was famous for, among other things, a banquet he prepared to celebrate the first year of the reign of Pope Pius V. Scappi provides some wonderful evidence of what civilization was like in the time of the Renaissance. It is enlightening in relation to the customs of the time that in the first volume of his works there is a description not only of the kitchen, but of where it should be located in relation to the rest of the house. "I believe first of all that the kitchen must be at a distance, rather than in a public area. This is so for various reasons, and particularly to avoid the nuisance created by crowds of people, and in order not to trouble the nearby living quarters of the building with the noise which must necessarily be made in this room."

The old recipe is for a rich, sweet pizza, but it should be remembered that the distinctions we make today between sweet and savory did not exist in the old days. The modern recipe is a Neapolitan classic.

You must have six ounces of shelled almonds and four ounces of soaked pine nuts and three ounces of fresh dates without the stones, and three ounces of fresh figs, three ounces of sultanas and you pound every thing in the mortar, sprinkling on rosewater so the mixture becomes like a paste. Add to these ingredients eight raw fresh egg yolks, six ounces of sugar, one ounce of crushed cinnamon, one and a half ounces of *mostaccioli* [small hard biscuits with candied fruit and grape must] ground to a powder, four ounces of rosewater, and when all this is well blended, cover a tart dish with marzipan, line the edges all around with a twist of the paste (not too thick), and put the mixture into it, mixed with four ounces of butter, making sure that it is not more than one inch high. Bake it in the oven without covering it, and serve it hot or cold as desired. Almost any spiced thing may be put on this pizza.

*3 tablespoons raisins, soaked in water*
*6 garlic cloves, chopped*
*3 tablespoons extra virgin olive oil*
*6 anchovy fillets packed in oil*
*1 lb (500 g) endive (or lamb's lettuce), sliced*
*salt and freshly ground pepper*
*1 oz (30 g) fresh yeast*
*¾ cup (6 fl oz/180 ml) lukewarm water*
*3 cups (12 oz/350 g) all purpose (plain) flour*
*2 tablespoons pine nuts*

Soak the raisins in warm water for about 30 minutes. Drain and pat dry.

In a skillet fry the garlic gently in the oil. Add the anchovy fillets and cook until they dissolve. Add the endive and raisins. Season with salt and pepper. Cover and cook over low heat for about 10 minutes.

Dissolve the yeast in the warm water; set aside to proof for about 10 minutes.

Heap the flour in a mound on a board. Make a well in the center and pour in the water and yeast. Mix and knead for about 10 minutes into smooth, soft dough. Set aside to rise in a warm place until doubled in volume.

Punch down the dough on a floured board. Roll out into a circle ¼ inch (0.5 cm) thick.

*To make a pie with various ingredients, which the Neapolitans call pizza*
*— modern recipe*

4 cups (1 lb/500 g) all purpose (plain) flour
1 lb (500 g) onions, thinly sliced
¼ cup (2 fl oz/60 ml) extra virgin olive oil
salt

Dissolve the yeast in the water.

Heap the flour into a mound on a pastry board. Make a well in the center and pour in the dissolved yeast, adding water as necessary to mix into a soft dough. Knead for at least 10 minutes. Shape the dough into a ball, place in a floured bowl, cover and set aside to rise until doubled in volume.

Knead the dough for a few moments, then pat out into a circle about 8 inch (20 cm) diameter and ½ inch (1 cm) high on a floured oven tray. Set aside to rise for 30 minutes.

Meanwhile, in a skillet, saute the onions in the oil over moderate heat for a few minutes until translucent. Scatter the onions over the *schiacciata* and season with salt. Bake in a preheated 400°F (200°C) oven until it begins to brown on top.

Let cool a little before serving.

*The month of August* (detail), (fifteenth century), fresco; CASTELLO DEL BUONCONSIGLIO, TRENTO

Lay the dough on a floured pizza pan. Cover with the endive. Sprinkle on the pine nuts. Bake in a preheated 400°F (200°C) oven for about 25 minutes, until light golden in color. Transfer to a serving plate and serve.

# ONION SCHIACCIATA

*Schiacciata alle cipolle*

Another ancient form of bread or pizza is *focaccia*, sometimes called *schiacciata* in Tuscany. Like the pizza, it is made from the same dough as bread. However, its shape is flat, and the garnish is much simpler. In many regions of Italy *schiacciata* is also called *pizza bianca* (white pizza), because many things can be put on top of it but never tomato. The most traditional form of *schiacciata* is simply sprinkled with oil and salt, but there are many variations and among the most popular are those using chopped herbs such as sage or rosemary. In Tuscany when the *schiacciata* is particularly thin it is called *ciaccino*.

1 oz (30 g) fresh brewer's yeast
⅔ cup (5 fl oz/150 ml) lukewarm water

*Onion* schiacciata

# WHOLEMEAL GRISSINI

*Grissini integrali*

**P**iedmont has always been particularly famous for its bread sticks, which have now migrated not only to the rest of Italy but all over the world. In good bakeries Piedmontese *grissini* are still made by hand, and often still with whole-wheat flour. The semolina helps to make them light and easily crumbled. They are served along with bread, and like bread are usually eaten without butter.

*2 tablespoons (⅓ oz/10 g) fresh yeast*
*⅔ cup (5 fl oz/150 ml) lukewarm water*
*1 cup (4 oz/120 g) unbleached all purpose (plain) flour*
*1½ cups (6 oz/180 g) whole-wheat (wholemeal) flour*
*1 cup (4 oz/120 g) semolina*
*1 teaspoon salt*
*2 tablespoons extra virgin olive oil*

Dissolve the yeast in the water.

In a bowl, mix the flours, ¾ cup (3 oz/90 g) of the semolina, the salt, olive oil, and water and yeast. Knead for 10 minutes, until the dough is smooth. Set aside to rise in a floured bowl until doubled in volume.

Punch down the dough and shape into long sticks like thick pencils. Roll them in the remaining semolina.

Bake in a preheated 400°F (200°C) oven for 15 minutes, or until slightly golden.

*Banquet scene*, Marcello Fogolino (1480–1548); CASTELLO, MALPAGA

# SALT CRACKERS

*Biscotti salati*

**T**his old recipe, discovered by a baker named Bianchi in the little village of Gaiole in the Chianti area, is one of the major successes of my cooking school. The biscuits are delicious and will keep perfectly in an airtight container for at least 2 weeks. They are an excellent accompaniment to a glass of good white wine as an appetizer, and may be varied in many ways, for example, by adding to the dough very finely chopped herbs such as rosemary, sage or thyme, or cumin or fennel seeds.

*2 tablespoons (⅓ oz/10 g) fresh yeast*
*⅔ cup (5 fl oz/150 ml) lukewarm water*
*2 cups (8 oz/250 g) unbleached all purpose (plain) flour*
*1 cup (4 oz/120 g) whole-wheat (wholemeal) flour*
*1 tablespoon salt*
*⅓ cup (3 fl oz/90 ml) extra virgin olive oil*

Dissolve the yeast in the warm water.

In a bowl combine the flours, salt, 3 tablespoons of the olive oil and the yeast mixture. Knead the dough until smooth. Shape into a ball, place in a floured bowl and set aside to rise until doubled in volume and the surface is slightly cracked.

On a floured surface, roll out the dough into a ¼ inch (0.5 cm) thick rectangle. Score it into squares with a knife and prick each with a fork.

Brush the squares with the remaining olive oil and sprinkle a little salt on top. Bake in a preheated 400°F (200°C) oven for 10 minutes. Separate the crackers and bake for 5 more minutes. Let cool completely.

*Wholemeal* grissini

*Salt crackers*

*Still life with fruit*, Vincenzo Campi (1536–91); BRERA GALLERY, MILAN Sauces have played an important role in Italian cooking since Roman times. Apicius wrote recipes fo

# SAUCES, PICKLES AND PRESERVES

...auces made from fruits and nuts, flavored with spices and herbs.

# SAUCES, PICKLES AND PRESERVES

While the Renaissance cooks thoroughly indulged themselves with heavy, laborious sauces, modern Italians prefer to appreciate the natural fresh flavors of the foods and their ingredients.

There is no doubt that Italians will relish a tingling green sauce or a piquant and hearty tomato sauce, but Italian cuisine does not extend to the complex and sophisticated sauces of the French. Despite the fact that some of these simple, deft sauces have become all-time classics, the usual practice is for Italian cooks to reserve a light hand when applying sauce to pasta and to serve roast meats with only their deglazed cooking juices. Many of the groaningly rich sauces of yesteryear owed their origin to outside influences.

In another Renaissance manuscript by a Venetian, there is a recipe with the mysterious name *salsa Sarasinesca* (Saracen sauce), thought to have been brought back to Italy by the Crusaders. Its ingredients, the exotic flavors of Arabia, are typical of those that were to characterize the Renaissance — almonds, raisins, ginger, nutmeg and cloves mixed with *agresto* (the juice of unripe grapes).

A manuscript dating from the fourteenth century, by an anonymous Tuscan, titled *Libro della Cocina (Book of Cooking)*, has a recipe for a sauce made with fennel flowers and egg yolks, flavored with saffron, cinnamon, cloves and cardamom. The author quaintly recommends making it during the month of September and serving it with eggs. During the seventeenth and eighteenth centuries the cuisine that evolved in the kitchens of grand households employed showy, rich sauces, many of French and Austrian origin. This practice was especially common in the extreme northern and southern regions, which were subject to foreign influence owing to political or geographical circumstances.

One of the great Italian classics is *salsa di pomodoro* (tomato sauce). This tasty and enduring sauce is most characteristic of regional cooking from Tuscany in North-central Italy to southernmost Sicily. Home-made tomato sauce is prepared from fresh, ripe San Marzano plum tomatoes. These are peeled, quartered and simmered for a couple of hours with the usual aromatic herbs and vegetables, seasoned with a little salt and sugar. It is most important to continue cooking until all the water in the tomatoes has evaporated. This concentrates the juices and the result is a full-flavored sauce of perfect consistency that does not even have to be put through a food mill. It can be seasoned with a handful of fresh basil or marjoram leaves but the freshness and fragrance of the tomatoes must always prevail. Late in the summer the provident country cook picks a supply of specially cultivated cherry tomatoes and hangs them high in the rafters of a storage room, where they slowly mature and provide fresh ingredients for *salsa di pomodoro* through the winter.

*Still life with fruit and flowers* (detail), Giovan Battista Ruoppolo (1629–93); CAPODIMONTE MUSEUM, NAPLES
During the Renaissance, Italian sauces became thicker and heavier, often incorporating both sweet and savory ingredients.

With today's modern conveniences a supply of plum tomatoes can be frozen and, when required, thawed out in boiling water before preparing the sauce.

Mostly, however, Italian cooks adhere to tradition and use their flavorsome *pomodori in conserva* (tomato preserve). This is prepared every year during August and September, when the fleshy San Marzano tomatoes are fully matured. They are peeled, put together whole with some basil leaves into hermetically sealed jars, which are then wrapped in paper and allowed to set in boiling water for about half an hour. When the jars have cooled they are stored in the larder until their contents are needed to add the color and flavor of summer to a variety of pasta, vegetable and meat dishes. There are a number of high-quality commercially produced *pomodori in conserva* available should this tomato preserve, regrettably not last the winter.

A splendid ancient sauce that has come down through the centuries in various permutations is *salsa verde*. This agreeably pungent green sauce is a classic of northern Italy. Embodying two basic ingredients — parsley and vinegar — it traditionally accompanies boiled meats, fish and eggs but is delicious on many other dishes as well. It appears in a fourteenth-century manuscript, written by an anonymous Venetian, called *Libro per Cuoco (Book for the Cook)*, where it is flavored with ginger, cloves and cinnamon and is recommended as an accompaniment for boiled foods. In another anonymous parchment of the early fifteenth century entitled *Due Libri di Cucina (Two Cookbooks)*, written by a southern Italian, the recipe includes garlic, "a few breadcrumbs" and mint. By the nineteenth century the spices have long been eliminated and Artusi has a recipe for a sauce that is sharply seasoned with anchovy, capers, a little onion, "very little" garlic and olive oil, to which he also adds a few fresh basil leaves.

In a class of its own is the rare and romantic *balsamico*, which comes from Modena and Reggio Emilia in the Emilia-Romagna region. This is not a sauce, although it is some-

*Still life*, Tommaso Salini (1575–1625); MUNICIPAL MUSEUM, MILAN
The foundations of most Italian sauces are wine and oil, which make them much lighter than the heavy sauces of other European cuisines.

times referred to as a vinegar. It is in fact a rather singular condiment that acts as a superb complement to many dishes. *Balsamico* is made from the unfermented must of sweet Trebbiano grapes, which is boiled very slowly in copper pots until reduced to a thick syrup; to this, vinegar is then added. The wonderful *balsamico tradizionale* is then aged for a minimum of ten years in a series of casks, all of different aromatic and hard woods, and blended with much older vintages as it is aged. This lengthy aging process involves the exercise of considerable skill in a tradition that goes back to the high Middle Ages. In 1046 Duke Bonifacio di Canossa presented the Emperor Henry III with a barrel of fine vinegar which was possibly of the *balsamico* type. During the Renaissance the Dukes of Este reportedly had their own *aceto ducale* (ducal vinegar), which they used in cooking and for

*Children picking fruit*, tapestry;
PITTI PALACE, FLORENCE
A classic condiment from Emilia-Romagna is *balsamico*, a vinegar made from the unfermented must of sweet trebbiano grapes.

239

*Basket of fruit*, Michelangelo Merisi,
known as Caravaggio (1571–1610);
AMBROSIANA GALLERY, MILAN
This picture is renowned for being
possibly the first still life ever painted.
Caravaggio was proclaiming nature to be
as profound a subject for painting as the
human figure.

drinking as an elixir and cordial. Today *balsamico tradizionale* is still made by a few
devoted producers. There are also less rare, and less costly, products that attempt to imitate
the genuine flavor by adding caramel to red wine vinegar.

Authentic *balsamico* is almost syrupy in consistency, with a gleaming dark-brown
color. It has a complex, penetrating aroma that is both fragrant and pleasingly acidic and
a taste that is a combination of sweet and tart. The flavor of many dishes is greatly enhanced by the addition of *balsamico*. It can be diluted in a little wine vinegar to dress a
salad; for a dessert with a difference and it is excellent over strawberries. It is also splendid as a seasoning for meats; it can be added to marinades for roasts or to the pan while
deglazing the juices; or a couple of drops can be added to cuts as they come off the grill.

Another accompaniment to boiled meats, which Elizabeth David describes as "ancient
and beautiful", is *mostarda di Cremona*, from the North (especially Lombardy). A preserve
rather than a sauce, this Cremonese mustard is an unusual and delicious combination of
whole fruits — cherries, figs, pears, plums, apricots, slices of melon — preserved in a thick,
sugar syrup of seasoned mustard, honey and white wine. Mustard seeds, from the plant
*Sinapis nigra*, have been one of the most important and popular spices (along with pepper)
since Roman times. According to medieval herbalists, mustard has numerous medicinal
qualities: it stimulates the appetite, helps digestion and prevents constipation. In the sixteenth century Domenico Romoli recommended the mustard seed not only as a cure for
toothache and flatulence but also as a formidable aphrodisiac.

Renaissance cooks applauded mustard for its hot, rich pungency and mixed the
pounded seeds with honey, vinegar and other spices to season their dishes. They combined

it with *mosto* (grape must), and then with other fruits cooked in sugar. The ancient taste for this sweet, hot preserve has also survived through the centuries in the *mostarda Veneta*, made with quince and served with pork dishes. These preserves are still made at home but today are more usually bought commercially prepared.

The numerous Renaissance *confetture* (jam) made from fruit and sugar, were predecessors to sweet preserves such as jam and marmalade. Cristoforo di Messisbugo cites for example *zuccheri di monache* (nuns' confections), which are fruit and nuts, citron, lemon peel, oranges, pears, almonds and other fruits cooked in a sugar syrup. At banquets these formed part of the *piatti di credenza* (cold dishes served from a sideboard). Today both *confettura* and *marmellata* (marmalade) are made with smaller pieces of puréed fruit and are prepared at home. But, because Italians do not widely partake of eating toast or bread with butter and jam for breakfast, these are not as popular in Italy as they are in other parts of the world.

An unusual Italian fruit and sugar delicacy is called *cotognata*: this is a quince preserve that is made by reducing the puréed fruit to a delicious paste that is spread about an inch (or 24 mm) thick on trays and dried in the sun. It is bought packed in little boxes and can be sliced and served as an exquisite after-dinner sweet.

*Still life with copper jug, roses, grapes, elder flowers, cedars and apples,* anonymous Florentine painter (seventeenth century); PITTI PALACE, FLORENCE The *confetture* (jams) of the Italian Renaissance, made from fruit and sugar, were the predecessors of modern-day jams and marmalades.

# GREEN SAUCE

*Salsa verde*

There is a recipe by an anonymous Venetian author for *"savore de ruga"* or rocket-lettuce sauce, which is very similar to the modern *salsa verde* and dates back to the fourteenth century.

This is the basic sauce for serving with *bollito misto* (a mixture of boiled meats). Leaving out the vinegar and the bread, it also makes a very good summer sauce for spaghetti. Green sauce is usually made with parsley, but Sienese cooks make it with tarragon, "the herb of Siena", when in season. Sometimes finely chopped pickled cucumber or a couple of chopped pickled onions are added to a green sauce.

*1 tablespoon stale country-style bread*
*¼ cup (2 fl oz/60 ml) red wine vinegar*
*¼ cup chopped parsley*
*salt and freshly ground pepper*
*1 hardboiled egg, chopped*
*1 tablespoon capers, drained and chopped*
*2 cups (16 fl oz/500 ml) extra virgin olive oil*

Soak the bread in the vinegar for 10 minutes. Drain and squeeze dry.

Combine the bread with the parsley, salt, pepper, egg and capers. Add the olive oil and mix well. Pour into a sauce jug and serve.

# WHITE, BLACK, GREEN AND YELLOW GARLIC SAUCE

*Agliata bianca, morella, verde e gialla*

At one time sauces were an almost obligatory accompaniment to many meat and fish dishes, and they were invariably very rich. This sauce from Cristoforo di Messisbugo is very similar to the walnut sauce still served on *pansoti* (a triangular type of ravioli) in the Liguria region today; it also has the variations of color and flavor that the taste of the time demanded. Sauces were nearly always a blend of sweet and savory ingredients, with the addition of the spices so fashionable in that period (partly because they had recently arrived in Italy, brought from the East by the seafaring Venetians, and before that by the Crusaders).

*Green sauce*

*White, black, green and yellow garlic sauce — modern recipe*

Take shelled walnuts and clean them, and white bread without crusts soaked in some good broth and garlic, as much as you like, and salt, and pound all these things together well. Then dilute with good meat or fish broth, depending on your preference, and if you do not want garlic put in pepper and juniper and if you want it yellow you put in saffron and if you want it brown or pinkish take some carob beans and scrape them and put them in water to boil and take the top part that is colored and put it through a sieve with some broth and put it in a cooking pot and bring to boil. Then mix more color or less into your *agliata* according to whether you wish it to be light or dark. Likewise if you want it green, take parsley juice or chard juice and when the greens are well cooked and thick, put them through a sieve and dilute with broth, then mix into your sauce. And it can be served alone or used in dishes of meat or large boiled fish or on *maccheroni*.

*1 handful crustless bread*
*1 cup (8 fl oz/250 ml) clear chicken stock*
*6 garlic cloves*
*6 oz (180 g) shelled walnuts*
*⅓ cup (3 fl oz/90 ml) extra virgin olive oil*
*salt and freshly ground pepper*

Soak the bread in the stock, then squeeze dry.

Put the garlic and walnuts in a mortar and mix in the bread. Pound with a pestle, and continue pounding as you add the oil little by little.

Season with salt and pepper. Dilute with additional stock if the sauce is too thick.

243

# FENNEL SAUCE

*Salsa al finocchio*

In ancient times more than today, it was usual to enrich meat and fish by the addition of a sauce. The practice is not so fashionable today, but if it is desired to use a sauce to give greater importance to a meat dish, the tendency is to make something much lighter, often with vegetables. Sauces of zucchini (courgettes), artichokes, broccoli or bell peppers (capsicums) may be made using the same method as for this fennel sauce, which is especially good with roast loin of pork.

*1 fennel bulb, roughly chopped*
*3 tablespoons (1½ oz/45 g) butter*
*1 tablespoon extra virgin olive oil*
*1 cup (8 fl oz/250 ml) dry white wine*
*½ cup (4 fl oz/120 ml) milk*

Put the fennel in a covered casserole with 2 tablespoons (1 oz/30 g) of the butter, the oil and a little water. Add wine and cook over low heat until tender.

Transfer to a blender and add the remaining butter and the milk. Blend until creamy. Reheat gently, pour into a sauce jug and serve.

*The greengrocer*, Giuseppe Maria Mitelli (1634–1718);
NATIONAL LIBRARY, FLORENCE

244

*Madonna dell' Imbevera Day* (nineteenth century), lithograph;
PRINT COLLECTION, MILAN

# TOMATO SAUCE

*Salsa di pomodoro*

Before the sixteenth century, when the tomato was still unknown, the seeds of the pomegranate were used to make sauces with the sharpness of this one.

The *salsa di pomodoro* (tomato sauce) is perhaps the most classic and traditional of all Italian sauces. Properly made, without too much seasoning, it is also very light and nutritious. The tomatoes must be fully ripe and simply peeled — the seeds are retained because not only are they an important source of fiber, they also contribute to the flavor and help to achieve just the right consistency. The longer the sauce is cooked over low heat, the better, because the longer it takes to reach the right consistency (the point when the liquid from the tomatoes is completely evaporated), the more flavor it will have. It is not always necessary to put it through a sieve at the end of cooking; you only need to do this when you want the sauce for some specially refined dish.

*2 lb (1 kg) plum (egg) tomatoes*
*2 garlic cloves, chopped*
*1 tablespoon chopped onion*
*1 tablespoon chopped parsley*
*1 tablespoon chopped carrot*
*1 tablespoon chopped celery*
*⅓ cup (3 fl oz/90 ml) extra virgin olive oil*
*1 tablespoon sugar*
*salt and freshly ground black pepper*
*1 handful fresh basil leaves, torn into small pieces*

Plunge the tomatoes into boiling water for 10 seconds. Peel and quarter.

Sauté the garlic, onion, parsley, carrot and celery in ¼ cup (2 fl oz/60 ml) of the olive oil until the onion is translucent.

Add the tomatoes and sugar; season with salt and pepper. Cover and cook over low heat, stirring from time to time, for about 2 hours until all of the water evaporates. Remove from the heat and stir in the basil leaves. Pour into a sauce jug and serve.

*Fennel sauce (bottom left)  Tomato sauce (top)  Tuna mayonnaise (bottom right)*

# TUNA MAYONNAISE

*Salsa tonnata*

Although mayonnaise is now one of the most typical sauces in Italian cooking, it was introduced into the local cuisine only a little over a century ago from France. Once again, many variations have been created using it as a base. This version is especially useful for a quickly prepared *vitello tonnato* (the classic sauce for this dish is made using the veal cooking liquid mixed with tuna). It is also excellent served in the center of a molded ring of boiled rice (cold). Another elegant summer dish is made by filling the center of raw tomatoes with this sauce, after the seeds and some of the flesh have been scooped out.

*2 egg yolks*
*1 whole egg*
*pinch of salt*
*1 cup (8 fl oz/250 ml) extra virgin olive oil*
*8 oz (250 g) canned tuna, drained*
*6 anchovy fillets packed in olive oil*
*2 tablespoons capers, drained*
*juice of 2 lemons*
*¼ cup (2 fl oz/60 ml) milk*

In a blender, combine the egg yolks, whole egg and salt. Process while adding the oil in a slow, steady stream, until it becomes a mayonnaise.

Add the tuna, anchovies, capers and lemon juice and blend. Gradually add the milk and blend to a thick and creamy consistency.

Pour into a sauce jug and serve.

245

# PRESERVED WHOLE ROSES

*Conserva di rose intiere*

This recipe is taken from *L'Arte di Ben Cucinare et Istruire i Men periti in Questa Lodevole Profession (The Art of Cooking Well and Teaching Those Less Expert in This Admirable Profession)*, a book written by the Bolognese cook at the Gonzaga Court, Bartolomeo Stefani. It was published in Mantua in 1662 with the subtitle *In which it is also taught how to make pies, relishes, sauces, jellies, tarts and other things*; the print is somewhat damaged and the facsimile copy is therefore not perfect — a few pages are difficult to read. At the end of the book the author gives a series of suggestions for banquets, both meatless (for the fast days observed in the Catholic religion) and with meat.

For the modern recipe it is suggested that you use the hips of the dog-rose which, although bitter, have an excellent flavor.

Take three pounds of clarified sugar and two pounds and six ounces of whole roses with an inch of the stalk, taking care to remove the seeds and scrape the stems, and moisten with rosewater. When the sugar is half cooked, take the roses which have first been washed and tied in bunches of three, and plunge them into said sugar for a period of one-eighth of an hour or a little less, then put them in small shallow cups of equal width top and bottom, arranging said roses with the stalk upwards, in such a way that they do not touch each other. When the sugar is cooked to perfection, as above, pour it over the roses. At banquets one or two may be served per guest, and over them a sauce of jasmine flowers; they can be used to make pastries with other ingredients according to your judgement; this preserve is extraordinarily comforting to the stomach.

*Kitchen utensils*, from Bartolomeo Scappi's book *Of the Art of Cooking with the Master of the House and Carver*, from Scappi's *Opera* (1570); LEVY PISETSKY COLLECTION, MILAN

*1 lb (500 g) dog-rose hips*
*1¼ cups (10 oz/300 g) superfine (caster) sugar*
*juice of 1 lemon*
*1 tablespoon almond oil*

Leave a small piece of stem on each rose-hip. In a heavy saucepan, heat the sugar with the lemon juice until it caramelizes and is a light brown color. One at a time, dip the rose-hips into it, holding them by the stems with tweezers. Lay them on a plate coated with the almond oil, not touching one another. When they are cooled, transfer to a serving plate and serve.

*Rural Party Reggio Calabria*, Vincenzo Morani (1809–70)

*Preserved whole roses — modern recipe*

*Strawberry sauce*

# STRAWBERRY SAUCE

*Salsa di fragole*

The earliest reference to light, fruit-based sauces is found in Francesco Leonardi's *L'Apicio Moderno* (*The Modern Epicurean*). Fruit sauces like this one are suitable for creamy desserts, their lightness contrasting with the heavier texture of rich cakes and puddings. This strawberry sauce is particularly suitable for serving with desserts made from cream or chocolate, and with *zabaglione* (a dessert made with eggs, sugar and Marsala). The same method can be used for other fruit such as raspberries, blackberries, mulberries, blueberries, cherries, peaches or apricots. Churned in an electric ice-cream maker, this sauce becomes a delicious refreshing sorbet.

*⅓ cup (3 oz/90 g) superfine (caster) sugar*
*¼ cup (2 fl oz/60 ml) water*
*1 lb (500 g) strawberries, hulled*
*¼ cup (2 fl oz/60 ml) kirsch*

Put the sugar in a saucepan. Add the water and bring to a boil. Cook for about 10 minutes to make a thick syrup that will coat the spoon.

Push the strawberries through a sieve. Mix with the syrup and the kirsch. Let cool to room temperature. Serve from a sauce jug.

*Strawberry* (1534),
from the *Herbal* of Leonhart Fuchs

# CREMONA FRUIT MUSTARD

*Mostarda di Cremona*

A typical Renaissance sweet-and-sharp sauce, Cremona fruit mustard is commercially made and sold in jars. Making it at home does not require a great deal of experience, only a certain amount of time, but the results are excellent and can be used in many recipes — particularly with boiled meats. In the Veneto region a very good mustard is made with apples, cooked and passed through a sieve: it is mainly served with roast goose, pork dishes, and of course baked ham.

*2 Martin, Bosch, or other small cooking pears, peeled*
*2 plums, pitted (stoned)*
*2 fresh apricots, pitted (stoned)*
*2 fresh figs*
*10 oz (300 g) pitted (stoned) cherries*
*2 cups (1 lb/500 g) superfine (caster) sugar*
*juice of ½ lemon*

*½ cup (4 fl oz/120 ml) dry white wine*
*1¼ cups (10 oz/300 g) honey*
*½ cup (2 oz/60 g) dry mustard*

Put the pears, plums, apricots, figs and cherries in a saucepan and add water to just cover. Add the sugar and lemon juice. Bring to a boil. Cook over low heat for about 10 minutes. Drain the fruit, reserving the syrup.

Dry the fruit with care. Leave it in the sun for a few days, turning it frequently, to dry out completely. Alternatively, dry it in the oven at 120°F (50°C).

Pour the wine into a saucepan and stir in the honey and the reserved syrup. Boil over moderate heat for about 5 minutes. Add the mustard, mix well, and remove from the heat.

Put the fruit into sterilized jars. Pour the syrup over to barely cover it. When the mustard is completely cooled, seal carefully and store in a cool, dry place.

*Cremona fruit mustard*

# APPLE AND LEMON JAM

*Marmellata di mele e limoni*

The first writer to give a recipe for jam was an anonymous Venetian writer of the fourteenth century, who advised using quinces and, of course, plenty of spices which were much in use at that time.

Italian cooks are very proud of their jams and conserves. Many housewives pick their fruit in autumn, or buy good-quality fruit from the markets, and make jams (with sieved fruit) and conserves (using the fruit cut in pieces). Lemons give a special flavor to jams, but do not use lemons that have been treated with diphenyl, otherwise the skins will always have a bitter taste, even after boiling.

*2 lb (1 kg) lemons*
*2 lb (1 kg) apples*
*2 lb (1 kg) superfine (caster) sugar*

Prick the lemons all over. Boil them in 3 changes of water for 5 minutes each time. (This takes away the bitterness.)

Cut the apples into wedges, removing the seeds but not the peel. Put them in a saucepan.

Thinly slice the lemons. Remove the seeds and add the lemons to the apples, cover with the sugar and set aside overnight.

Boil the fruit gently over very low heat for about 1 hour. Put the fruit through a food mill. Cook again, stirring often, until the mixture has the desired consistency and a small amount of it dropped onto a sloping plate remains where it is.

Pour the jam into sterilized jars. Top with a circle of waxed paper moistened with some liqueur. Seal. Store in a cool, dry place.

*Lemons and cedars*, Bartolomeo Bimbi (1648–1725);
PITTI PALACE, FLORENCE

# PRESERVED TOMATOES

*Pomodori in conserva*

In August and September when tomatoes are ripe, Italian cooks preserve them in quantity so there will be plenty for use during the winter to add flavor to spaghetti, meat and fish. The bottles of bright red fruit are kept in the dark, if possible, in a cool place but not in the refrigerator. Prepared in this way they will last a whole year. Other vegetables can also be prepared in this way — vegetables like bell peppers (capsicums), small onions and pickling cucumbers, but before bottling these must be boiled for a minute in a mixture of half water and half vinegar to acidify them and prevent fermentation. One of the first cookery writers to give recipes for preserving vegetables was the fifteenth-century Maestro Martino da Como, although at the time he was writing, tomatoes were unknown and he suggested preserving other vegetables and fruit.

*2 lb (1 kg) fully ripe plum (egg) tomatoes*
*6 basil leaves*
*salt*
*1 tablespoon superfine (caster) sugar*

Bring a saucepan of water to a boil. Immerse the tomatoes in this for 30 seconds. Peel. Put them into a jar which has been boiled for a couple of minutes, alternating with the basil leaves, a small amount of salt and the sugar.

Seal airtight with a lid. Wrap the jar in a sheet of newspaper and put it in a saucepan. Add cold water to barely cover the jar. Bring to a boil, and boil for 30 minutes.

Leave the jars in the water until cooled. Dry the jars and store in a cool place to keep until winter.

*Apple and lemon jam*

*Preserved tomatoes*

# BIBLIOGRAPHY

Agnoletti, Vincenzo  *La Nuovissima Cucina Economica (The New Economical Cuisine)*  Parma: 1814, reprinted Bologna: Arnaldo Forni, 1983

Anon.  *Libro della Cocina (Book of Cooking)*  Tuscany: fourteenth century, reprinted Bologna: Arnaldo Forni, 1970

Anon.  *Libro per Cuoco (Book for the Cook)*  Venice: fourteenth century

Anon.  *Liber de Coquina (Book of Cooking)*  Southern Italy: fifteenth century

Anon.  *La Cuciniera Piemontese (The Piedmontese Cook)*  Turin: Soffretti, 1798, reprinted Bologna: Arnaldo Forni, 1980

Anon.  *Libro Contenente la Maniera di Cucinare e Vari Segreti e Rimedi per Malattie e Altro (Book Containing the Manner of Cooking and Various Secrets and Remedies for Illness and Other Matters)*  Reggio: eighteenth century

Artusi, Pellegrino  *La Scienza in Cucina e l'Arte di Mangiar Bene (The Science of Cooking and the Art of Eating Well)*  Florence: 1891

Bettelli Candela, Enza  *Marmellate e Confetture (Marmalades and Jams)*  Milan: Idea Libri, 1983

Biaggi, Beatrice  *C'è un Fungo nel Bosco (There's a Mushroom in the Woods)*  Milan: Idea Libri, 1988

Bonetti Tocco, Silvia  *Antichi Dolci di Casa (Old-fashioned Home-made Desserts)*  Milan: Idea Libri, 1983

Bonetti Tocco, Silvia & Schiaffino, Mariarosa  *Pasta Fresca (Fresh Pasta)*  Milan: Idea Libri, 1987

Buonassisi, Vincenzo & Torre, Silvio  *Stoccafisso e Baccalà*  Milan: Idea Libri, 1988

Cavalcanti, Ippolito  *Cucina Teorico Pratica (Cooking Theory and Practice)*  Naples: 1839

Cervio, Vincenzo  *Il Trinciante (The Carver)*  Venice: 1581, reprinted Bologna: Arnaldo Forni, 1980

Corrado, Vincenzo  *Il Cuoco Galante (The Gallant Cook)*  Naples: 1773

David, Elizabeth  *Italian Food*  Harmondsworth: Penguin, 1969

Davidson, Alan  *Mediterranean Seafood*  Louisiana: Louisiana State University Press, 1972

Del Conte, Anna  *Gastronomy of Italy*  New York: Prentice Hall Press, 1988

Della Croce, Julia  *Pasta Classica (Classic Pasta)*  New York: Chronicle Books, 1987

Faccioli, Emilio  *L'Arte della Cucina in Italia (The Art of Cooking in Italy)*  Turin: Einaudi, 1987

Felici, Costanzo  *Del' Insalata e Piante che in Qualunque Modo Vengono per Cibo dell'Homo (Concerning Salad Greens and Plants that are Used in Any Way as Food for Man)*  Pesaro: sixteenth century

Field, Carol  *The Italian Baker*  New York: Harper and Row, 1985

Giovannini, Francesco  *La Tavola degli Anziani (The Table of the Ancients)*  Lucca: Maria Pacini Fazzi, 1987

Gosetti della Salda, Ada  *Le Ricette Regionali Italiane (Italian Regional Dishes)*  Milan: Solares, 1967

Hazan, Marcella  *The Classic Italian Cookbook*  London: Macmillan, 1980

————— *More Classic Italian Cooking*  New York: Ballantine Books, 1984

Lamma, Giuseppe  *Libri di Cucina (Books of Cooking)*  Bologna: fifteenth century

Laniado, Nessia  *Pizza*  Milan: Idea Libri, 1988

Leonardi, Francesco  *L'Apicio Moderno (The Modern Epicurean)*  Rome: 1790

Lotteringhi della Stufa Incontri, Maria Luisa  *Pranzi e Conviti (Dinners and Feasts)*  Florence: 1965

Luraschi, Giovan Felice  *Nuovo Cuoco Milanese Economico (The New Economical Milanese Cook)*  Milan: Motta, 1829, reprinted Bologna: Arnaldo Forni, 1980

Maestro Martino da Como  *Libro de Arte Coquinaria (Book of Culinary Art)*  Rome: fifteenth century

di Messisbugo, Cristoforo  *Banchetti Composizione di Vivande e Apparecchio Generale (Banquets, Composition of Meals and General Equipment)*  Venice: sixteenth century, reprinted Bologna: Arnaldo Forni, 1973

Parazzoli, Vittorio  *Sapore di Pane (Taste of Bread)*  Milan: Idea Libri, 1984

Pisanelli, Baldassare  *Trattato della Natura de' Cibi et del Bere (Treatise on the Nature of Foods and Drinks)*  Venice: 1584

Platina, Bartolomeo  *De Honesta Voluptate ac Valetudine (Concerning Honest Pleasure and Well-being)*  Rome: 1474

Portinari, Folco  *Voglia di Gelato (Craving for Ice-Cream)*  Milan: Idea Libri, 1987

Riveccio Zaniboni, Maria  *Polenta, Piatto da Re (Polenta, a Dish Fit for a King)*  Milan: Idea Libri, 1986

Romoli, Domenico  *La Singolar Dottrina (The Particular Doctrine)*  Florence: 1560

Root, Waverley  *The Food of Italy*  New York: Vintage Books, 1977

Roversi, Giancarlo  *La Tavola Imbandita da Giuseppe Lamma (The Banquet Table of Giuseppe Lamma)*  Bologna: Grafis, 1988

Santi Puppo, Pietro  *Il Cuciniere Moderno Ossia la Vera Maniera di Ben Cucinare (The Modern Cook or the True Method of Cooking Well)*  Lucca: Baroni, 1849

Scappi, Bartolomeo  *Opera (Work)*  Venice: 1570, reprinted Bologna: Arnaldo Forni, 1980

Stefani, Bartolomeo  *L'Arte di Ben Cucinare (The Art of Good Cooking)*  Mantua: 1662, reprinted Bologna: Arnaldo Forni, 1983

Tanara, Vincenzo  *L'Economia del Cittadino in Villa (Economy in the City Home)*  Venice: 1687

Touring Club Italiano  *Guida all' Italia Gastronomica (Guide to Gastronomic Italy)*  Milan: 1984

Urbani, Ada  *Ritratto di Tartufo (Portrait of a Truffle)*  Milan: Sugar, 1985

Vesco, Clotilde  *Cucina Fiorentino fra Medioevo e Rinascimento (The Cuisine of Florence from the Middle Ages to the Renaissance)*  Lucca: Maria Pacini Fazzi, 1984

Vialardi, Giovanni  *Trattato di Cucina Pasticcera (Treatise on Cake and Pastry Cooking)*  Turin: Favale, 1854, reprinted Bologna: Arnaldo Forni, 1986

# INDEX

# ACKNOWLEDGMENTS

The author wishes to acknowledge the assistance of John Meis in researching the text.

HISTORICAL PICTURES

Weldon Russell Pty Ltd would like to thank the following photographic libraries for supplying pictures for reproduction from their collections:

*AFE, Rome:* p. 53

*Agenzia L. Ricciarini, Milan:* pp. 45, 46, 47, 51, 55, 194 (top), 196 (bottom), 197 (bottom)

*Archivio Fabbri, Milan:* pp. 24–5, 32 (top), 48, 92 (bottom), 105, 107, 146, 162 (bottom), 212–13, 236, 246 (bottom)

*Giancarlo Costa, Milan:* pp. 20, 23, 60 (bottom), 82 (bottom), 92 (top), 141 (bottom), 142 (bottom), 166 (top), 170, 178 (bottom), 180 (bottom), 198 (bottom), 200 (bottom), 226 (top), 248 (bottom)

*Scala, Florence:* front cover, back cover, endpapers, opp. title page, title page, 4–5, opp. contents page, pp. 8–9, 10, 12, 13 (top & bottom), 14, 15, 16, 17, 18–19, 26, 28, 29, 30, 31, 40–1, 42, 52, 72–3, 74, 77, 78 (top), 96–7, 98, 101, 102, 103, 104, 120 (top & bottom), 124–5, 126, 128, 129, 130, 131, 133, 134, 135, 148 (top & bottom), 156–7, 158, 160, 161, 163, 164, 165, 166 (bottom), 167, 168 (bottom), 169, 183 (bottom), 186–7, 188, 190, 191, 192, 193, 194 (bottom), 195, 197 (top), 205, 211 (top), 214, 216, 217, 218 (top & bottom), 219, 222, 223, 231 (top), 232 (top), 234–5, 238, 239, 240, 241, 244 (bottom), 250 (top)

*Studio Pizzi, Milan:* pp. 22, 36 (top & bottom), 49, 65 (bottom), 68 (top & bottom), 76, 100, 106, 108, 132, 138 (top), 162 (top), 168 (top), 177 (bottom), 206 (bottom), 220, 221 (top & bottom), 226 (bottom), 229, 244 (top), 246 (top)

FOOD PHOTOGRAPHY

*John Sims* (home economist: Laura Brezzi Caponetti; location: Sian and Carlo Petrucci; ceramics: Ubaldo Grazia): pp. 35, 37, 56, 69, 87, 93, 121, 149, 153, 179, 183 (top), 203, 207, 227, 233, 247, 251

All other food photographs by Archivio Fabbri (photographer: Romano Vada; art director: Lella Guelfi)

## OVEN TEMPERATURE CONVERSIONS

| ° Celsius | ° Fahrenheit | Gas Oven Marks |
|---|---|---|
| 110°C | 225°F | ¼ |
| 130 | 250 | ½ |
| 140 | 275 | 1 |
| 150 | 300 | 2 |
| 170 | 325 | 3 |
| 180 | 350 | 4 |
| 190 | 375 | 5 |
| 200 | 400 | 6 |
| 220 | 425 | 7 |
| 230 | 450 | 8 |
| 240 | 475 | 9 |